U0869152

National Sailing Scheme Instructor Handbook

国家航海计划教练手册

英国皇家游艇协会 著
黄乙能 杨 玉 译

The Royal Yachting Association, RYA House, Ensign Way, Hamble,
Southampton, Hampshire SO31 4YA
www.rya.org.uk

哈爾濱工程大學出版社
Harbin Engineering University Press

Technical Editing

Amanda Van Santen, Laurence West, Grahame Forshaw.

Contributions

Mike Hart, Andy Carley, Nic Wymer, Debbie Blatchford, Simon Davies, David Ritchie, John Thorn.

Photo Credits

Laurence West, Grahame Forshaw, Richard Langdon/Ocean Images, Paul Wyeth.

The RYA is committed to encouraging both men and women to participate in sailing. For clarity only, this book is written using the masculine gender e.g. man overboard.

Illustrators

Doug Bishenden, Richard Lloyd, Phil Twining and Jake Kavanagh.

Cover Design

Jude Williams.

CONTENTS 目录

CONTENTS 目录

Foreword 前言

Sailing is a wonderfully diverse sport with so many types of boats to suit everyone, regardless of age or ability. The RYA National Sailing Scheme offers one of the best ways into the sport and the progressive training programme, made up of a series of two day courses, enables participants to progress quickly from beginner to expert in a controlled, safe and fun environment.

帆船是一项丰富多彩的运动，各种船型不胜枚举，无论你是儿童，还是年长者，又或者是从未接触过帆船的新手，甚至是航海行家，你都能找到适合自己的船型。RYA（英国皇家游艇协会）制定的国家航海计划为学习帆船者提供了最优方案，该航海计划由为期两天的一系列课程组成，让初学者能够在安全、可控且有趣的环境下学习帆船，逐步成为航海高手。

Participants can choose to learn in dinghies, multihulls or small keelboats, offering a level of activity and adrenaline to suit any taste.

参与者可选择学习小帆船、多体船或者小型龙骨船，大家能够在相应水平的运动中找到自己的乐趣，充分刺激你的肾上腺素。

The Youth Sailing Scheme is closely aligned to the adult National Sailing Scheme, but with even more emphasis on fun and games in the early stages. It is delivered in smaller bite sized chunks to build confidence and skills.

青少年航海计划与成人国家航海计划基本一致，但青少年航海计划前期的课程更注重游戏和娱乐，课程更加细化，旨在培养学员的水上自信和航海技能。

Both the youth and the adult schemes offer parallel routes through learning the basics before embarking on the more advanced courses, where more specialist skills are taught and individual coaching is provided.

青少年航海计划和成人航海计划的基础部分和进阶部分的课程基本相同，后期的高级单元会包含更多专业技术和对学员的单人指导内容。

The RYA sailing schemes are taught in a vast number of locations from the open sea to small lakes, from the north of Scotland to the shores of the Mediterranean. The boats vary from Optimists and Picos to keelboats and multihulls. In spite of this variation, the process of learning to sail has remained largely unchanged during the forty plus years that the RYA has run a national training scheme.

RYA航海计划里的课程可在各种地方开展，从开阔的海洋到狭小的湖泊、从苏格兰北部到地中海沿岸。可采用OP和Pico，或龙骨船和多体船。尽管教学地点和船型多种多样，但是RYA在过去40多年开展国家航海计划期间，提供的教学流程只有很小的改动。

The RYA method known to every dinghy instructor has stood the test of time with few modifications and remains as effective today as it was at its inception. This book explains the techniques and progressions that make up the method along with all the other skills and knowledge required by RYA instructors. It assumes you are already a competent sailor who would like to become involved in an RYA training centre, teaching dinghy, multihull or keelboat sailing.

RYA的教学方法为每一名小帆船教练所熟知，经得住时间的考验，一直以来仅需做少量修改，却始终卓有成效。本书阐明了构成RYA教学方法的技术和发展，以及RYA教练需掌握的知识和其他技能。本书适合合格的水手，且有志愿在RYA培训中心从事小帆船、多体船或者龙骨船教学的人。

This instructor handbook is for all those working, or volunteering, as instructors, senior instructors and coaches within the RYA National Sailing Scheme and Youth Sailing Scheme. This publication also includes an explanation of who can teach the scheme and where, and space to include your log of instructional experience and courses attended.

本教练手册适用于RYA国家航海计划和青少年航海计划的所有工作者，无论是初级教练、高级教练、教官，还是志愿者。本书还阐述了教学资质以及教学场所，同时书中还留有笔记页，可供记录教学经验以及完成的课程。

Amanda Van Santen阿曼达·范·萨腾

Chief Instructor — Dinghy & Windsurfing

主教练——小帆船和帆板

2 Equal Opportunities 机会平等

POLICY STATEMENT 政策声明

The Royal Yachting Association is committed to equality of opportunity and aims to ensure that all present and potential participants, members, instructors, coaches, competitors, officials, volunteers and employees are treated fairly and on an equal basis, irrespective of sex, age, disability, race, religion or belief, sexual orientation, pregnancy and maternity, marriage and civil partnerships, gender reassignment or social status.

RYA秉持机会平等的原则，致力于确保所有现有和未来的参与者、会员、教练、教官、参赛者、赛事官、志愿者和职员等都能受到平等公正的待遇，不论其性别、年龄、身体状况、种族、宗教信仰、性取向、怀孕生育状况、婚姻及伴侣状况、变性行为或者社会阶层。

Objectives 目标

- To ensure boating is accessible and attractive to the widest audience.
  确保帆船驾驶简单易学且对广大观众具有吸引力。。
- To ensure that the RYA's services, including training schemes, are as accessible as possible, including to people with disabilities.
  为了确保RYA的服务（包括培训计划），尽可能地包括残疾人在内。
- To increase the diversity of our Instructors, Coaches and Race Officials.
  为了增加我们的教练、教官和竞赛官员的多样性。
- To identify and promote more role models at all levels from under-represented groups, including women and girls, people with disabilities, people from BAME backgrounds and LGBT+ people.
  在代表性不足的人群中，从各个级别中挑选并推广更多适合的运动形式，包括女性、女童、残疾人，以及不同种族及具有少数民族背景的人。
- To attract new participants from under-represented groups through targeted initiatives.
  通过有针对性的举措吸引代表性不足的群体的新参与者。
- To maintain the Advanced level of the Equality Standard for Sport.
  体现高级水准的体育平等标准。

Implementation 实施

- The RYA encourages its affiliated clubs and organisations, recognised training centres and other stakeholders to adopt similar policies, so that they offer an experience to participants that is friendly, welcoming and open to all.
  RYA鼓励其附属俱乐部、组织、认证的培训中心和其他利益相关者采取类似的政策，以便为参与者提供友好、热情和开放的体验。
- Appointments to voluntary or paid positions with the RYA will be made on the basis of an individual's knowledge, skills and experience and the competences required for the role.
  RYA在录用志愿者或带薪员工时，会考察申请者的个人知识、技能、经验及相应职位所需的能力。
- The RYA will tailor requirements in relation to RYA training schemes which may inhibit the performance of candidates with special needs, provided that the standard, quality and integrity of schemes and assessments are not compromised.
  在不损害计划、评估标准、质量和完整性的前提下，RYA将针对RYA培训计划量身定制要求，这些要求可能会限制有特殊需要的申请者的发挥。
- The RYA will develop further policies for specific subject areas where appropriate (e.g. instructing, race officials).
  RYA将会在适当的情况下针对特定主题领域制定进一步的政策（例如，教练、竞赛官员）。
- The RYA reserves the right to discipline any of its members, qualification holders, appointees, volunteers, or employees who practise any form of discrimination in breach of this policy, in line with the relevant articles, rules, codes of conduct and disciplinary procedures.
  RYA对任何违反本政策进行任何形式歧视的成员、资格持有人、任命者、志愿者或雇员保留根据相关条款、规则、行为守则和纪律程序进行纪律处分的权利。
- The effectiveness of this policy will be monitored and evaluated on an ongoing basis by the RYA Safeguarding and Equality Manager reporting to the RYA Board and the Sports Council Equality Group.
  政策的有效性将由RYA保障和平等经理持续监控和评估，并向RYA理事会和体育理事会平等小组报告。

RYA TRAINING CENTRES RYA培训中心

RYA recognised training centres can issue RYA certificates in the disciplines for which they have been approved. These centres fall into three main categories:
RYA认证的培训中心可通过认可的途径颁发RYA证书。这些培训中心主要有以下三类：

- Sailing centres open to the public.
向公众开放的航海中心。
- Sailing clubs providing tuition for their members and prospective members.
向其会员和潜在会员提供教学的帆船俱乐部。
- Organisations such as local education authorities, Scouts and HM Services, teaching their own groups or members.
各类教授内部群体或会员的组织，如地方教育机构、童子军培训、军事服务。

RYA training centre recognition is vested in the Principal. They are responsible for issuing RYA certificates and ensuring that the requirements of RYA recognition are maintained at all times.
培训中心的RYA认可资格归属于该培训中心的总负责人。他/她们负责颁发RYA证书，并负责确保RYA认可资格所需要的必要条件长期有效。

Guidelines for the recognition of RYA training centres are available in a separate document from the RYA or from the website at www.rya.org.uk.
RYA培训中心的认证准则列在一份单独的文件上，其也可在RYA官网www.rya.org.uk上查询。

RYA AFFILIATED CLUBS RYA附属俱乐部

Affiliated clubs have been at the very heart of the RYA since its foundation in 1875, and a large part of RYA work is still devoted to their promotion and protection. Any club with an RYA-specified boating interest may apply to the RYA for affiliation, namely:
自1875年RYA成立以来，附属俱乐部就是RYA的核心组成部分。RYA的大量工作均致力于对附属俱乐部的推广和保护。任何对RYA的船类运动感兴趣的俱乐部，均可申请RYA认证。这些运动包括：

- Windsurfing. 帆板。
- Dinghy Sailing (cruising and racing). 小帆船（巡游及竞赛）。
- Yacht Sailing (cruising and racing). 大帆船（巡游及竞赛）。
- Motor cruising. 机动艇巡游。
- Sportsboats and RIBs. 赛艇及橡皮艇。
- Personal watercraft. 摩托艇。
- Inland waterways. 内陆运河船只。

It is normally a requirement that a club applying for affiliation has at least 30 members. For full affiliation, a club must have democratically elected officers and a constitution showing that no outside body has control over its affairs. Fully affiliated clubs have one vote for each £1 of affiliation fees paid in voting rights on RYA matters. Clubs that cannot demonstrate democratic process or independence may apply for restricted affiliation, a separate category with no voting rights. For further information about becoming affiliated to the RYA or the benefits of doing so, please contact the RYA at info@rya.org.uk.
按照常规要求，申请认证的俱乐部至少有30名会员。对于完全附属的俱乐部，则必须有经选举出来的负责人和俱乐部章程，说明其事务没有受到任何第三方的干涉。完全附属俱乐部每交纳一英镑会费，就会获得一个RYA事务的投票权。无法确定其是否为民主或独立的俱乐部，可申请成为不完全附属俱乐部，此类俱乐部将没有投票权。关于成为RYA附属俱乐部及其权益的更多信息，请通过info@rya.org.uk 联系RYA。

3 RYA Organisations RYA组织机构

BRITISH YOUTH SAILING (BYS) RECOGNISED CLUB英国青年帆船俱乐部

The BYS Recognised Club Programme accredits and supports those clubs that have made a commitment to put the development of Junior Racing at the forefront of club activity. They are safe and effective places to develop your skills and there will almost certainly be one in your area. Team 15 clubs encompass the same values but focus on the windsurfing rather than dinghy sailing. The process is run by the RYA High Performance Managers. All details are listed in the RYA website..
BYS认可的俱乐部计划认可并支持那些承诺将青少年竞赛的发展放在俱乐部活动最前沿的俱乐部。 它们是发展您的技能的安全有效的场所，几乎可以肯定的是您所在的地区都将会有这样一个俱乐部。 15队俱乐部的价值观相同，但侧重于帆板运动，而不是小帆船航行。 该过程由RYA 高级绩效经理执行。 所有详细信息都在RYA网站上列出。

A BYS Recognised Club is required to BYS俱乐部须具备的条件:

- Provide a structured Junior Race Training Programme.
  提供完善的青少年竞赛培训项目。
- Guide their promising youngsters into the recognised youth classes following their period in a junior class.
  引导少年队里面有潜力的学员进入经过认可的青少年队当中。
- Have sufficient numbers of a recognised junior class of boat (members or club owned), equipment and qualified personnel to achieve the aims of partnership.
  有足够数量的基础级别认证船只（会员或俱乐部拥有均可）、装备及合格工作人员来实现合作关系。

ONBOARD “上船”计划

RYA OnBoard gives young people the opportunity to gain a range of skills and benefits through learning to sail or windsurf in a safe, fun, and structured environment. OnBoard is co-ordinated by the RYA and delivered all across the UK by RYA Recognised Training Centres. The programme complements the National Curriculum and supports a variety of valuable life skills that help to build confidence and shape personal development. Sailing and windsurfing can also spark a young person's creativity, improve their communication skills, and help them develop a growth mindset.

RYA “上船”计划让年轻人有机会在安全、有趣且结构化的环境中学习航行或驾驶风帆从而学到各种技能和能力。 “上船”计划由RYA协调，并由RYA认可的培训中心在英国各地开展。 该计划是对国家课程的补充，并提供各种有价值的生活技能训练，这有助于建立信心和促进个人发展。 帆船和帆板运动还可以激发年轻人的创造力，提高他们的沟通能力，并帮助他们养成良好心态。

Since its launch in 2005, RYA OnBoard has introduced over 800,000 young people to sailing and windsurfing, with over 100,000 becoming regular participants, and the programme continues to grow. OnBoard is a fantastic opportunity for us to introduce 8–18-year-olds to sailing and windsurfing, and promote our sport to new audiences. For more information visit rya.org.uk/onboard.

自2005年推出“上船”计划以来，RYA “上船”计划吸引了80万年轻人参加帆船和帆板运动，其中有10万人成为这项运动的常客，并且该计划还在继续发展中。 对于我们来说，“上船”计划是一个绝佳的机会，可以将8～18岁的孩子吸引到帆船和帆板运动中，并向新的受众群体推广我们的运动。 想要获得更多“上船”计划信息，请访问rya.org.uk/onboard。

THE DUKE OF EDINBURGH'S AWARD 爱丁堡公爵奖励计划

The RYA is recognised as a National Operating Authority for The Duke of Edinburgh's Award (DofE).
The DofE is a voluntary, non-competitive programme of activities for anyone aged 14 to 24, giving the opportunity to experience new activities or develop existing skills.
RYA是爱丁堡公爵奖励计划（DofE）认证的国营权威机构。DofE是一个自发的、非竞争性的活动项目，目的是为14～24岁之间的青少年提供体验新活动和提高现有技能的机会。

There are three progressive levels of programmes which, when successfully completed, lead to a Bronze, Silver or Gold Award.
该项目设有三个级别，参与者在成功完成任务后，即可获得铜奖、银奖或金奖等相应的奖励。

DofE Timescales 爱丁堡公爵奖励计划时间表

BRONZE (14+ years) 铜奖（14岁+）			
VOLUNTEERING 志愿者	PHYSICAL 体能	SKILLS 技能	EXPEDITION 探险
3 months 3个月	3 months 3个月	3 months 3个月	Plan, train for and undertake a 2 day, 1 night expedition 计划、训练进行两天一夜的探险
All participants must undertake a further 3 months in the Volunteering, Physical or Skills sections 在此基础上，所有参与者都需再参加一次为期3个月的志愿服务、体能或技能版块的活动。			

Silver (15+ years) 银奖（15岁+）			
VOLUNTEERING 志愿者	PHYSICAL 体能	SKILLS 技能	EXPEDITION 探险
6 months 6个月	3 Once section for 6 months and the other section for 3 months 三次为期一共6个月的项目和一个3个月项目	Plan, train for and undertake a 3 day, 2 night expedition 计划、培训、进行三天两夜的探险	Plan, train for and undertake a 3 day, 2 night expedition 计划、培训、进行三天两夜的探险
Direct entrants must undertake a further 6 months in either the Volunteering or the longer of the Physical or Skills sections 直接申请银奖项目的参与者，需要在此基础上再参加为期六个月的志愿服务，或者参加更长时间的体能和技能版块的活动			

Gold (16+ years) 金奖（16岁+）			
VOLUNTEERING 志愿者	PHYSICAL 体能	SKILLS 技能	EXPEDITION 探险
12 months 12个月	One section for 12 months and the other section for 6 months 参加一次12个月的项目和一个6个月的项目	Plan, train for and undertake a 4 day, 3 night expedition 计划、培训、进行四天三夜的探险	Undertake a shared activity in a residential setting away from home for 5 days and 4 nights 进行团体活动，离家外宿五天四夜
Direct entrants must undertake a further 6 months in either the Volunteering or the longer of the Physical or Skills sections 直接申请金奖项目的参与者，需要在此基础上再参加一次为期6个月的志愿服务，或者参加更长时间的体能和技能版块的活动			

Doing your DofE 参与爱丁堡公爵奖励计划

Achieving a DofE Award can be made an adventure from beginning to end. Within an RYA club or training centre, there are already so many activities young people could take part in which can count towards their DofE. These could range from:
从开始参与爱丁堡公爵奖励计划到最后获得奖励，这整个过程由始至终都是一场探险。在RYA俱乐部或培训中心，有各种可以让青少年获得爱丁堡公爵奖励的活动。这些活动有：

- **Volunteering**: Helping out at your local Training Centre, club or Team 15 night on a regular basis, this could be as an assistant, in the kitchen or maybe even on the committee!
  志愿者：夜间定期去当地的培训中心、俱乐部或Team15帮忙，可作为助理或厨房后勤，甚至是在组委会帮忙！

- **Physical**: Regularly taking part in Sailing or windsurfing activity, why not set yourself a goal to gain a certain certificate in the RYA National Sailing or Windsurfing scheme or maybe participate in regular club racing.
  体能：经常参加帆船帆板活动，给自己定下一个目标，争取拿到RYA国家航海计划或帆板计划的证书，或定期参加俱乐部比赛。
- **Skill**: All about developing your skills, whether practical, social or personal. You may choose to sharpen up your powerboating, learn a new skill such as boat repair work, become an instructor or perhaps increase your theory knowledge and learn all about meteorology!
  技能：提升你的各项技能，不论是实践技能、社会技能还是个人技能。你可以选择提高机动艇操作技术，学习新的技能。例如，帆船维修，成为一名教练，或者是提高你的理论知识水平，学习气象学！
- **Residential and Expedition**: You may never have been away from home before, let alone using your board or boat to go on an exciting adventure with friends, so now is the time! • Dinghy Sailing (cruising and racing).
  外宿探索活动：你之前可能从未离家外宿过，更别说用帆船或帆板跟朋友一起去探险了，但是，现在是时候啦！小帆船航行（巡航和竞赛）

Getting involved as an Instructor, Coach or Trainer 成为教练、教官或教员

There is a considerable amount of interaction between the participants and the adults who are supporting them, with specific DofE roles such as Centre Coordinators, Leaders, Supervisors and Assessors. If you are interested in helping, further information on these roles can be found by visiting the DofE website.
在DofE项目中，活动参与者和支持他们的成人之间会有很多互动，例如，培训中心协调员、领队、监管员和测评官。如果你有兴趣参与，请登录DofE官网，查询各职位的详细信息。

Further information can be found, explaining the opportunities available, on the DofE website www.dofe.org, and the RYA website www.rya.org.uk/go/dofe.
更多信息和工作机会，请登录DofE官网www.dofe.org和RYA官网www.rya.org.uk/go/dofe获取。

General Considerations 总体考虑　4

DUTY OF CARE 关爱义务

Instructors and Coaches must always remember that they are usually teaching relatively inexperienced sailors, who may not be able to make a sound assessment of the risks inherent in the sport. Instructors and particularly Senior Instructors should not hesitate to make prudent decisions in unfavourable conditions to ensure the safety of the students in their care.

教练和教官必须时刻谨记，学员通常是缺乏经验的，学员可能无法估计帆船运动存在的风险。教练们尤其是高级教练，在不利条件下，要当机立断，谨慎决定，确保学员们的安全。

INSTRUCTOR HEALTH DECLARATION 教练健康声明

RYA Instructors and Coaches must declare any medical condition which might affect their duty of care as an instructor. They also undertake to inform the RYA of any relevant change in their medical situation after qualifying.

RYA教练和教官必须说明在任何有可能影响他们履行关爱义务的医疗情况。而且，在获得教练资格后，如自身健康状况发生任何变化，应告知RYA。

The RYA reserves the right to withhold or suspend qualification from anyone who is considered unlikely to fulfil this requirement.

任何没有履行这一要求的人，RYA有权扣留或吊销其证书。

STUDENT HEALTH DECLARATION 学员健康声明

In order that they are informed as to any additional risk to students, RYA training centres are strongly advised to include a health declaration in their booking forms. The Principal/Chief Instructor must pass on such information to the individual instructor responsible for the student.

为了清楚地了解学员可能存在的健康风险，RYA培训中心强烈建议，在学员的报名表中须添加健康声明。校长/主教练必须把信息告知相关负责教练。

The declaration should say that the student is, to the best of their knowledge, not suffering from epilepsy, disability, giddy spells, asthma, angina or other heart condition, and is fit to participate in the course. It should be signed and dated by the student and include details of any medical conditions or injuries and medication being taken. If there is doubt as to someone's fitness to take part, medical advice may be sought.

在声明中应说明，在学员所知范围内，不存在癫痫、残疾、头晕、哮喘、心绞痛或者其他心脏疾病，而且身体条件达到了参加课程的标准。健康声明应该由学员签字，注明日期，其中还包括身体状况或受伤情况，以及正在服用的药物。如果不确定学员是否适合参与，应参考医嘱。

SWIMMERS 游泳者

It is recommended that all those participating in the sport of sailing should be able to swim.No minimum level swimming ability is stipulated, but students should be able to demonstrate water confidence. It is essential that the instructor in charge of a course knows if any course members are non-swimmers. Non-swimmers may be required to wear life jackets instead of buoyancy aids.

所有参与帆船活动的人都应会游泳。无最低游泳等级要求，但学员应能展示自己在水上的自信。尤其重要的是，如果负责课程的教练清楚哪些是不会游泳的学员，其会要求他们穿着救生衣，而不是助浮衣。

5 RYA Instructor Awards RYA教练认证

RYA Coach Assessor
(Appointed by RYA)
RYA 教官测评官
(由RYA指定)

↑

RYA Senior Instructor
RYA 高级教练

↑

Keelboat/Multihull/Dinghy Instructor Endorsements
龙骨船/多体船/小帆船教练认证

↑

RYA Advanced Instructor Endorsement
RYA 高阶教练认证

← RYA Instructor
RYA 初级教练 →

RYA Racing Instructor Endorsement (RCL1)
RYA 竞赛教练认证
(一级竞赛教练)

↑

RYA Assistant Instructor
RYA 助理教练

RYA ASSISTANT INSTRUCTOR RYA助理教练

The Assistant Instructor is trained to assist qualified instructors to teach beginners up to the standard of the National Sailing Scheme Level 2 and the Youth Sailing Scheme Stage 3. They must only work under the supervision of a Senior Instructor. The award is centre specific.
培训中心需对助教进行培训，使其能够协助已认证的教练，教授从初学者到国家航海计划级别二和青少年航海计划第三阶段的课程。助教必须在高级教练的监督下工作。助教资格由培训中心认证即可。

Role 角色

- Assists RYA Instructors.
  协助RYA教练。
- Instructs up to National Sailing Certificate Level 2 and Stage 3 of the Youth Sailing Scheme.
  协助国家航海计划级别二和青少年航海计划第三阶段课程。

Eligibility for the Training Course 培训资格

- Sailing Standard — Pass one of the National Sailing Scheme Advanced Modules.
  航海技能标准——至少通过国家航海计划中的一项高级课程模块。
- Recommendation by Principal of training centre.
  培训中心负责人推荐函。

Training 助教培训

Training will cover the centre's safe operating procedures and the teaching points related to teaching beginners shown later in this book.
The award is centre specific. Training is based on a two day (or modular) course of 20 hrs duration at the centre, run by the Principal/Chief Instructor who holds a valid RYA Senior Instructor certificate.
培训内容包括培训中心的安全操作程序，以及教授初学者的教学要点（本书在之后会提到）。助教资格由所在培训中心认证。助教培训由持有有效RYA高级教练资格证的培训中心负责人/主教练负责，时间为两天（或更长时间），约20小时。

Assessment 测评

Candidates will be assessed on their practical teaching ability with beginners. Successful candidates will be awarded an RYA Assistant Instructor certificate by their Principal.
测评是测试助教候选人实际教授初学者的水平。通过测评的候选人由其所在受训的培训中心负责人授予RYA助理教练资格。

Certificate Validity 资格证有效期

The centre specific Assistant Instructor certificate is awarded to successful candidates by their training centre and is valid for five years.
培训中心给通过助教测评的学员颁发助教资格证，有效期为五年。

Assistant Instructor Training Course 助教培训课程

- Attend either a specific training course over 20 hrs, or receive 1:1 'on-the-job' training over a similar period.
  参加一次超过20h的助教培训课，或是接受同等时间"一对一"的实战培训。
- Training is primarily afloat covering teaching points from each session.
  培训主要是在水上进行，每节课都会进行教学要点的讲解。
- Will be based around the centre's main fleet (double or single handers).
  课程采用所在培训中心的主要用船（单人艇或双人艇）。
- If double handers, the AI will helm initially then hand over to the students as quickly as possible.
  如使用双人艇，首先由助教掌舵，然后尽快让学员掌舵。
- If single handers, the AI will mainly be a helper, rigger, catcher etc.
  如使用单人艇，助教则负责协助，帮忙装船、接船回岸等工作。
- After training, AI candidates will be assessed on their ability to teach beginners effectively.
  培训结束后，评估助教候选人是否能够有效地教授帆船初学者。

Important Note 重要提示

The AI does not need to hold a first aid or powerboat certificate, therefore AIs must never be allowed to work without direct supervision.
助教不需要持有急救证或机动艇证书，所以助教不允许在没有监督的情况下工作。

The award is centre specific. Thus if an Assistant Instructor moves from one training centre to another, it is likely that his new Principal will issue a new Assistant Instructor Award after retraining.
助教资格由所在培训中心认证。所以如果一名助教到新的培训中心工作，就需要在当地进行二次培训，由新的负责人给他颁发新的助教资格证。

RYA INSTRUCTOR PRE-ENTRY SAILING ASSESSMENT
RTA教练帆船技能课前测评

Before being accepted onto an instructor training course, candidates need to pass this assessment of sailing skills. This is a practical test conducted by an RYA Coach/Assessor not more than one year in advance of their proposed course. This will determine whether they have the required sailing ability to become an instructor, as there is little time on the course for training input to improve their sailing skills.

小帆船教练候选人须通过帆船技能测评后，才能参加教练培训课程。该测评是一项实践帆船技能的测试，由一名RYA教官/测评官执行，有效期为一年。该测评将评定候选人是否具备成为教练所需的航海技能，因为教练培训课程的重点是教学，不是航海技能培训。

It is recommended that, prior to taking the assessment, candidates satisfy themselves that they can sail confidently and to the standard detailed below. They should also have the appropriate background knowledge and understanding of requirements.

建议在参加测评前，候选人要对自己的航行水平有足够的自信，并能达到以下标准。同时，应具备相应的理论知识和对各项要求的熟知。

During the assessment, the candidate will be judged on his preparation for and execution of each of the tasks, including awareness of others. The assessment will be made in a boat of the candidate's or coach's choice, with a Portsmouth Yardstick of less than 1230. If the assessment is conducted in a keelboat or multihull, the rudderless sailing section should be omitted.

测评会对候选人的个人准备和每个任务的执行能力，包括其他意识等进行评定。测评在候选人或教官选择的船上进行，用船的朴茨茅斯数应小于1230。若选择龙骨船或多体船，则应去掉无舵航行环节的测评。

The assessment may be undertaken during a skills course run by an RYA Coach/Assessor. Candidates for a coastal instructor certificate should undertake the sailing assessment on coastal waters.

测评可能会在RYA教官/测评官负责的技能课上进行。沿海教练资格证候选人则须在沿海水域进行这项测试。

The candidate should be able to complete the following tasks, sailing at all times with an awareness of 'the Five Essentials' i.e. sail setting, balance, trim, centreboard and course sailed. The Assessor will be seeking to confirm that the candidate can sail in a controlled and competent manner, considering preparation, communication, approach and execution for each exercise.

候选人要能够完成以下任务，在航行的任何时刻都有运用“五要素”的意识：调帆，船的左右，船的前后，稳向板的位置和最佳航线。测评官需要看到候选人在每个练习中都能有效地控制帆船，操作流畅且非常自信，并且考查候选人的课程准备情况、沟通能力、教学方法以及执行能力。

1 Sail around a triangular course 绕三角标

- Each leg of the course will be a minimum of 100 metres.
  每个航段最短100 m。
- Close mark rounding.
  贴标绕。
- Allow for tide if appropriate.
  如适用，考虑潮汐的影响。
- Use all the boat's equipment to best advantage including spinnaker if carried.
  充分运用船上所有的设备(包括球帆，如有配备)。

2 Sail a tight circular course 绕小圈航行

- Circle less than three boat lengths' radius around a stationary (free floating) boat. 在停止的船（摩托艇挂空挡）附近绕圈航行，圆圈半径不小于三倍船长。
- Make only one tack and one gybe.
  仅用一次迎风转向和一次顺风转向完成一次绕圈。
- Sail trim and boat balance/trim suited to the manoeuvre.
  合理地调整船帆以及船的左右/前后平衡。

The circle should be as small as you can safely make it, but the Assessor will accept that, in doing this, you might have to leave the centreboard in one position.

绕圈的半径越小越好，但要保证你能够安全地完成任务。在操作过程中，为了达成目标，你可能只能将稳向板保持在一个位置，这点测评官是可以接受的。

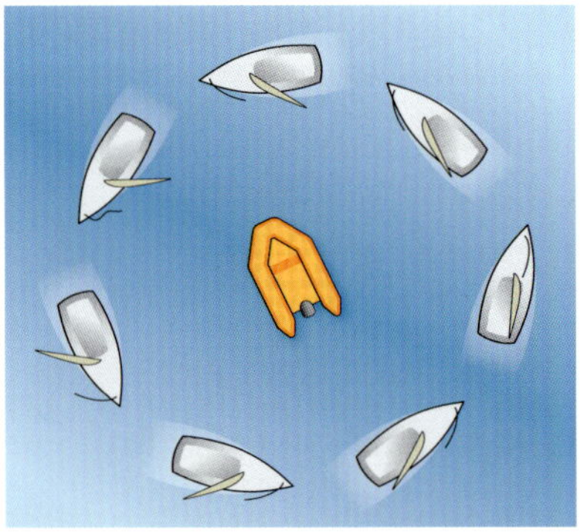

3 Sail a follow-my-leader course 跟船航行

- On all points of sailing.
  能够在任何航行角度跟船。
- Speeding up/slowing down (up and down wind).
  迎风和顺风航行时加速或减速。
- Maintain a constant distance (1-2 boat lengths).
  保持距离（1～2倍船长）。

4 Pick up a man overboard dummy 救助落水假人

- Boat must be stopped dead in the water when you pick up the dummy.
  在救起假人时，船必须处于完全停止的状态。
- Pick up at the windward shroud.
  从上风侧支索处救起。
- Do not tack while you pull it aboard.
  在把假人救上船之前，不要迎风转向。
- Pick up on the first attempt.
  要能够在首次尝试时将“人”救起。

You may also be asked to complete some of the following:
测评官也可能会要求你完成以下一些任务:

1 Sail rudderless, or with rudder in place and the tiller on loose elastic (class dependent)
无舵航行——拆掉舵或用弹性绳将舵松散地固定在中间（取决于船型）

- Sail a triangular course.
  绕三角标。
- Demonstrate effective sail trim/boat balance.
  能够有效地演示对船帆的调整，调节船的左右。
- Modifications to sail area, sheeting purchase and centreboard setting are permitted during the exercise.
  在该练习中，允许改变航行区域，改变机械效率比，调整稳向板。
- Consider other water users and apply the ‘Rules of the road’.
  注意其他的水上人员，应用航行规则。

2 Lee shore landing and departure
背风岸的上岸与离岸

- Use correct sail plan, jib only if necessary.
  合理用帆，如有必要，仅用前帆。
- Land in a controlled fashion.
  让船在完全受控的状态下靠岸。
- On departure, clear the shore successfully in a controlled way on the first attempt.
  初次尝试离岸时，控制好船离开岸边。

3 Pick up a mooring or anchor 系泊或抛锚

- Correct sail plan.
  合理用帆。
- Boat should be stopped next to the buoy.
  船要停在浮标旁。
- Pick up buoy first time.
  要能在初次尝试时就捡起浮标。
- When mooring buoy is on board, the boat should remain under control.
  浮标在船上后，要能保持船在控制之中。
- Anchoring to take place in the area designated by the Assessor.
  在测评官指定的地方抛锚。
- Anchoring should be successful on the first attempt.
  要做到在初次抛锚就成功。
- After the anchor has held, the boat should remain under control.
  在锚抓地后，依旧保持船在控制之中。

4 Come alongside a moored boat 靠船

- Approach under control.
  控好船，靠近抛锚的船。
- Stop alongside on the first attempt.
  要做到初次靠船就成功。
- Remain in control thereafter.
  成功靠船后，依旧保持船在控制之中。

The Coach/Assessor will use an appropriate selection of these exercises to make a judgement of the candidate. Preparation and execution of the task will be judged as well as the factoring in of an ‘escape’ route. He will use the tasks most suited to the location and conditions.

教官/测评官会从这些练习中选出一些来测试候选教练。任务的准备和执行以及“脱离”路线都会被纳入评估范围。测评官会选择最适合考察地点和条件的任务。

Throughout this section the phrase ‘on the first attempt’ should not be taken to mean that you cannot make a seamanlike decision to break off at a reasonably early stage and try again. It merely means that once you have become committed to a task, it should be successfully completed.

本部分里“初次尝试”这个词语，不是理解为：你不能在执行操作的早期阶段中止任务，然后再次尝试。该词语的意思是说一旦你确定要正式执行任务，就要能够顺利完成。

5 Recover a capsized dinghy and sail away
正船并继续航行

- Recover the dinghy on the first attempt.
  在初次尝试时，就能将翻覆的小帆船正过来。
- No external help permitted.
  不允许外部协助。
- The recovery should be controlled and seamanlike.
  候选人要能控制好正船的全过程，就像一个熟练的水手。
- Ensure that the boat and the candidates are fully prepared for the event.
  确保候选人为测评已经做好了准备，而且培训用船适合进行该项测试。

Throughout the pre-entry sailing assessment, the Coach/Assessor will try to obtain an overall impression of your sailing ability and whether it is of the required RYA standard. As a result, you might technically fail one task and still pass the assessment. The Coach/Assessor may also take into account previous sailing experience.
在整个测评过程中，教官/测评官会对你的航行能力以及是否达到RYA的标准做一个整体评估。因此，你可能没有完成一项技术性的任务，但仍会通过测评。教练/测评官可能也会把你以前的航海经历作为测评结果的参考。

You should not attempt the pre-entry assessment without practising all the tasks in the boat in which you or the Assessor intends you to use to take the test, or one similar.

在参加测评前，一定要提前做好准备。在你或者测评员打算使用的船型或类似船型上练习所有可能的任务。

Finally, please remember that although the pre-entry is likely to be conducted in a double handed dinghy, the instructor course will include practical work in single handlers. All instructors are therefore expected to be capable of sailing the single handers commonly used within training centres such as Picos, Toppers and Lasers. Any instructor candidate unfamiliar with these boats is recommended to gain some experience of them prior to the training course.
最后，请记住虽然可能会在双人船上进行测评，但是教练培训课程包含在单人船上的实操。因此，所有的教练都应具备驾驶单人船的能力。在培训中心常用的单人船，例如Picos、Topper和激光。我们建议对这些船型不熟悉的候选人，在课程开始前，用自己不熟悉的船型多多练习。

RYA DINGHY/KEELBOAT/MULTIHULL INSTRUCTOR

RYA小帆船/龙骨船/多体船教练

It is possible to complete the National Sailing Scheme in dinghies, keelboats or multihulls. Therefore instructors teaching the scheme must be qualified for the type of boat in which they will be teaching i.e. only RYA Dinghy Instructors can teach in dinghies, and only RYA Keelboat Instructors can teach in keelboats although Dinghy Instructors can broaden their qualification to include keelboats and vice versa. The instructor certificate is endorsed accordingly and will also show whether the instructor is qualified to teach on inland or coastal waters (depending on where they completed the pre-entry sailing assessment and course).
可以采用小帆船、龙骨船或多体船完成国家航海计划的课程。因此，教授该计划课程的教练必须取得相应船型的教练资格证。即：只有取得RYA小帆船教练资格的教练才可以使用小帆船教学，取得RYA龙骨船教练资格的教练才可以使用龙骨船教学。当然，小帆船教练可以考取龙骨船教学的资格证，反之亦然。教练证书上会体现出新的认证资格，并且注明认证的教学水域是在内陆还是沿海（取决于候选人参加测评和课程的地点）。

Role 角色

- Competent, experienced sailor able to sail in strong winds.
  经验丰富、技术强的水手，能在强风条件下航行。
- Qualified powerboat handler to RYA Powerboat Level 2.
  持有RYA机动艇级别二的证书。
- Can teach in dinghies, keelboats or multihulls depending on previous experience and training.
  根据之前的经验和培训，教授小帆船、龙骨船或多体船。
- Can teach RYA National Sailing Scheme Levels 1, 2, 3, Seamanship Skills, Day Sailing, Sailing with Spinnakers (where appropriately experienced and approved by the centre principal) and Youth Sailing Scheme Stages 1-4.
  可教授RYA国家航海计划级别一、二、三的课程，以及航海技术技能、日间航行、球帆航行（需具备适当的经验以及培训中心负责人的许可）单元和青少年航海计划阶段1～4的课程。

Eligibility for the Training Course 参加培训资格

- Minimum age 16 (no candidates will be accepted for training under this age).
  最小年龄16岁（不接受低于此年龄的候选人）。
- A valid RYA First Aid certificate, or another acceptable first aid qualification as detailed on the RYA website (www.rya.org.uk/go/firstaidcertificates).
  有效的RYA急救证书或其他RYA接受的急救能力证明，详细信息可在RYA网站上查询（www.rya.org.uk/go/firstaidcertificates）。
- RYA Powerboat Level 2 certificate.
  RYA机动艇级别二证书。
- Pre-entry sailing assessment completed within one year prior to the instructor training course.
  在参加教练培训课程前一年内须通过航海技术测评。
- RYA membership.
  RYA会员。

Training 教练培训

Throughout your training, it is important to remember that the RYA teaching methods used have been developed successfully over many years. You will be introduced to some techniques which have become standardised because it is important that RYA instruction should follow broadly the same pattern in every training centre.

在整个培训过程中，请记住非常重要的一点：RYA的教学方法经过多年的实践与发展，已经形成了一套成功的教学方法。你将学习到的各种教学技能都是标准化的，因为RYA使每个RYA培训中心保持教学同步非常重要。

It is equally important, however, that you should not follow certain drills slavishly without considering that certain boats will require variations of the 'method'. Without scope for minor variations, there would be no room for development and improvement.

还有一点同等重要的是：不能盲目地按照既定的操作步骤来执行教学，要根据不同的船型调整教学。不能根据具体情况做出改善，就无法取得进步。

- Course staffed by RYA Coaches/Assessors.
  课程由RYA教官/测评官负责。
- Training includes teaching techniques ashore and afloat.
  培训包括岸上和水上教学技巧的教授。
- Course duration is normally 50hrs/5 days week but could be modular over a number of weekends or single days. This approach may actually take longer.
  课程时间通常为50个小时/一星期5天，也可以是几个周末或单独几天的课程。采用后者可能占用的时间更长。
- A list of courses running can be obtained from RYA HQ, RDOs and Regional Coaches.
  可以从RYA总部、区域发展负责人和区域教官获取课程列表。
- The structure and content of the National Sailing Scheme and Youth Sailing Scheme.
  国家航海计划和青少年航海计划的结构及内容。
- Training in RYA teaching methods to the Seamanship Skills Module including teaching those with special needs.
  RYA教学方法教授航海技术技能单元，包括教授有特殊需求的学员。
- Instructing techniques for adults and children.
  教授成年人和孩子的技巧。
- Preparation and presentation of a lesson.
  课程的前期准备和教授。
- Preparation and use of visual aids.
  可视化教具的准备和使用。
- The assessment of students' abilities.
  学员能力评估。
- A form of written paper (or oral test) covering teaching methods and background.
  包含教学方法和理论知识的书面材料（或口头测验）。
- The use of powered craft in a teaching environment.
  在教学环境中使用机动艇。
- Safeguarding, child protection, Health & Safety, and cold water shock.
  安全监管、儿童保护、健康与安全和冷水刺激。

Throughout the course, evidence of competence in these areas will be noted by the training Coach/Assessor and credited towards the candidate's final moderation/assessment.

在整个课程中，培训教官/测评官会考查候选人以上各方面的能力，其直接影响测评官最后的审核/测评。

Certificate Validity 证书有效期

- Instructor certificates valid for 5 years from date of issue if supported by a valid first aid certificate.
  在候选者持有有效急救证书的前提下，教练证从发证日起，有效期为五年。
- Certificates can be revalidated by obtaining and returning a completed revalidation form accompanied by a log of teaching experience in an RYA training centre, valid first aid certificate, valid RYA membership number.
  延长证书有效期的方法是：获取延期表格，将自己在RYA培训中心的教学经历填写完整，同时提交有效的急救证书和RYA会员号。
- A minimum of 30 hours' teaching experience is required.
  教学时长不得少于30个小时。
- Little or no logged experience may require a re-assessment to ensure the instructor is still up to date.
  对于教学少或教学经历没有记录在案的教练，为确保其教学水平，可能需要重新测评。
- Revalidation should normally include all existing instructor endorsements.
  延长有效期通常包括教练现有的所有认证。

RYA Instructor Course Moderation/Assessment 教练课程的审核/测评

Instructor courses are moderated by an outside moderator (coach/assessor) who has not been involved in the training. Their task is to confirm that all RYA standards expected on the course have been upheld by the training coach and the candidates and they will do this partly by observing the candidates deliver teaching in as realistic conditions as possible.

教练课程由没有介入过培训的外部审核员（教官/测评官）进行审核。他们的任务是确保教官和候选人在培训中都能达到RYA的标准。他们采取的一部分审核措施是，在一旁观察候选人在实际教学情境中的教学表现。

The moderation will follow the pattern below 审核须按照以下模式开展：

- Moderation will take place immediately following the training course.
  审核与培训课程应同步进行。
- Moderation elements will include practical teaching afloat, a teaching session ashore, teaching a land drill and giving a short 5 minutes presentation (optional).
  审核包括在水上的实践教学，一节岸上理论课，一次岸上教学和一次5分钟教学演讲（可选）。
- Your training coach will take the role of the Senior Instructor and outline the order of the day to you.
  你的培训教官会担任高级教练的角色，给你概述一天的流程。
- If possible, there may be 'real students' to teach.
  如可行，可在培训中安排"真正的学员"。
- If teaching in a double hander, it is likely that the moderator will join you in the boat.
  如在双人船上教学，审核员可能会和你一同上船。
- They are able to form an accurate opinion in a short time, so don't be concerned if they don't spend long with you.
  他们能在短时间内得出准确的判断，所以不必担心他们观察你的时间不长。
- In the unlikely event that a candidate is not considered ready to be moderated, a separate time for moderation will be suggested, along with an action plan.
  很少有候选人会被视为没有做好被审核的准备，如果有这种情况，审核员会建议进行另一次审核，并给你一个改善计划。

The moderator will be looking for 审核员的考查点：

- The ability to plan the session according to the needs of your students.
  根据学员需求计划课程的能力。
- A friendly, supportive manner towards your students, from their arrival to departure.
  从学员抵达直到学员离开，是否一直保持积极友好，支持学员的状态。
- Briefing and debriefing skills.
  培训前简述与培训后总结的能力。
- The boat rigged according to weather conditions and the abilities of your students.
  根据天气情况和学员的能力设置帆船。
- Adequate boat control at all times.
  始终保持对船的合理控制。
- Teaching according to the methods outlined on your course and in this book, progressing according to the students' abilities.
  根据课程类型和本书中的说明进行教学，根据学员的能力调整教学的难度。
- Correct positioning of instructor and students.
  教练和学员在教学时所处的位置是否正确。
- Successful demonstrations and clear explanations.
  成功的演示和清楚的说明。
- Correct diagnosis and tactful correction of students' faults.
  能够准确地判断学员的错误，并有分寸地纠正他们。

- Use of lying-to position for crew changes and briefings.
  利用飘帆停船来调换船员或进行简述。
- Running a safe session.
  课程安全。

It is far more natural for you to be teaching 'real students', usually beginners, than for another instructor or the moderator to play the role of a student, but if the latter is necessary the moderator will take account of the false situation.

对你来说，给真正的学员上课，比给教练或审核员扮演的学员上课要自然得多，但是如果只能适应后者，审核员会将这种模拟的因素考虑在内。

When beginners are used, the moderator will also be assessing you through their reaction, looking for the three key factors which are important for successful teaching:

如果是给真正的初学者上课，审核员会根据他们的反应来评估你的教学，有三个关键点对于成功教学至关重要：

- Are the students safe?
  学员安全吗？
- Are they enjoying themselves?
  他们开心吗？
- Are they learning anything valuable?
  他们学到有价值的东西了吗？

Although all these points are important, safety remains the highest priority.

虽然这三点都非常重要，但安全永远是首要考虑的。

Five Minutes Presentation 五分钟教学演讲

During the training course, candidates will have given a presentation on a topic chosen by the training coach and, prior to giving it, will have had training input on how best to deliver it. In order to achieve a definite outcome, the moderator may ask candidates to deliver a short presentation, possibly unprepared, on an aspect of sailing. Candidates may also be asked to deliver a presentation of this type if their initial presentation did not come up to the required standard.

在培训中，培训教官会给候选人指定一个题目，让候选人进行一次教学演讲。在教学前，教官会对候选人进行培训，教他们如何讲到最好。为了确认候选人的理论教学能力，审核员可能会要求候选人做一个跟帆船相关的简短教学演讲，这很有可能是没有事先让你准备的。如果第一次演讲没有达到标准，候选人可能会被要求进行第二次演讲。

Practical Demonstration of Land Drills 岸上练习演示

The moderator may expect you to cover land drills for aft and/or centre mainsheet boats. Before doing so, he will have discussed with your training coach the techniques used during the course, in case there are any local differences from the drills outlined in this handbook.

审核员可能会希望你用后置主缭和/或中置主缭的帆船演示岸上练习。在演示前，审核员会与你的培训教官商讨，确定在培训中应使用的技巧，了解可能存在的地区性差异，以及与本书的叙述不同之处。

The moderator is not trying to catch you out by minute attention to detail, but he will be looking for:

审核员不会锱铢必较地去抠每个细节，但是他会重点观察：

- A brief explanation of why drills are used.
  简要说明为什么要进行岸上练习。
- Adequate preparation (and explanation) of equipment.
  器材准备充足（器材讲解得当）。
- Good positioning of students.
  教学时，让学员站在适当的位置。
- Clear accurate demonstrations, both at normal speed and slowly with commentary, then again at normal speed.
  分别使用常速与慢速进行清晰准确的动作演示和口头讲解，最后再进行一次常速演示与口头讲解。
- Ability to identify and correct students' faults.
  识别并纠正学员错误的能力。

Overall Assessment 整体测评

It is usual for a number of candidates to be assessed on the same day and this will result in a period when you are not directly under the attention of the assessor, but he may still be keeping a distant eye on your work.
多名候选人在同一天进行测评的情况非常普遍。所以在某段时间内，你可能不在测评员的直接关注下。但是，他仍有可能在远处观察你。

Throughout the moderation, in addition to considering the detailed points outlined above, the moderator will be making an overall (or holistic) judgement, based on the criteria and measured against his experience of the sport. The qualities sought can be summarised as:
在整个审核的过程中，审核员除了关注以上所列的具体要点外，还会根据他自己对该项运动的经验和标准，做出整体判断。他关注的要点可总结为以下几条：

- Enthusiasm for the sport 对运动的热情；
- Confidence in the subject 对讲解主题的信心；
- Teaching ability 教学能力；
- Anticipation 预测；
- Awareness of safety throughout 自始至终的安全意识。

At some point he will seek comments from the training coach, who has been monitoring your progress throughout the course and so has a good idea of your ability. This will help the moderator to take account of any particular circumstances on the day.
在某些阶段，他会征寻培训教官的意见，因为培训教练在整个课程中一直在监督你的进展，对你的能力有更多的了解。这将会帮助审核员了解白天发生的特殊情况。

The moderator and training coach will review your performance with you. This debrief may include several more questions to ensure that you have sufficient understanding of different aspects of work as an instructor.
审核员和培训教官会跟你一起评价你的表现。他们可能会询问一些问题，确保你对教练这份工作的各方面能够充分地理解。

Finally, the training coach and moderator will confirm whether or not you have yet proved your competence as an RYA Instructor and complete the necessary paperwork. If for some reason the candidate is not entirely successful then an action plan will be drawn up and agreed to help overcome any gaps in knowledge or ability.
最后，培训教官和审核员会确认，你是否证明了自己具备RYA教练的能力，并且填写相关书面文件。如因某些原因，候选人没能完全通过测评，那么他们会给你拟定一个改善计划，帮助你提高在理论知识或能力上的不足。

If you disagree with the decision, they will discuss the possibility of a re-assessment or the procedure for appeal to the RYA.
如果你不认同最后的决定，他们会讨论重新测评的可能性，或者告知你向RYA申诉的流程。

RYA INSTRUCTOR ENDORSEMENTS RYA小帆船教练认证

An RYA Instructor can teach students the module Level 1 Start Sailing, Level 2 Basic Skills, Level 3 Better Sailing, and Seamanship Skills of the National Sailing Scheme, and Youth Sailing Scheme up to Stage 4. He can also teach Sailing with Spinnakers with the approval of the Principal and Day Sailing under the supervision of a coastal SI. The following endorsements are designed to extend the scope of an instructor's ability and will increase his value to the Principal of a training centre.
RYA小帆船教练可教授航海计划里的多种课程，包括级别一"航海起步"，级别二"基础技能"，级别三"进阶航海"和航海术技能单元，以及青少年航海计划第1～4阶段的课程。如取得航海中心负责人的许可，教练也可教授球帆课程；在有沿海水域教学认证的高级教练的监督下，教练可教授日间航行课程。以下认证的目的是为了拓展教练的能力范畴，提升他对于所在培训中心负责人的价值。

COASTAL ENDORSEMENT 沿海水域教学认证

Role 角色

- Instructors and Senior Instructors wishing to operate at a coastal venue must hold a coastal award.
  在沿海水域教课的教练及高级教练，必须持有沿海水域教学的证书。

- Mediterranean training centres are classified as coastal.
  地中海的培训中心属沿海水域。
- A coastal endorsement applies to all other instructor endorsements, including the Advanced Instructor award.
  沿海水域教学认证适用于所有教练，其中也包括高阶教练的认证。

Training/Assessment 培训/测评

- Candidates should apply to a coastal centre or their Regional Development Officer for details of courses.
  候选人须向沿海水域培训中心或当地的区域负责人获取课程的详细内容。
- Training/assessment will be given by an RYA Coach/Assessor either by:Two day training course with continuous assessment or 1 day assessment.
  培训/测评由一名RYA教官/测评官组织执行，或通过两天的培训课程和期间的连续测评或单独一整天的测评。
- Assessment will be based on the pre-entry skill test and sailing techniques on tidal waters.
  测评基于候选人的课前技能测试结果以及在潮汐水域的航行技能水平。

ADVANCED INSTRUCTOR ENDORSEMENT 高阶教练认证

The Advanced Instructor (ADI) must have the background knowledge, technical ability and skills to demonstrate any of the Sailing with Spinnakers or Performance Sailing techniques. Teaching people how to sail performance boats requires a subtle change in the attitude of the instructor. There are many different skills to learn from a coaching point of view. While many people will wish to receive coaching or instruction in race standard Wayfarers or GP14s, many of the newer boats will be a lot faster, so an appropriate coaching style will be required. While students will know the basic skills required to get the boat from A to B, instructors have to be able to analyse their performance, give positive feedback and coach them progressively. ADIs must be confident in sailing the boats in which they are coaching so they can provide effective demonstrations.

高阶教练必须具有充足的理论知识储备和达到一定标准的专业技术技能，能够展示“球帆航行”或“高阶航海”单元的任何技能水平。教授学员驾驶高性能帆船，需要教练在教学态度上做一些改变。从教练的角度来说，学员有很多不同的技能要学习。但是，对于大多数学员来说，有的人想接受标准赛船Wayfarers或GP14s的培训，有的人可能更喜欢接受新型的快速帆船的培训。所以，教练应根据不同的船型调整自己的教学风格。这个阶段的学员已经具备了将船从A航行到B的基本技巧，高阶教练要能够分析他们的表现，给出积极的反馈，让他们不断地进步。高级教练要对自己教学的船型有充分的自信，这样才能做出高效的展示。

There are a number of areas that the ADIs' endorsement will focus on.
关于高阶教练的认证，有几个方面须重点关注。

Role 角色

- An Advanced Instructor is an experienced instructor with a broad background of sailing experience.
  高阶教练须具备丰富的教学经验和航海经历。
- Has been trained to teach Performance Sailing and Sailing with Spinnakers from the RYA National Sailing Scheme.
  接受过（RYA国家航海计划）“高阶航海”和“球帆航行”单元的教学培训。

Eligibility 资格

- Candidates will hold the RYA Instructor certificate.
  候选人持有RYA小帆船教练证。
- Have at least 1 season's teaching experience.
  至少有一个航海季度的教学经验。
- Possess skills to at least the Performance Sailing and Sailing with Spinnakers modules.
  至少具备“高阶航海”和“球帆航行”这两个单元的航海技能。
- Will have powerboat handling skills in a teaching environment.
  具备在教学环境中驾驶机动船的技能。

Training/Assessment 培训/测评

- Candidates should apply to their Regional Development Officer for details of courses.
  候选人须向当地区域负责人获取课程信息。
- Attend a two day training/continuous assessment course covering the following content:
  参加一个为期两天/连续测评的课程，内容包括：
- Performance boat handling, spinnaker handling, 5 essentials coaching, use of powerboats.
  高性能帆船操作、球帆操作、航行五要素教学、机动艇的使用。
- The course may include a theory test.
  课程可能包含理论测试。
- A certificate will be issued by the RYA upon successful completion.
  成功完成课程后，RYA会给教练颁发证书。

DINGHY/KEELBOAT/MULTIHULL ENDORSEMENT

小帆船/龙骨船/多体船教学认证

Role 角色

Instructors who completed their initial training course and assessment in one boat discipline, but who subsequently want to instruct in another, should obtain these endorsements.

已完成了一种船型的培训课程和测评的教练，如希望有资质教授其他船型，应取得相应的认证。

- Candidates should apply to their Regional Development Officer for details of courses.
  候选人应向当地区域发展负责人获取课程信息。
- Training will be given by an authorised RYA Coach/Assessor.
  由一名RYA教官/测评官进行培训。
- Candidates will attend a two day training/assessment course during which they will be asked to demonstrate pre-entry test skills and teaching techniques in the new discipline.
  候选人须参加一次为期两天的包含培训和测评的课程，在此期间，候选人也要进行课前测评，并演示操作相应船型的教学技巧。
- A certificate will be issued by the RYA upon successful completion.
  成功完成课程后，RYA会给教练颁发证书。

Eligibility 资格

- Candidates will hold the RYA Dinghy/Keelboat/Multihull Instructor certificate.
  候选人须持有RYA小帆船/龙骨船/多体船的教练资格证。
- Have at least one season's teaching experience.
  至少有一个季度的教学经验。
- Possess skills to at least the Seamanship and Sailing with Spinnakers modules.
  至少具备"航海技术"和"球帆航行"这两个单元的航海技能。
- Will have powerboat handling skills in a teaching environment.
  具备在教学环境中，驾驶机动艇的技能。

Training/Assessment 培训/测评

- A pre-entry assessment with appropriate modifications for each boat discipline will be included.
  每一种船型对应的课前测评。
- Attend a 2 day training/continuous assessment course.
  参加一个为期两天/连续测评的课程。
- The course may include a theory test.
  培训可能会包括一次理论测验。

- A certificate will be issued by the RYA upon successful completion.
  成功完成课程后，RYA会给教练颁发证书。

RACING INSTRUCTOR ENDORSEMENT(RACING COACH LEVEL 1) 竞赛教练认证(一级竞赛教练)

The majority of dinghy sailing in Britain takes place in clubs; most clubs organise racing which is a main focus of their activities. Many people learn to sail each year but can be put off the sport when faced for the first time with the apparent complexities of club racing.

在英国，大多数的小帆船活动都是在俱乐部进行的，而且大部分俱乐部都会把竞赛作为其主要活动。每年都会有大量的学员开始学帆船，但是在他们参加完第一次帆船赛后，可能会因为觉得比赛很复杂，而打消继续学帆船的积极性。

The Racing Instructor course is designed to enable instructors to introduce relatively inexperienced sailors to club racing. All RYA Instructor courses should include approximately half a day of practical training in the subject.

竞赛教练课程的目的是让教练具备足够的将帆船比赛介绍给经验相对较少的学员的能力。所有RYA的教练课程包括半天左右的竞赛实践训练。

Role 角色

This endorsement can be obtained by instructors with experience of club racing who wish to teach racing skills through the Start Racing module of the RYA sailing schemes. Racing Instructors with sufficient personal racing experience will also be permitted to teach the Intermediate and Advanced Racing courses.

有俱乐部比赛经验，且希望教授RYA航海计划中“初级竞赛”单元课程的教练可获得竞赛教练认证。个人比赛经验丰富的竞赛教练如经许可，也可教授中级和高级竞赛课程。

Eligibility 资格

RYA Instructors who have experience of club racing (minimum completed 9 races plus assisted race officer) may qualify during their instructor training course. Alternatively, qualified instructors may undertake further training at a later date with a Coach/Assessor.

有俱乐部比赛经验（至少参加过9场比赛，并曾协助过赛事官）的RYA教练可能在教练培训课程期间，取得竞赛教练资格。或者获得认证的教练，可能会需要教官/测评官在之后进行进一步的培训。

Training/Assessment 培训/测评

The one day course will include the organisation of club racing, preparation and management of the Start Racing course and instructional techniques afloat including the use of race training exercises. On successful completion, a record card will be completed by an RYA Coach/Assessor and sent to the RYA. Assessment is continuous.

一天的课程包括俱乐部竞赛的组织，“初级竞赛”课程的前期准备和管理，以及水上教学技巧和竞赛培训练习的运用。顺利完成此课程后，RYA的教官/测评官会填写候选人的培训记录卡，并提交给RYA。培训中会有连续测评。

The course should include the following characteristics:

这项课程应包含以下特征：

- An emphasis on racing as fun.
  强调比赛的趣味性。
- Ensuring that starts and rules are not intimidating.
  不因为严格的起航要求和相关规则而使人望而却步。
- The provision of enough information for Level 2/3 standard sailors to get round a club racing course safely, without presenting a hazard to other sailors.
  给级别二和级别三的学员提供足够的信息，确保她/他们能安全地完成俱乐部的一般比赛航线，且不会威胁到其他参赛者的安全。

- Encouragement to sailors to start racing, join a club and progress within the sport.
  鼓励学员去参加比赛，加入俱乐部，提高自己的航海技能。

RACING COACH LEVEL 2 二级竞赛教练

Role 角色

A qualified RYA Racing Coach Level 2 is a good club racer with personal knowledge of club and/or regional racing and a broad basis of coaching skills. They will be able to deliver Start, Intermediate and Advanced Racing where appropriate, working at affiliated clubs or recognised training centres.

RYA二级竞赛教练必须具备良好的俱乐部竞技水平，对俱乐部和/或者地区范围内的比赛有良好的认识，同时也具备各种基础的教学技能。其能够在RYA附属俱乐部或认证中心教授“初级、中级和高级竞赛”的培训课程。

Eligibility 资格

- Appropriate racing experience (guide = good club racer).
  拥有一定的比赛经验（例如，良好的俱乐部竞技水平）。
- Appropriate current racing knowledge (classes/pathways).
  对现今的比赛有一定的认识（ 帆船级别/进阶体系 ）。
- RYA Powerboat Level 2 certificate.
  持有RYA机动艇级别二的证书。
- A valid RYA First Aid certificate, or another acceptable first aid qualification as detailed on the RYA website (www.rya.org.uk/go/firstaidcertificates).
  持有有效的RYA急救证书或在RYA官网上列出的其他可接受的急救证书。(www.rya.org.uk/go/firstaidcertificates)
- Minimum age 16. Level 2 Coaches aged under 18 should be appropriately supervised by an adult who is either a Senior Instructor or a Racing Coach Level 2 or above.
  二级竞赛教练最小年龄为16岁。小于18岁的二级竞赛教练，须在成年的高级教练或二级及以上级别的竞赛教练监督下进行教学。
- Previous instructing experience is preferred but is not essential if the candidate has suitable alternative experience.
  有教学经验者优先，但如果候选人有适当的其他经验也可。

Training/Assessment 培训/测评

The course to become an RYA Racing Coach Level 2 is an intense weekend/two days course looking at the theory of coaching and applying it in a practical series of on the water exercises.

RYA二级竞赛教练培训课程强度很大，时间为2天/周末。课程主要包括教学理论，以及在水上实践课程中的应用。

Each candidate will be expected to run complete sessions including a brief, on the water exercises with feedback and a debrief. The aim of the course is to provide candidates with skills and techniques to coach racing to youth and adult sailors. Assessment is continuous.

每个候选人都要进行一些不同的练习，每个练习都包括下水前简述、水上训练和反馈以及总结。该课程的目标是培训候选人的竞赛教学技能技巧，让他们具备教授青少年和成年人竞赛的能力。培训期间会有连续测评。

Revalidation 证书延期

Racing Coaches are requested to revalidate every 5 years to ensure their continued effectiveness as a coach.
竞赛教练每五年须申请资格证延期，以确保竞赛教学资格的持续有效性。

- Complete the Revalidation Form on the Racing Coaches section of the RYA website and send it to:
  在RYA官网上填写竞赛教练资格证的延期申请表，并邮寄至：Racing Department, RYA House, Ensign Way, Hamble, Southampton, Hants SO31 4YA

You also need to send a copy of:A valid First Aid certificate.
连同一份有效的急救证书复印件。

- To see if your first aid certificate is valid go to:
  查看急救证书是否有效，请登录下面的网站：

http://www.rya.org.uk/coursestraining/resources/Pages/Firstaidandmedical.aspx

RYA SENIOR INSTRUCTOR RYA高级教练

The Principal of an RYA Training Centre carries the formal responsibility for ensuring that all training complies with RYA guidelines, laid down in the current Guidance Notes for inspection of RYA Recognised Training Centres. The Principal may himself be a Senior Instructor or may appoint a Senior Instructor to act as sailing manager, and to ensure that sailing tuition is organised according to RYA methods and standards.
RYA培训中心负责人的职责是确保所在培训中心的所有培训都符合RYA的指导方针。RYA指导方针列在最新的指引摘要中以供RYA认可的培训中心查阅。负责人本人可能也是一名高级教练，或者他可以任命一名高级教练来担任经理，确保所有的教学都依照RYA的方法和标准进行。

The qualities required of a Senior Instructor are patience, resourcefulness, and the ability to deal with students and instructors. SIs should also have the organisational ability to ensure that courses are safe, enjoyable, and informative.
高级教练应具备的素质：耐心、足智多谋、知道如何应对学员及其他教练，除此之外还应具备一定的组织能力，确保课程的安全性、趣味性及内容的充实性。

Quite apart from his responsibility to his students, the Senior Instructor has a responsibility to his instructors, to his club or employer and the RYA.
高级教练除了要对学员负责以外，也要对手下的教练、其所在俱乐部或雇主以及RYA负责。

Senior Instructor training is a combination of teaching and work experience. Courses are organised on a regional basis with minimum numbers in order to bring together candidates with a variety of backgrounds and instructing experience.
高级教练课程是培训与工作相结合的。课程是根据地区的不同来组织的，应达到人数下限，要能使不同背景，不同教学经验的候选人共同参与。

The course may be split into two weekends or a number of days, with the separate sessions being run at different centres within a region. This gives candidates the opportunity of working at different places and hence being introduced to different operational problems.
本课程可分成两个周末或几天在同一地区的各培训中心开展。这样可以给候选人在不同地方工作的机会，从而使他们了解各培训中心的运营情况。

Those wishing to apply for a SI course should do so to their Regional Development Officer, who will have information regarding where courses are being run in their particular region. They will group together applicants in order to ensure that the course runs. The course will only run if there are sufficient candidates to make it viable.
有意愿参加高级教练课程的教练应向区域发展负责人提出申请，负责人知道在本地区的哪些地方会开这个课程。他们会把申请人集中在一起，本课程只有学员数量满足人数下限才能开课。

Once accepted, the candidate will receive the ‘SI workbook’. This must be completed before attending the course as well as any preparation set by the training coaches. Failure to do so will have a direct effect on the outcome.
一旦申请通过了，候选人会拿到一本《高级教练工作手册》，并需要做一些培训教官布置的前期准备工作，且必须在开课前完成。如未能完成，将会直接影响认证结果。

An RYA recognised dinghy/keelboat/multihull training centre must have a current Senior Instructor as its Principal or Chief Instructor.
在RYA认证的小帆船/龙骨船/多体船培训中心，必须有一名高级教练担任负责人或主教练。

Role 角色

The SI is an experienced instructor who has been trained and assessed to be competent in the following areas:
高级教练要经验丰富，经过培训和测评，能够胜任以下各方面的工作：

- Organise and manage RYA National Sailing Scheme and Youth Sailing Scheme sailing courses.
  组织并管理RYA航海计划和青少年航海计划课程。
- Organise and control group sailing tuition of all ages and abilities.
  组织并管理好所有年龄段和所有级别课程的教学。
- Supervising, directing and assisting a team of Instructors and Assistant Instructors.
  监督、指导并协助教练和助教团队。

Eligibility 资格

Candidates must first be an RYA Dinghy/Keelboat/Multihull Instructor and must fulfil the following criteria before taking part in the Senior Instructor training course:
首先，候选人必须是RYA认证的小帆船/龙骨船/多体船教练，并且在参加高级教练培训课程前，满足以下条件：

- Correct teaching ratios.
  正确的教学比例。
- Correct student/instructor matching (father/son, husband/wife).
  学员与教练的正确搭配（父子、夫妻）。
- Group control ashore and afloat.
  管理好岸上和在水上的活动。
- The ‘house rules’ of the centre including equipment stowage.
  培训中心的“家规”应说明设备的存放。
- Safe slipway and launching procedures.
  安全的下水坡道及船只下水流程。
- Safe and effective use of safety boats and their allocation.
  安全而有效地使用安全艇及其合理的分配。
- Ensuring all staff including visiting ones know what is expected of them.
  确保所有职员和访客都了解培训中心的要求。
- Students learning, content and pace of sessions.
  学员的学习、培训内容和节奏。
- An awareness of weather conditions and calling a halt to on-water activities.
  有留意天气情况的意识，在必要时暂停水上活动。
- Alternative teaching programme in the event of adverse weather (high/no wind).
  在不利天气（强风或无风）情况下，用其他活动代替。
- In the case of postponement, re-programming staff and facilities.
  在工作推迟情况下，重新组织安排员工工作和设备。
- The SI should have an overall awareness of what is happening on the water amongst all the fleets operating to anticipate potential problems and avoid them.
  高级教练应全面掌控水上所有船只的活动，预测潜在问题并及时采取措施。

Before each practical session, the SI must be confident that each of his instructors has a clear idea of the aim and purpose of that session, so that they can confirm that the aims have been met during the debriefing.

在每次实操课开始前，高级教练要能确定每名教练都对自己的课程目标非常清楚。这样在总结时，教练就能明确是否达到课程目标。

It should already be clear that an SI has a great deal of responsibility, relying on resourcefulness to solve problems as they arise. Apart from directing the work of instructors, the SI should assist and support them, particularly when they need advice. The following summary of brief questions might provoke further thoughts. How should these be answered?

很明确的一点是，高级教练需要承担多种责任，问题出现时，要依靠自己的才智来解决。除了安排教练的工作外，高级教练还应协助并支持初级教练，尤其是当他们需要建议的时候。下面总结了一些问题，可能会启发你的思考。应该如何回答这些问题呢？

Ten Questions from Instructors 教练十问

1. One of my students is learning far more quickly that the others. What do I do?
   课上有一名学员比其他学员学得都快，我应该怎么办呢？
2. It's blowing Force 5 out there, what do I do? (Day 2 of a beginner's course)
   风力5级，怎么办？（初学者课程第二天）
3. What should I do with my hands when I'm lecturing?
   教学时，手放在哪里好？
4. You've asked me in to cover for Robin whilst he's away, how do I know what his students have covered so far? (Third day of a Seamanship course)
   罗宾请假了，由我帮他代课，我如何了解他的学员学到了什么程度？（航海技术技能课程第三天）
5. How do I tell when my students are ready to move on to the next stage of the syllabus?
   我该如何判断我的学员是否准备好了进入下一阶段的教学？
6. Bob and Sally say they're too old to take part in the capsize drill. What can I tell them?
   鲍勃和萨利说，他们年龄太大无法参与正船练习。我该怎么跟他们说？
7. What do I do if three of my Toppers capsize at once?
   如果教学时有三条船同时翻了，我该怎么办？

8. Why should I shave? (From a 22-year-old male instructor.)
我为什么要刮胡子? (问题出自一名22岁的男教练)
9. Why should I bother with the kill cord on the outboard? It only gets in the way.
为什么在驾驶发动机外挂的救生艇时，要用安全绳? 这东西让我在船上行动很不方便。
10. How do I teach Jenny to sail? She's only got one hand.
我如何教授珍妮学帆船? 她身体有缺陷，只有一只手。

Some of those questions should never arise, but instructors will always look to the SI for advice. **This should be encouraged.** Even though they should know the answers, the SI must treat questions from instructors in just the same way that they should treat questions from students. It could be considered that instructors are also the SI's customers.

这其中有些问题根本就不需要问，但是教练们总是会希望向高级教练寻求建议。高级教练应鼓励教练们多提问。即使教练们理应知道答案，但是当他们问起时，高级教练必须像对待学员一样为他们解答。高级教练应把教练们也当作自己的顾客。

Catastrophe Clinic 灾难诊所

One of the advantages of a large Senior Instructor course is that it brings together candidates with a wide, varied collective experience of teaching sailing. One useful way of sharing that experience is by the exercise known as Catastrophe Clinic.

人数多的高级教练课程有一个很大的优势，就是能将拥有各种不同帆船教学经验的候选人聚集到一起。有一种让大家可以共享这些经验的练习方法，该方法叫作灾难诊疗法。

Each candidate writes a short outline of the worst things which have happened to them whilst teaching sailing. The outline should contain details of:

每个候选人简要写出在教学时遇到的最严重的情况。其中应包括以下细节:

- The type of venue (inland, estuary, open sea). 教学区域类型（内河、河口、开放海域）。
- The size of fleet and type of boats. 船数和船型。
- The number of students and the level of course. 学员数量和课程级别。
- The number of instructors and teaching or rescue boats. 教练数量以及教练艇或救生艇数量。
- What happened. 事情发生的经过。

The group leader then collects all the examples and introduces them one by one for group discussion, with the author of each scenario remaining silent when his 'catastrophe' is discussed.

由小组长将所有的事件收集起来，逐一介绍给大家，然后进行小组讨论。在讨论某一名教练的“灾难”时，该教练应保持沉默。

After the group has discussed the problem and decided what they would have done in the circumstances, the author then explains what he actually did and why.
在讨论完问题并商议出解决办法后，由该事件教练说明情况发生时他是如何处理的，以及这样处理的原因。

Some problems may result from the unexpected behaviour of instructors or students and will call upon the SI's resources of tact and diplomacy in finding a solution.

有些问题可能是由于教练或学员的一些意外行为导致的。这时，就需要高级教练运用自己的处事技巧和手段迅速地找出解决方法。

The real epics usually result from not one single problem but a string of circumstances, each one of which on its own might not have been so serious. The horror of multiple capsizes in deteriorating weather conditions, possibly with dangerous lee shore or commercial shipping nearby, calls for clear thinking to establish priorities and act decisively. The two Golden Rules in such circumstances are:

意外的发生往往不是因为某一个问题，而是由一系列看似没有严重后果的小问题造成的。在恶劣天气下，多条船倾覆的情况是很棘手的，如果是发生在背风岸或者周围有商船时就更麻烦了。这就需要高级教练思路清晰，当机立断，判断事情的优先次序，果断行动。这种情况发生时，有两条黄金法则:

- **Count heads** 清点人数;
- **Save people before property.** 先救人，再救物。

One recurring theme, which is not highlighted above, is that of the student with a health problem, either unknown or undisclosed. Examples range from the teenage diabetic on a residential course who forgets his medication in the excitement of the activity, to the middle aged man who suffers a suspected heart attack during a capsize recovery session and the woman who collapses in the hot shower after sailing, for reasons totally

unconnected with the activity.
有一个常见的问题上文未强调，就是学员的健康问题，学员可能不知情，或未被诊断出来。比如，问题小的，患有糖尿病的孩子，报的是寄宿课程，由于参加活动太兴奋，忘记吃药；问题严重的，中年人在正船时，疑似心脏病突发。还有女学员在洗热水澡时，突然晕倒。事情发生的原因有可能与参加的活动毫无关联。
All have specific lessons for the Senior Instructor but the overall message is that the SI in control of the group must know of any health problems. The usual way of finding out is to require all students to complete a health declaration.
高级教练可以从以上所列举的事件中，学到很多经验，但是总的来说，负责某一团队的高级教练必须清楚学员的所有健康问题。最常用的方法是要求所有的学员填写健康声明。

Senior Instructor Assessment 高级教练测评

Throughout your SI course you will be assessed on your ability to plan, organise and run practical sessions, and on your input to shorebased sessions. In particular, the training coaches are looking for:
在整个高级教练课程中，测评官会考查候选人计划、组织和执行实践课程的能力，以及岸上教学水平。培训教练会特别关注以下方面：

- Aims clearly stated (did the session have clear objectives?).
  清晰地阐明教学目标（学员们都知道你对他们的要求吗？）。
- Briefing was complete and clear (did the group know what was required?).
  活动前的简述清晰完整（学员们清楚你的要求吗？）。
- Sailing area identified. 明确航行区域。
- Could the leader be clearly identified? 学员能很容易就认出你来吗?
- That the whole group was involved. 团队共同参与。
- Enthusiasm was maintained. 保持热情。
- Problems were solved. 解决问题。
- Signals (two way) were established including ‘Abandon.
  建立（双向）信号，包括“终止”。
- On-water coaching took place. 水上教学的开展。
- Group control was maintained (no unnecessary delays) ashore and afloat.
  在岸上和水上都能管理好学员（没有不必要的延误）。
- Each student was carefully debriefed and problems discussed and solved.
  仔细地对每个学员的表现进行总结，讨论并解决他们的问题。
- Session achieved all objectives.达成所有的课程目标。
- Students’ questions were answered. 解答学员提出的所有问题。
- Students were informed of their successes. The follow-on session was described.
  表扬学员们做得好的地方，并简要说明后续课程。
- The equipment was carefully put away after the session.
  课程结束后，设备应小心收起。

Good Relationships with Others 建立良好的关系

In addition, the training coaches will be applying an assessment based on their experience of the RYA Coaching Scheme to decide whether the candidate meets the requirements of a Senior Instructor. If they are unable to confirm that they have successfully completed the course, the Coaches will outline the reasons for that decision and an action plan will be set for future success.
另外，培训教官将根据他们对RYA教学计划的经验对学员们进行测评，决定候选人是否符合高级教练的标准。如果教官觉得候选人没有达到要求，他们会说明理由，并为学员制订改善计划，使学员能在下次顺利通过测评。

RYA COACH/ASSESSOR 教官/测评官

An RYA Coach/Assessor is an experienced Senior Instructor with an Advanced Instructor Endorsement who has been trained and assessed as competent to themselves train and assess Instructors and Senior Instructors, and appointed to deliver such training by the RYA Chief Instructor. Coaches/Assessors are appointed on an annual basis, and attend a reassessment every five years.

RYA教官/测评官一定是资深的高级教练，而且其通过了高阶教练的认证，并且已通过了拓展培训和测评，证明了他们具有培训和评估初级教练和高级教练的能力。由RYA主教练指派进行小帆船教练的培训与测评。

Eligibility 资格

A Senior Instructor with proven ability and extensive experience of the National Sailing Scheme and Youth Sailing Scheme in a variety of training centres. These qualities are expected to include a thoroughly competent level of personal sailing ability, good teaching, motivating and leadership skills, good fleet management, excellent coaching skills and a positive enthusiastic approach based on good communication skills.

首先，候选人必须是高级教练，并且其能力得到了认可，有大量在多个培训中心教授"国家航海计划"和"青少年航海计划"课程的经验。候选人须具备的能力包括：优秀的航海技能，良好的教学水平，激励并领导他人的能力，优秀的船只管理能力，出色的教授技能和良好的沟通技巧，且总是保持积极热情的态度。

A mature approach is necessary. Training candidate instructors can be a challenging business, demanding delicate judgement.

成熟的沟通方法十分必要。培训候选教练是一项高难度的工作，需要测评官时刻保持敏锐的判断力。

Regional Development Officers and Regional Coaches nominate potential Coaches/Assessors to the RYA Chief Instructor.

区域发展负责人和教官向RYA主教练提名有潜力的教官/测评官候选人。

Coaches/Assessors based overseas are occasionally trained where a requirement can be demonstrated. In this case the first approach should be to the RYA HQ.

RYA有时会组织进行非英国国籍教官/测评官的培训。这种情况应直接向RYA总部申请。

It is a requirement to be an RYA member on application and for the duration of your appointment.

申请人在提交申请以及被任命阶段都必须是RYA的会员。

Preparation/Selection (2 days) 准备/选拔（两天）

Candidates should be able to:

候选人应具备：

- Demonstrate and teach any part of the National Sailing Scheme including all the modules.
  演示并且教授国家航海计划所有模块里的任何内容。
- Sail competently in a variety of boats including single handers and high performance craft.
  能够出色地驾驶各种船型，包括单人船和高性能帆船。
- Plan and manage a course involving sessions ashore and afloat.
  计划并管理一次课程，包含岸上和水上的培训。
- Demonstrate effective safety boat and coach boat skills.
  演示驾驶安全艇和教练艇进行教学的技能。
- Give a formal presentation including the use of visual aids, and chair a discussion.
  利用教具，做一次正式的教学演讲，并主持一次讨论。
- Show enthusiasm, motivation and leadership.
  展现积极热情、激励人心的特质以及领导力。

Training Course 培训课程

The five-days training course will include:

五天的培训包括以下内容：

- The skills of teaching and assessing RYA Instructors.
  教授和评估RYA教练的技能。
- The RYA National Sailing Scheme and Youth Sailing Scheme and standards required for instructional awards.
  RYA国家航海计划和青少年航海计划，以及获得教练认证的标准。

- Administration of the scheme.
  航海计划里涉及的行政内容。
- Advanced seamanship techniques.
  高级航海术。
- High performance sailing.
  高阶航海技能。
- Teaching students with special needs, safeguarding and child protection.
  特殊学员教学，安全防护及儿童保护。

Apprenticeship 实习期

Candidates who complete the training course successfully will normally be expected to organise and run their first instructor course with the help and mentoring of a more experienced Coach/Assessor. On successful completion of this they will be appointed as an RYA Coach/Assessor.

通常在候选人成功完成课程后，须在一名经验更丰富的教官/测评官的帮助和监督下，组织并执行自己的第一个教练课程。成功完成本课程后，候选人就正式成为RYA的教官/测评官。

Coaches/Assessors wishing to train Instructors in other boat disciplines such as keelboat or multihull should normally have suitable experience and/or the relevant instructor endorsement.

如果教官/测评官想使用其他船型来培训教练，例如龙骨船或多体船，通常需要有此类船型的驾驶经验，和/或者相关的教练资格证。

Coaches/Assessors wishing to become RYA Training Centre Inspectors should attend a one-day training course organised by the RYA.

教官/测评官如希望成为RYA培训中心的巡视官，则须参加由RYA组织的为期一天的培训。

Coach/Assessor Updating
教官/测评官进修

After five years Coaches/Assessors must attend a practical revalidation organised by the RYA. An update will be delivered on changes to the schemes as well as giving an opportunity to feed back to the RYA. The day will also include an assessment of your ability and current knowledge in the following areas to a role-model delivery:

被任命五年后，教官/测评官需参加一次由RYA组织的证书延期实践培训。将更新关于航海计划的改进，并给予教官们一个向RYA反馈的机会。培训日也将包含一次对于教官能力和现阶段知识的实际展示测评，测评内容包括：

- Techniques for teaching and assessing instructors.
  教授和评估教练的技巧。
- Peer-to-peer reviewing.
  同行互评。
- Delivery of a practical, on-water session.
  实际讲解一次在水上的课程。
- Personal sailing ability.
  个人航海能力。
- Powerboat discipline and role-model delivery.
  机动艇纪律和作为榜样式的实际授课。

WHO TEACHES WHAT IN THE RYA NATIONAL SAILING SCHEME AND YOUTH SAILING SCHEME RYA国家航海计划及青少年航海计划课程与教练对照表

	National Sailing Scheme in dinghies 国家航海计划小帆船项目	National Sailing Scheme in keelboats 国家航海计划龙骨船项目	National Sailing Scheme in multihulls 国家航海计划多体船项目	Youth Sailing Scheme 青少年航海计划
Dinghy Instructor 小帆船教练	Levels 1, 2, 3, Day Sailing, Seamanship Skills, Sailing with Spinnakers* 级别一、二、三，日间航行，航海技术技能，球帆航行*			Stages 一、二、三、四 in dinghies 小帆船课程第一、二、三、四阶段
Keelboat Instructor 龙骨船教练		Levels 1, 2, 3, Day Sailing, Seamanship Skills, Sailing with Spinnakers* 级别一、二、三，日间航行，航海技术技能，球帆航行*		Stages 1, 2, 3, 4 in keelboats 龙骨船课程第一、二、三、四阶段

	国家航海计划 小帆船项目	国家航海计划 龙骨船项目	国家航海计划 多体船项目	青少年 航海计划
Multihull Instructor 多体船教练			Levels 1, 2, 3, Day Sailing, Seamanship Skills, Sailing with Spinnakers* 级别一、二、三、四日间航行，航海技术技能，球帆航行*	Stages 1, 2, 3, 4in multihulls 多体船课程第一、二、三、四阶段
Advanced Instructor 高阶教练	As Dinghy Instructor plus Sailing with Spinnakers, Performance Sailing 小帆船教练培训，以及球帆航行和高阶航海	As Keelboat Instructor plus Sailing with Spinnakers and Performance Sailing 龙骨船教练培训，以及球帆航行和高阶航海	As Multihull Instructor plus Sailing with Spinnakers and Performance Sailing 多体船教练培训，以及球帆航行和高阶航海	As Dinghy Instructor plus Sailing with Spinnakers, Performance Sailing 小帆船教练培训，以及球帆航行和高阶航海
Senior Instructor 高级教练	As Dinghy Instructor plus Sailing with Spinnakers 小帆船教练培训，以及球帆航行	As Keelboat instructor plus Sailing with Spinnakers 龙骨船教练培训，以及球帆航行	As Multihull Instructor plus Sailing with Spinnakers 多体船教练培训，以及球帆航行	As Dinghy Instructor plus Sailing with Spinnakers 小帆船教练培训，以及球帆航行
Racing Instructor/ Racing Coach Level 1 竞赛教练/一级竞赛教练	As Dinghy Instructor plus Start Racing, Intermediate Racing, Advanced Racing* 小帆船教练培训，以及初级、中级和高级竞赛课程*	As Keelboat Instructor plus Start Racing, Intermediate Racing, Advanced Racing* 龙骨船教练培训，以及初级、中级和高级竞赛课程*	As Multihull Instructor plus Start Racing, Intermediate Racing, Advanced Racing* 多体船教练培训，以及初级、中级和高级竞赛课程*	As Dinghy Instructor plus Start Racing, Intermediate Racing, Advanced Racing* 小帆船教练培训，以及初级、中级和高级竞赛课程*
Racing Coach Level 2 二级竞赛教练	Start Racing, Intermediate Racing, Advanced Racing 初级、中级和高级竞赛课程	Start Racing, Intermediate Racing, Advanced Racing 初级、中级和高级竞赛课程	Start Racing, Intermediate Racing, Advanced Racing 初级、中级和高级竞赛课程	Start Racing, Intermediate Racing, Advanced Racing 初级、中级和高级竞赛课程
Racing Coach Level 3 三级竞赛教练	Start Racing, Intermediate Racing, Advanced Racing 初级、中级和高级竞赛课程	Start Racing, Intermediate Racing, Advanced Racing 初级、中级和高级竞赛课程	Start Racing, Intermediate Racing, Advanced Racing 初级、中级和高级竞赛课程	Start Racing, Intermediate Racing, Advanced Racing 初级、中级和高级竞赛课程
RYA Coach/ Assessor 竞赛教官/测评官	All NSS and YSS courses plus Dinghy Instructor/ SI Courses and endorsements 所有NSS和YSS课程，以及小帆船教练/高级教练员课程和认证	All NSS and YSS courses plus Keelboat Instructor/ SI Courses and endorsements 所有NSS和YSS课程，以及龙骨船教练/高级教练课程和认证	All NSS and YSS courses plus Multihull Instructor/ SI Courses and endorsements 所有NSS和YSS课程，以及多体船教练/高级教练课程和认证	All NSS and YSS courses plus Dinghy Instructor/ SI Courses and endorsements 所有NSS和YSS课程，以及小帆船教练/高级教练员课程和认证

*Instructor who is suitably experienced and approved by the Principal or Chief Instructor.
*课程由拥有适当经验，且经航海中心负责人或主教练许可的教练负责。
A dinghy Senior Instructor holding RYA Day Skipper Practical or above may teach and supervise the NSS in keelboats.
拥有RYA日间船长（水上实践认证）或以上资格的小帆船高级教练，可教授或监督龙骨船的NSS课程。
N.B. All RYA tuition should be supervised by an RYA Senior Instructor.
注意：所有RYA的课程都应在RYA高级教练监督下进行。

TEACHING RATIOS WITHIN THE NATIONAL SAILING SCHEME/ YOUTH SAILING SCHEME
国家航海计划和青少年航海计划的教学比例

TYPE OF CRAFT 船型	STUDENT:INSTRUCTOR RATIO 学员与教练比例
Crewed dinghies and multihulls 多人小帆船和多体船	3:1 for beginners with instructor onboard. Maximum 9:1 but not more than 6 boats per instructor (e.g. 3 Wayfarers with 3 students in each, or 4 Picos with 2 students in each) 3:1 初学者且教练在船指导。最大比例为9:1，但是不能超过6条船（例如：3 Wayfare，每条船上有3名学员，或4条Pico，每条船上有2名学员）
Single handed dinghies and multihulls 单人小帆船和多体船	6:1 (applies only whilst the boats are used as single handers) 6:1 （仅适用于只使用单人船的情况）
Keelboats 龙骨船	Day boats/keelboats without accommodation: 4:1 (instructor on board) 1 instructor must be responsible for no more than 9 students (e.g. 3 boats with 3 students in each) 龙骨船日间航行（无床铺）：4:1（教练在船） 每个教练负责的学员不得超过9人（例如：3条船，每条船上有3名学员）

TEACHING RATIOS FOR INSTRUCTOR TRAINING COURSES
教练培训课程的教学比例

DELIVERED BY 执行者	COURSE 课程	Ratio 比例	Moderated 有无审核
Senior Instructor 高级教练	Assistant Instructor 助教	1:6	NO
Coach Assessor 教官 测评官	Dinghy Instructor 小帆船教练	1:6	YES
Coach Assessor 教官 测评官	Keelboat Instructor* 龙骨船教练*	1:6	YES
Coach Assessor 教官 测评官	Multihull Instructor* 多体船教练*	1:6	YES
Coach Assessor 教官 测评官	Dinghy Instructor Endorsement 小帆船教练认证	1:6	YES
Coach Assessor 教官 测评官	Keelboat Instructor Endorsement* 龙骨船教练员认证*	1:6	NO
Coach Assessor 教官 测评官	Multihull Instructor Endorsement* 多体船教练员认证*	1:6	NO
Coach Assessor 教官 测评官	Coastal Endorsement 沿海教学认证	1:6	NO
Coach Assessor 教官 测评官	Advanced Instructor Endorsement 高阶教练认证	1:6	NO
Coach Assessor 教官 测评官	Racing Instructor Endorsement/Racing Coach L1 竞赛教练认证/一级竞赛教练	1:6	NO
Coach Assessor 教官 测评官	Senior Instructor 高级教练	Min. 6 candidates 最少6名	YES Throughout 有，由始至终
Racing Coach Tutor 竞赛教练导师	Racing Coach Level 2 二级竞赛教练	Max. 6 candidates 最多6名	NO
Coaching Development Manager 教学发展经理	Racing Coach Level 3 三级竞赛教练	Max. 12candidates 最多12名	YES Throughout 有，由始至终
Coaching Development Manager 教学发展经理	Racing Coach Tutor 竞赛教练导师	Individual 一对一评估	NO

*Coach/Assessor approved by RYA Chief Instructor.
*主教练批准的教官或测评官。

6 Techniques for Instructing and Coaching 教学和指导技巧

INSTRUCTING AND COACHING SKILLS 教学和技能指导

As an RYA Instructor you will deliver teaching material as both an instructor and coach. Which one it is will depend on a number of factors:
作为一名RYA教练，你会以教练和指导这两个身份来进行教学。具体是何种身份取决于以下几个因素：

- The type of session (practical or theory). 课程类型（实践或理论）。
- The subject (new subject or developing existing techniques and skills).
  课程主题（新主题或是提升已学过的技术技巧）。
- The teaching method (discussion, demonstration or student practise).
  教学方法（讨论、示范或学员实践）。
- The environment (ashore or afloat). 教学环境（岸上或水上）。
- Number of students. 学员数量。
- Where they are in the RYA scheme. 学员水平达到RYA航海计划中的哪一阶段。

Your role as an instructor is to help students learn through teaching them practical and theoretical aspects of the activity. It mostly involves explaining and demonstrating techniques that are new to them.
作为教练，你的职责是通过理论和实践的教授来帮助学员学习。教学中涉及大量新技巧的讲解和演示。

However, coaching implies a shift towards helping students develop those techniques into skills. It might involve more observation, feedback and questioning to check their understanding of the skills.
然而，教授意味着你在帮助学员把技术变成其自身的技能。该过程涉及更多观察、反馈以及提问，来考察学员对技术的理解。

A simple, well-used model for this input is shown below. It is by no means the only teaching model, but it has stood the test of time and addresses a number of learning styles that the students will have.
下面介绍一个易于掌握、使用良好的教学模板。这个教学模板不是唯一的，但经过时间检验，该模板能够有效帮助学生学习。

TEACHING MODEL—EDICTS 教学模板——EDICTS

E—Explanation. The instructor gives a verbal description of the task to be taught. (Instruction)
解释。教练员口头解释将要学习的任务。（授课）

D—Demonstration. The instructor then demonstrates the skill to be taught. Before handing over the controls, they will check the students' understanding of the task. (Instruction)
演示。教练员演示将要学习的技能。在让学员操控时，教练员要检查确认学员对于任务的理解。(授课)

I—Imitation. The students then attempt to 'copy' the skill that the instructor has just shown them. (Coaching)
局限。学员随后尝试练习教练演示的技能。（指导）

C—Correction. The instructor will give any corrective feedback required to improve student performance. (Coaching)
纠正。教练员给学员纠正反馈。

T—Training. Or more correctly, practice. The student can then apply the feedback they have just received. If no feedback was required they can repeat the skill, thereby developing positive reinforcement. (Coaching)
训练。或者更准确地说应该是练习。学员练习教练给予的反馈建议。如果不需要反馈，学员就练习技能、巩固技能。（指导）

S—Summary. Before moving on to the next excercise, the instructor summarises the skill with the student, the lessons learned and confirms understanding. (Coaching)
总结。在开始下一项练习之前，教练与学员总结技能和课程的学习情况，确认学员是否理解了。（指导）

As can be seen from the model, the RYA instructor does much more than simply instruct. If they are comfortable and able, after the instructing stage they can use coaching to help their students to develop their own performance.
从模板中可以看出，RYA教练做得要比一般教学要求的多。如果他们感到舒适并有能力，在教学阶段完成后，他们可以使用指导建议来帮助学生提高他们自己的水平。

If you coach your students effectively their performance should improve and any problems that prevent them progressing can be solved.
如果你能有效地指导学生，他们的表现就会有所改善，任何阻碍他们进步的问题都能得到解决。

Techniques for Instructing and Coaching
教学和指导技巧

Effective Coaching Needs 切实有效的指导所需要的必要条件

- A mutual desire to coach/be coached.
  培训者和受训者目标一致。
- Empathy towards your students.
  对学员保有同情心。
- Good communication between coach and student.
  保持良好的交流。
- A focus on clear achievable goals.
  专注于清楚可达到的目标。

There are three main processes involved in coaching:
指导中涉及的三个主要过程:

Communication 沟通
Listening, questioning, responding and giving feedback.
听、提问、回应和反馈。

Influencing 影响
Increasing confidence and independence in your students.
增强学员的自信心和独立性。

Positively reinforcing things done well.
提出并表扬学员完成的出色的技术。

Helping 帮助
Expressing concern for, and empathy with, their development.
关心并同情学员的进步。

Establishing support for your students.
成为学员的支柱。

Identifying students' needs and linking this to their goals.
了解学员的需求，并与他们的目标结合起来。

Remember that we are communicating all the time. Our thoughts and emotions can often 'leak' out through our verbal and non-verbal communication.
要记住，我们无时无刻不在沟通，我们的想法和情绪通常会通过语言和非语言的沟通流露出来。

Instructors and Coaches should therefore:
指导官因此应:
Develop their verbal and non-verbal communication skills.
提高自身语言和非语言的沟通技巧。

Ensure that they provide positive feedback during sessions.
确保在课程中给予积极的反馈。

Give all students equal or appropriate attention.
给予所有学员同等或适当的关注。

Ensure that they listen to their students, not just talk!
确保不要一味地说教，要聆听学员的声音!

Helping your Students to Learn 帮助学员学习

Sailing is a fun, practical and exciting sport which requires experiential learning—in other words **learning through doing**. It helps to break it down into four stages. In simple terms this means:
帆船运动是一项有趣、实践性强且令人兴奋的运动，须采用体验式的学习方式。换句话说，就是从实践中学习。具体可分为四个阶段，简单来说:

- Run a structured activity or session.
  进行有组织的活动或课程。
- Review and discuss what happened during the session.
  在培训时，进行回顾和讨论。

6 Techniques for Instructing and Coaching
教学和指导技巧

- Help your students learn and be sure about what they know.
  帮助学员学习，确认他们掌握的内容。
- Encourage students to apply their learning to future sessions.
  鼓励学员将所学内容应用到以后的课程中。

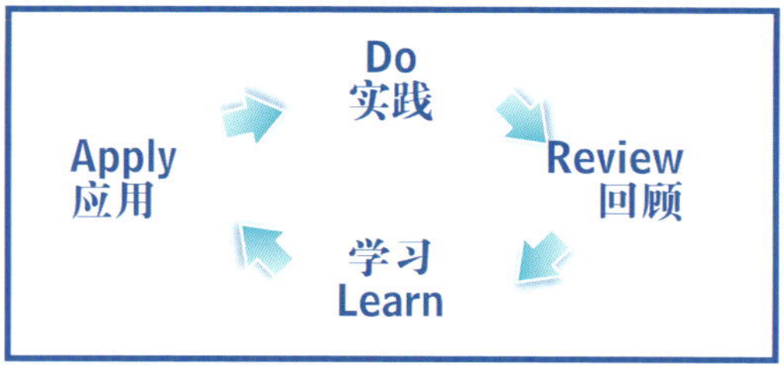

Throughout this process students need:
在该过程中学员需要：

- Positive and constructive feedback.
  积极、有建设性的反馈。
- Time to reflect.
  反应理解的时间。
- Structured sessions that build on each other.
  培训内容结构清晰，紧密联系。

Exactly how you tackle these four stages can be determined by understanding how your students absorb information and learn new skills.
对于这四个阶段的进度安排，应根据学员接收信息和学习新技巧的能力而定。

Absorbing Information 汲取信息

Not everyone sees and experiences the world in the same way. We take in information through our senses:
不是每个人都以同样的方式看待和体验世界。我们通过自身的感官来获取外界信息：

- Visual—eyes. 视觉感官——眼睛。
- Auditory—ears. 听觉感官——耳朵。
- Kinaesthetic—touch, feel and movement. 运动感知——触摸，感觉和动作。

These senses are pathways to our brains. None of us use one pathway exclusively—there is significant overlap between them, but your students are likely to have a preference:
这些感觉是我们的大脑接收信息的途径。没有人只使用某一个途径，各途径在使用中有明显的重复。但是你的学员可能会有所偏好：

Visual Learners 视觉型学习者

They like 他们喜欢：
- Written information. 文字信息。
- Pictures and observation. 图像和观察。
- Sessions that have a lot of content to observe i.e. demonstrations and visual aids.
  涉及大量观察类的培训，比如：演示和视觉教具的使用。

Auditory Learners 听觉型学习者

They like 他们喜欢：
- Information contained in the spoken word.
  通过说话传递信息。
- Clear verbal explanations/briefings.
  清晰的口头说明/简要介绍。
- Verbal feedback.
  口头反馈。
- Discussions.
  讨论。

Top Tip 小贴士

What I hear, I forget. 我听到的，我会忘。
What I see, I remember. 我看见的，我会记住。
What I do, I understand. 我做过的，我会理解。

Kinaesthetic Learners 运动感知型学习者

They like 他们喜欢:

- Learning through touch and movement.
  通过肢体触摸和动作来学习。
- To have a go and see what happens.
  凡事先试一试，看会发生什么。

So, by adapting your teaching style to suit these three preferences, you should be able to create a learning environment with something for everyone.
因此，通过调整你的教学风格，来适应这三种不同的偏好，你就能创造出适合所有人的教学环境。

Once we have absorbed information, we need to process it in order for us to learn. In the same way that we have a preference for absorbing information, we also tend to have a preference for how we learn from this information. Just as people have a tendency towards left or right handedness, which influences how they tackle manual tasks, many people have a particular learning style which influences how they approach mental tasks.
接收信息后，为了学习这些信息，我们的大脑会对这些信息进行处理。我们接收信息的方式有偏好，同样地，学习信息的方式也存在偏好性。就像我们使用左右手的倾向，会影响我们动手的方式。很多人有特定的学习方式，这也会影响他们大脑的工作方法。

As instructors or coaches, by being aware of different learning preferences or styles we are able to modify our own teaching style to suit that of our students.
作为教练或指导，通过了解学员不同的学习偏好或方式，可以调整自己的教学风格来适应他们。

Tips for Reinforcing Learning 巩固学习的建议

- Always put new techniques into context—understanding is helped if you see the ‘big picture’.
  在教授新技巧时，解释学习它的原因——从整体看，有助于学员的理解。
- The average person can deal with approximately seven chunks of information—don’t overload them.
  每个人一次平均可以处理大约7个信息板块——不要给学员过多的信息。
- People remember the beginning and end, but often miss the middle—keep demonstrations and explanations short and structured.
  人们通常会记住开头和结尾，而忽略中间部分——所以，要注意保持演示和说明简洁而有结构。
- Keep information memorable—use unusual, funny or unexpected ways to illustrate your teaching.
  加深印象——使用不寻常的、有趣的或者出乎意料的方法来教学。
- Use a range of methods to teach important skills in order to cater for your students’ range of learning styles —i.e. explaining, showing a video, visualizing, reading, looking at pictures etc.
  运用多种方法来教授重要技能，以适应学员不同的学习风格——比如讲解、播放视频、肉眼观察、阅读和观看图像等。
- Ensure that new skills become well-established with plenty of practice and reinforcement.
  确保通过大量练习和加强训练完全掌握新技能。
- Focus your students on what they should do, rather than what they should not do, or they might end up doing the very opposite to what they should! Positive coaching!
  积极教学！强调学员应该做什么，而不是不应该做什么，否则可能会适得其反。

Demonstrations are particularly important and useful in sailing, so demonstrate whenever possible. People will need time to identify what is being taught, so link the parts into a smooth skill that becomes automatic.
在帆船教学中，演示是非常重要而且有效的手段，所以要尽可能多演示。学员需要时间消化学习的内容，然后把各部分结合成流畅的技巧，最后形成条件反射。

This leads us to the ‘whole – part – whole’ demonstration method, where the skill is executed at normal speed, then broken into detailed parts, then redone at normal speed. In this way both a mental picture and a detailed understanding can be conveyed.
以上内容将我们导向“整体—分解—整体”的演示方法，先用正常速度演示一遍，然后分部演示，最后再以正常速度演示一次。这样便于学员形成对整个技术和细节的理解。

Use of Land Drills 运用岸上练习

It is possible to teach the entire syllabus without ever using any land drills, providing a number of factors are present. These are, good/perfect sailing conditions which include the venue, a dinghy that the student(s) are comfortable in, receptive student(s) able to act immediately and consistently on input and effective communication between student(s) and instructor.
如满足以下因素，完全无须岸上教学就可教完教学大纲里的所有内容。首先，航行条件良好/完美，包括场地和教学用船；其次，学员理解能力强，可快速并持续地完成教学任务，学员和教练沟通良好。

Only one of these elements needs to be missing to 'break the chain', therefore instructors should consider using land drills where they will enhance/accelerate or reinforce student learning.
如其中某个因素无法满足，学习链就会被打破，此时，教练应考虑在岸上教学，这样有助于提高/加速或巩固学员的学习。

LAND DRILLS 岸上教学

- Land drills introduce clarity and simplicity. They enable students to achieve more in less time afloat. They are not an end in themselves, nor are they always necessary or appropriate.
  岸上教学应清楚简明，能让学员在条件不允许的情况下，花较少的水上时间，学到更多内容。岸上教学并不是教学的结束，而且也不总是必须的或适用的。
- Land drills work particularly well after a demonstration afloat to convey the 'big picture'.
  通过水上演示，使学员有一个总体认识后，再进行岸上教学效果会非常好。
- Introduce the session by explaining why the land drill may be useful.
  在本培训一开始会向学员讲解岸上教学的作用。
- Make it as real as possible. Boats are much better than ropes and chairs.
  场景越真实越好。用真船比用绳子和椅子的效果会好很多。
- If using a boat, make sure it is safe on its trolley with people aboard, or put it on grass or even in the water.
  如果确定用实体船，应确保船安放在船车上，保证船上人员的安全或是把船放在草地上，甚至是水里。
- Position the students where they can see clearly but are safe. Be aware of any distractions.
  学员所处的位置要安全，且能清楚地看到你的操作。注意其他干扰因素。
- What you do is more important than what you say. Use few words and demonstrate smoothly at normal speed, before breaking the manoeuvre down.
  你的操作比讲解更重要。在将技能分解之前，先用正常速度流畅地演示一遍，演示时讲解要尽量简洁。
- Most instructors talk too much as they demonstrate.
  很多教练在演示时会讲得过多。
- Involve your students where possible e.g. in moving the boom or balancing the boat.
  尽可能地让学员参与进来，比如：移动帆杆或协助保持船的平衡。
- When teaching children, consider increasing entertainment by turning the drill into play by the use of songs or other ideas.
  在教授儿童时，应提高课程的趣味性，可运用歌曲或其他方法将岸上教学变成游戏。
- Land drills are useful for a number of skills e.g. spinnaker work, anchoring, reefing etc., where a complicated series of actions have to be co-ordinated.
  将一系列复杂的动作协调起来，采用岸上教学非常有效，比如：球帆操作、抛锚、缩帆等。

THE FOUR STAGES OF LEARNING—UNCONSCIOUS INCOMPETENCE TO UNCONSCIOUS COMPETENCE
学习的四个阶段——无意识不胜任到无意识胜任

You can expect your students largely to follow the same stages when learning any new technique. Indeed, as they progress up through the stages with one technique they may begin again at the bottom with new techniques or skills.
一般来说，学员在学习新技能的时候都会经历相同的阶段。在他们学习某个技术时经历了这些阶段，在学习其他新技能时，可能会再经历一遍。

Techniques for Instructing and Coaching 6
教学和指导技巧

Four Stages of Competence
掌握技能的四个阶段

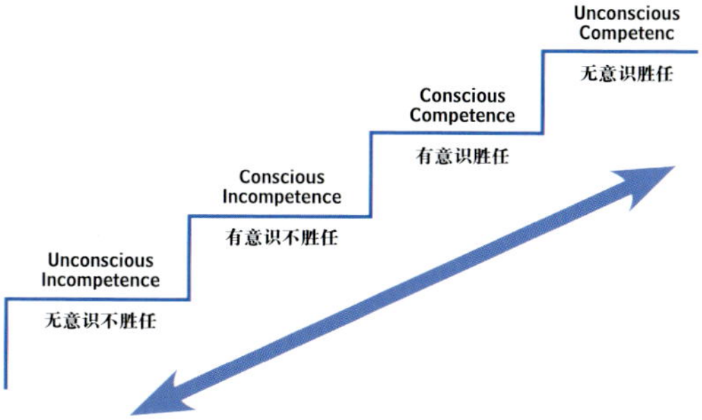

Unconscious Incompetence:
Students don't know what they don't know.
无意识不胜任:
学员不知道自己不知道什么。

Conscious Incompetence:
Students are aware of what they don't know. For some this adds clarity, others find it daunting and frustrating.
有意识不胜任:
学员开始意识到自己不知道哪些知识。对有些学员来说，这个阶段让他们更清楚，有的人会觉得气馁和沮丧。

Conscious Competence:
Students are becoming competent but still have to think about what they are doing and how they do it. Following simple sequences will be useful at this stage.
有意识胜任:
学员开始能够胜任，但仍须思考他们在做的事情以及如何去做。在该阶段，遵照简单的操作步骤很有效。

Unconscious Competence:
Students now do things with very little conscious thought. Things flow and are effortless.
无意识胜任:
在该阶段，学员做动作时很少会有意识地主动思考。操作流畅且毫不费劲。

BASIC SKILLS MODEL
基本的技能学习模式

Unconscious Competence 无意识胜任
(Self-reliant achiever 独立自主)

↑

Conscious Competence 有意识胜任
(Capable but cautious performer 有能力但谨慎)

↑

Conscious Incompetence 有意识不胜任
(Disillusioned learner 大失所望)

↑

Unconscious Incompetence 无意识不胜任
(Enthusiastic beginner 热情的初学者)

Coaching 指导
Developing the sailor's own analysis
开发学员的自我分析能力
SUPPORTIVE BEHAVIOUR
支持行为

Instructing 教学
Creating the building blocks
学习基础技能
DIRECTIVE BEHAVIOUR
引导行为

Instructors should adapt their approach as students develop competence and become more skilful, initially instructing and being directive in their approach to the development of good technique but eventually becoming less directive and more supportive as technique becomes more skilful and adopting a more coaching role.
在学员学习的不同阶段，教练应采用不同的教学方法。刚开始，要多教学、多指导，使学员掌握操艇技巧，之后随着学员的操作更加熟练，应逐渐减少指令，多去支持他们，逐渐转换成教官的角色。

Techniques for Instructing and Coaching
教学和指导技巧

HOW AND WHY PEOPLE LEARN? 人是如何学习的，为什么要学习?

Adults and young people often learn in different ways and for different reasons:
成年人和青少年的学习方式和学习理由通常大不相同:

THE WAY ADULTS LEARN 成年人的学习方式	TIPS TO HELP 教学建议
Typically more independent and self directed 更加独立，而且有自我导向的能力	Once given a task, they will get on with it and will not need 'watching' to complete it. Sometimes can be difficult to get them to stop 一旦接受了某项任务，就会全身心地投入，而且能在无人监督的情况下完成
Goal orientated and structured approach to learning. They have become used to being lectured. They can find the relaxed RYA session uncomfortable 目标导向型，学习有方。习惯了严肃的教学方式，对轻松的RYA课堂会感到不习惯	Encourage them to answer questions and to question the content of the session in general. Don't allow anyone to opt out 鼓励他们回答问题，并对课程内容进行提问。不要允许任何人保持沉默
Need to know why they are learning something 明确学习目的	Ensure that the purpose as well as the aim of the session is made clear at the start. 确保目标明确，在课程开始前就进行说明。
Accumulated life experience can be applied to the learning process for good and bad. They are also used to 'problem solving' 生活经验丰富，可运用到学习中。他们习惯了解决问题	Use this to advantage and incorporate it into sessions. It may make sessions longer, however 可将该优势运用到培训中，不过可能会使培训时间更长
Often reluctant to get things wrong and appear foolish, especially in front of the group and become frustrated when they do! 通常，他们会因为不安而犯错，使他们显得很愚钝，尤其是在很多人面前发生这种情况，会使他们变得十分沮丧	Reward correct answers/solutions and encourage those who answer incorrectly to find the right ones 奖励给出正确答案或解决方案的人，同时鼓励答错的人找到正确的答案

THE WAY CHILDREN LEARN 青少年的学习方式	TIPS TO HELP 教学建议
More random and instructor/coach led 更加随意，需要教练/教官的引导	Providing they are occupied and interested, they will respond to teaching input 让他们保持忙碌和感兴趣的状态，这样他们就会认真地听讲
Fun and experiential orientated approach 趣味和体验导向型	This doesn't include classrooms! Motivation can dip if too long is spent in one. Explore alternatives, work cards, models, constructive games, allow students to draw their understanding on the white board 不适合在课堂进行！在一个环节耗时过长，趣味性就降低了。多探索一些其他教学方法，如使用卡片、模型、益智游戏等，允许学员把自己的理解画在白板上

THE WAY CHILDREN LEARN 青少年的学习方式	TIPS TO HELP 教学建议
Need to know why they are learning something 明确学习目的	Ensure that the purpose as well as the aim of the session is made clear at the start 确保目标明确，在课程开始前就进行说明
Want to know 'what', 'where' and 'when' rather than 'why' 相比“为什么”，他们更想知道“什么”“在哪里”“什么时间”	They are much more 'active' in their learning 在学习时，更活跃
May be experiencing the skill for the first time. Not biased by other experiences, they're free learners 可能是第一次尝试，不受其他经历的影响，他们还是白纸一张	Often, young people make better students. They can learn faster and have better powers of retention 通常，青少年学员的学习能力更强。他们学习速度更快，记忆力也更好
A more natural approach with fewer inhibitions. Happy to get things wrong! 放得开、不拘束、不怕犯错！	Don't expect perfection in the sessions 不要期待他们做到完美
Youngsters can be shy and reluctant to participate, especially if they have few or no friends in the group 他们可能会很害羞，不愿意去参与，尤其是没有同伴或人少的时候	Involve them with simple questions and enthusiastically reward correct answers. Check understanding with a 'fun' quiz 可以提一些简单的问题，对回答正确的学员给予热情的奖励，以此让他们融入到课堂中来。用“小测试”的方法来检查他们的学习情况
Enthusiasm can lead to boisterous behaviour and even loss of control. Be vigilant of this 过于激动可能会让他们变得很闹腾，甚至失去控制。要注意控制好学员的情绪	Ensure that the youngsters know 'who is in charge' and check unruly behaviour early. A simple way to stop idle chatter is to sit the group down 让孩子们知道负责人是谁，尽早地发现不守规矩的行为。一个让大家停止闲聊的小方法：让所有人都坐下来
Use the Youth Sailing Scheme 采用青少年航海计划	It has advice on different approaches and learning styles. 它对不同的学习方法和学习方式给出了建议。

People often learn best through fun and enjoyment. Make your sessions fun and stimulating for all.
人在开心快乐时学习能力最强。所以在教学时，要让课程充满乐趣，让大家兴奋起来。

What Might Motivate our Students to Learn? 什么会鼓励学员学习？

- Making or maintaining social relationships. 建立或维系人际关系。
- Learning to engage others—parents often learn with a view to involving the rest of their family.
  为了让他人共同参与——通常父母们会考虑让家人一起参与。
- A desire to achieve awards and qualifications. 想获取认证和证书。
- Escape or stimulation from everyday life. 脱离日常生活或寻求刺激。
- Interest in the subject. 对课程主题感兴趣。
- Lifestyle aspiration. 生活方式的追求。

Being aware of your students' possible motivations for taking the course helps you to shape it, the materials you use and how you structure the groups in which they are placed for teaching.
了解学员参与培训的动机，有助于你构建课程，准备教学材料以及组建学习小组。

6 Techniques for Instructing and Coaching
教学和指导技巧

BARRIERS TO LEARNING 学习障碍

- Other responsibilities (families, careers, social commitments).
  其他责任（家庭、事业和社会责任）。
- Lack of time.
  缺乏时间。
- Environment—being wet and cold!
  环境——害怕湿冷！
- Feelings—looking or feeling silly.
  感觉——觉得自己看起来很傻。
- Scheduling problems—when courses take place.
  课程安排问题——课程时间不适合。
- Insufficient confidence.
  缺乏自信。
- Inappropriate teaching methods.
  教学方法不适合。
- Culture clash—young fit blond instructor vs. unfit, middle-aged student.
  文化冲突——如年轻健美的金发美女教练与发福的中年学员。
- Personality clashes—between student and instructor.
  个性冲突——学员与教练之间。
- Having to learn, if told by parent or spouse but not interested or ready.
  非自主学习，如在家长或配偶的要求下去学，但自己其实不感兴趣或没有事先准备好。
- Fear of failure (again).
  害怕失败（或再次失败）。

“本·艾恩斯利小的时候曾向我恳求诀窍。”
（本·艾恩斯利，英国帆船运动员，英国最成功的帆船帆板选手之一，五次奥运会奖牌得主，四次奥运冠军，现役美洲杯赛船船长）

Fear 恐惧

Fear is one of the main barriers which you, a good instructor, can help the students overcome.
恐惧是学员最主要的学习障碍之一，作为一名优秀的教练，你能够帮助学员克服这一问题。

Adults and children normally have three principal fears when trying something for the first time:
一般情况下，成年人和青少年在第一次尝试新事物的时候，有三种主要的恐惧：

Fear of failure—Be clear about their progress throughout the course. Encourage them to try things out, even if it means making mistakes. If the course is assessed, let your students know the outcome.
害怕失败——应对方式是，在课程中明确指出学员的进步。即使他们操作失败也要鼓励他们多尝试。如果你对学员作了评估，告知他们结果。

Fear of the unknown—Keep your students fully informed throughout the course, the stages they will go through and why you are structuring the course that way.
对未知的恐惧——应对方式是，让学员充分了解课程的安排，以及这样安排的原因。

Fear of not being liked or fitting in—Break the ice early and encourage groups to work together and get to know each other. Consider some games to help people relax.
害怕不被喜欢或无法融入——尽早帮助学员破冰，鼓励团队合作，让大家互相了解。可以考虑玩游戏让学员放松。

PEOPLE SKILLS FOR INSTRUCTORS 教练的人际交往能力

What your Students Think of You—Emotional Intelligence 学员如何看待你——情商

How you are perceived by others determines your credibility and therefore the influence you will have over them. First impressions are vital as it is estimated that up to 90% of people's opinions of you are formed in the first four minutes of meeting you. Therefore, you will start with a disadvantage if your students arrive for the course only to find you stressed and bedraggled, trying to open up the centre, tidy up the mess left by the previous group, getting equipment stores open and rescue boats afloat.
学员对你的看法决定了你的可信度，以及你对他们的影响力。第一印象十分重要，据估计，人们对你看法的90%都来自第一次见面的前4分钟。因此，如果学员第一次来上课，结果发现你邋里邋遢，还在紧张地准备上课；手忙脚乱地整理上节课留下的乱摊子，或还在想办法开器材室的门；整理水上的船只。那么对你来说就非常不利了。

Tips for gaining your students' trust:
获得学员信任的诀窍：

- The first four minutes of any encounter are the most important and set the scene.
  第一次见面的前4分钟非常重要，要做好铺垫。
- Always set up early and be ready for their arrival.
  务必提前做好准备，迎接学员。
- Pay attention to your personal appearance and grooming as this can exert an inordinate influence on their first impression of you.
  注意个人仪容仪表，这对你的第一印象有很重要的影响。
- Listen to your students and respect what they tell you—the more you listen, the more you can influence them.
  聆听学员，尊重他们说的话——你聆听得越多，你对他们的影响力就越大。
- Spend time with them to enable a rapport to develop.
  花时间与学员相处，建立良好的师生关系。
- Put their needs before your own.
  把他/她们的需求放在你的需求之前。

6 Techniques for Instructing and Coaching
教学和指导技巧

What you Need to Know about your Students 你需要了解关于学员的事项

Remember that amongst your students you are going to have widely differing ages, genders, backgrounds, skills, hopes, fears, expectations and aspirations.
要记住，你教授的学员当中，年龄、性别、背景、技能、希冀、忧虑、期待和追求都各不相同。
It's a good idea to gather as much information as possible on these areas from your students prior to the course. Some of this can be done on booking forms or simple questionnaires. Questions you might want to ask of beginners:
尽可能在课前了解学员的这些信息。有些信息可通过预定表或简单的问卷获得。对于初学者，你需要问的问题是：

- Why do you want to learn to sail?
  为什么想要学习帆船？
- Have you done any sailing before, when, where etc?
  以前玩过帆船吗？如有，在哪里，什么时候等。
- Do you take part in any other water sports?
  你还参与过其他什么水上运动吗？
- What will you do once you are able to sail?
  学会帆船之后想做什么？

...and so on.
等等。

Being prepared with this information can help you to:
了解了这些信息将有助于你：

- Create the right environment.
  营造合适的氛围。
- Be warm, welcoming and friendly.
  让学员感受到你的温暖、热情和友好。
- Tell them a bit about yourself.
  和他们分享一些你自己的事。
- Get them all talking about themselves.
  让他/她们都讲讲自己。
- Tell them what to expect (and what not to expect).
  告诉他们将会发生什么（不会发生什么）。
- Create the course (together).
  与学员一起创建课程。
- Break the ice.
  排除陌生感。

COMMUNICATION SKILLS 沟通技巧

Communication is more than just words. We are constantly communicating, even when we are saying nothing.

Research has shown that 55% of your communication is determined by your body language, posture and eye contact, 38% by your tone of voice, and only 7% by your actual words. Therefore, to get your message across, concentrate on how you talk, not just what you say.
沟通不仅仅限于语言。即使在我们不说话的时候，其实也在不断地沟通。研究表明，55%的沟通是由肢体语言、姿势以及眼神来传递的，38%是通过语音语调，只有7%是通过语言本身传递的。因此，在传递信息时，要注意说话方式，而不只是说话内容。

Whatever you say, typically your students will:

不管你说什么，你的学员可能都会：

- Filter: Pick out more or less important bits for themselves.
  过滤：选择对他们重要的信息。
- Distort: Interpret things for themselves.
  曲解：用自己的方式理解你所说的内容。
- Delete: Remove any bits that they find unclear or too difficult.
  删除：学员会自动删除他们认为不清楚或过于困难的信息。

Remember that often **less is more**—keep your messages simple and free of jargon, and back them up with demonstrations and practical examples.
要记住，少即是多。简化信息，避免使用术语，采用演示和实例进行说明。

Check your students' understanding of new information as often as possible, using open questions to enable them to confirm what you have said or what you want them to do.
尽可能频繁地检查学员对于新知识的理解程度，问一些开放性的问题，检查他们是否明白了课程要点或是你要求他们掌握的内容。

Remember the worst question in the world is...'Do you understand?' There will only ever be one answer - 'yes'.
记住，世界上最无用的问题是：“明白了吗？”回答永远都只是一个答案：“明白了”。

Non-verbal Messages 非语言信息

People use a variety of behaviour to maintain a smooth flow of communication, such as head-nods, smiles, frowns, laughter etc. Your students' facial expressions provide you with some feedback on the session. Glazed or down-turned eyes indicate boredom or disinterest, as does fidgeting. Fully raised eyebrows signal disbelief and half raised indicate puzzlement. The posture of the group enables you to judge their attitude and mood.
人在沟通时，除了运用语言外，还会使用各种行为来保持沟通的流畅。例如，点头、微笑、皱眉和大笑等。课堂上学员的表情通常能反映你上课的效果。

STUDENTS DON'T LIKE BEING TICKED OFF...
学员不喜欢被指责

Communication Blocks 沟通障碍

Communication difficulties between the instructor and the student can happen for a number of reasons:
教练与学员之间存在沟通障碍的原因可能是：

- The student's perception of something is not the same as yours.
  学员对某事的观念与你的不同。
- The student may jump to a conclusion instead of working through the process of hearing, understanding and accepting.
  学员可能会过早地下结论，没有经过听讲、理解和接受等过程。
- The student may lack the knowledge and understanding of what you are trying to teach.
  学员可能会缺乏一些相关知识，无法理解教练正在讲的内容。
- The student may lack the motivation.
  学员可能缺乏学习动力。
- The instructor may have difficulty in expressing what they want to say.
  教练可能表述不清。
- Emotions may interfere in the communication process.
  情绪因素可能会影响沟通。
- There may be a clash of personalities.
  也可能有性格冲突。

6 Techniques for Instructing and Coaching 教学和指导技巧

Effective Communication 有效沟通

Effective communication contains six elements: 有效沟通包含六个要素：

• CLEAR	Ensure that the information is presented clearly.
清楚	确保信息的呈现是清楚的。
• CONCISE	Be concise: do not lose the message by being long winded.
简洁	简明扼要：不要过于长篇大论而忽略了关键信息。
• CORRECT	Be accurate, avoid giving misleading information.
准确	准确，避免给出误导性信息。
• COMPLETE	Give all the information and not just part of it.
完整	给出全部信息，不要只是一部分。
• COURTEOUS	Be polite and non-threatening, avoid conflict.
礼仪	彬彬有礼，避免威胁和冲突等行为。
• CONSTRUCTIVE	Be positive, avoid being critical and negative.
建设性	积极正面，避免批评和负面。

Always check that: 时刻检查以下几点：

- You have your students' attention.
  学员注意力是否集中。
- Your students are accepting what you are saying.
  学员们是否在接收你的信息。
- You are giving clear explanations and demonstrations.
  你的解释和示范是否是清楚的。
- Your students have understood.
  学员是否理解了你讲的内容。

Always consider: 时刻思考以下几点：

- WHY you need to communicate?
  为什么需要沟通?
- WHO you are communicating with?
  沟通的对象是谁?
- WHERE and WHEN the message will best be delivered.
  信息传递的最佳时间和地点。
- WHAT you will be explaining or demonstrating?
  解释或演示的内容是什么?
- HOW you will get the information across?
  如何传递信息?

Communication whilst afloat is particularly important but often goes wrong, so remember:

水上沟通特别重要，但很容易出错，需谨记以下要点：

- Keep verbal communication to a minimum.
  尽可能减少语言交流。
- Project your voice towards your students – it gets lost in the wind.
  使学员能够听到你的声音，尽量避免你的声音被风减弱。
- Never shout—it implies that you are angry.
  严禁向学员喊叫——这会让学员以为你很生气。
- Position your students where they can hear you best.
  让学员处在能听清你说话的最佳位置。
- Call students to you frequently for feedback and further instructions (single handers).
  频繁地让学员靠到你的船的旁边，纠正他们的操作并给出进一步指导（单人船）。
- Use pre-agreed visual signals.
  使用预先商定好的视觉信号。
- Use an agreed signal to confirm understanding.
  使用预先商定好的信号确认对方是否理解。

PRESENTATION SKILLS 教学演讲技巧

It is normal for inexperienced instructors to be nervous about giving presentations, despite the fact that they know their subject matter well but, with the right frame of mind and a bit of practice, the nerves will soon start to disappear.
对于经验尚浅的教练来说，演讲的时候紧张是很正常的，即使他们对主题已经十分熟悉，但是稍加练习，把握好心态，紧张感很快就会消失。

The fear often revolves around things going wrong, such as:
通常出现问题的时候，很容易产生恐惧感，例如：

- I'll dry up. 我快没有话说了。
- No one will be interested. 没有人会感兴趣。
- I'll be boring. 我的讲述会很无聊。
- They won't like me. 他们不会喜欢我。
- I don't know enough about my subject. 我对主题不熟悉。
- They'll ask me difficult questions. 他们会问我很难的问题。
- I'll make a fool of myself. 我会出丑。

However, being aware of these fears can help you to ensure that they don't come true.
然而，意识到这些问题能够帮助你确保不出现以上问题。

Good Presentations Depend on Several Elements:
优秀的演讲取决于以下因素：

The Content 演讲内容

Write down what you need to cover from the syllabuses onto a large sheet of paper in the form of headings. If you can, try to group related things together. Even subjects which may not initially seem relevant to the presentation may help identify other things which are. Keeping your objectives in mind, sort out the relevant material using the need to know and nice to know group. Keep the 'need to know' and discard the 'nice to know' for now. Group the 'need to know' under three structured headings—a) introduction, b) main body, and c) summary and close.

将你要讲的大纲上涉及的要点以标题形式写在一大张纸上，如果可以，尝试把相关的内容组合在一起，甚至可以写下非直接关联的要点，帮助你联想到那些需要讲到的内容。关注“需要知道的”，暂时不要管“可以知道的”。

- Consider the time available for the presentation. After all the 'need to know' have been included can any of the 'nice to knows' be added in? If so, choose the most relevant first.
  考虑演讲的时间。在讲完了所有“需要知道的”信息之后，是否可以说一些“可以知道的”信息？如果可以的话，就先讲那些最重要的。
- Group the points you have decided to include under subject headings but do not consider the sequence at this stage.
  在每个主题下写出要点，该阶段先不要考虑讲解的顺序。
- Place the subject headings in a logical, interesting order.
  把主题按照逻辑性或者有趣的顺序排列。
- Put a time allocation on each subject and the use of each visual aid.
  设置好每个主题的演讲时间以及每一个视觉教具所需的时间。
- Make working notes for the presentation.
  准备演讲笔记。

The Words 措辞

- Clear, concise, jargon-free language.
  清晰、简洁和避免术语化。
- Think before you speak—don't 'think out loud'!
  整理好再说——不要边想边说！
- Emphasise the important bits. 强调重点。
- Summarise what you've said and ask questions.
  总结课程内容并提问。

Be aware of, but not too self-conscious of, your body movements: 注意自己的肢体语言，但也不要过分关注：	
Posture 姿势	Sit or stand up straight—but not rigid 坐直或站直——但不要让自己看上去很僵硬
Hands 手势	Don't be afraid of using them —as long as they are not distracting the audience 不要害怕使用手势——只要其不分散听众的注意力
Movement 移动	It is fine to move about as long as, once more, this does not become a distraction 可以适当走动，只要不分散听众的注意力
Position 位置	Avoid obstructions to the audiences' view of you 避免障碍物挡住听众的视线
View of your visual aids 视觉教具	Never turn your back on the audience—they won't hear you 永远不要背对听众，否则他们无法听到你说话
Eyes 眼神	Maintain eye contact with the whole audience 保持和听众的眼神交流
Notes 笔记	Do not talk to your notes or visual aids 不要对着你的笔记或是教具讲话

HANDLING QUESTIONS 处理问题

Set the Rules for Questions 设置提问环节

Set rules for questions in the beginning i.e. save questions for the end, or ask questions whenever you like (which might be more common and useful in an informal environment). Remember, you are the leader, so lead. Whichever rule you set, make sure it's followed. Reserve the right to stop taking questions in order to ensure you have sufficient time to cover all subjects.
在开场时就说明何时提问，比如：在最后提问，或是随时提问（在非正式环境下，这种方式更常用，更有效）。记住，你是领导者，要引导他们。定下了提问的时间，就要确保实施。保留停止提问的权力，让你有足够的时间将所有的内容都讲到。

What to Say when you don't Know the Answer 不知道答案时，如何处理

Honesty is the only policy when presenting to a group, but blatantly admitting 'I don't know' in response to a direct question can be disastrous. No one can know the answer to every question, but it's how the situation is handled that separates great presenters from amateurs.
在当众演讲时，诚实是最好的解决问题的方法，但直接承认“我不知道”会很糟糕。世界上没有人能知道所有问题的答案，但是如何处理这种情况的方式，决定了你是否是一名优秀的讲者。

Don't get lulled into thinking you have seen and heard it all on a particular topic. At any time someone can come out of left field with a question you have never thought of before.
不要以为你对某个特定的话题看过、听过的够多了，就以为什么都难不倒你。任何时候都有可能有人跳出来，问你一些意想不到的问题。

The following strategies can help you field even the toughest questions with confidence.
以下策略可以帮助你自信地解决最棘手的问题。

Reflection 反问

Repeat the question and toss it back to your audience. 'Does anyone here have any experience with that?' The audience can save you without ever realising it. In fact, they will love to be involved and share their knowledge. After you have fielded their contributions, summarise and add your own ideas.
重复该问题，然后抛回给观众："有人之前有过这样的经历吗？"观众可能会无意识地帮你解围。事实上，他们会很愿意参与进来，并且分享他们的知识。有了他们的答案后，总结一下，然后加上你自己的观点即可。

'I don't know the answer to that but I will find out for you.'
"我不知道这个问题的答案，但是我会尽快找到答案。"

This is an old standard and it works well. It is an opportunity to go the extra mile, expand your knowledge, and impress your audience.
这是一个很老套的标准回答，而且屡试不爽。每次遇到这种问题，都是一个让你自我增值的好机会，既可以拓展你的知识，还可以给学员留下深刻的印象。

Defer to the Expert
请专家来解答

This is a more sophisticated version of the 'Reflection' technique. Sometimes a question is legitimately outside of your area of expertise but there may be someone more experienced within the school or centre who you can pass it on to. You will need to decide who presents the answer—you or them.
该技巧比"反问"观众更高级。有时候，问题不在你的专业范围之内，但在培训中心或学校里可能有经验更丰富的人，可以询问他们。但是你需要决定，最后由谁来向观众们解答——你还是他们。

Compliment the Questioner
赞美提问者

For this to be effective, the compliment must be sincere. 'That's a good question. I've never thought about it that way. Does anyone here have any ideas on that?' You might also combine this technique with 'I'll Get Back to You'.
赞美要真诚才有效。例如，可以说"这是个好问题，我从来没这样考虑过。其他人有什么想法吗？"你也可以结合"我稍后为你解答"来回应。

USE OF VISUAL AIDS
视觉教具的使用

Skilful use of visual aids can greatly enhance your presentation, but don't let them take over. Always remember that your relationship with your audience is key and visual aids are just there to support you. They can take the attention off you periodically and allow you to think ahead.
熟练地使用视觉教具可为演示增色，但不要过度使用。要记住你和听众的关系才是关键，教具只是辅助。可偶尔转移大家的注意力，让你提前思考。

Some General Tips:
通用小贴士：

- The best visual aid is a live example of your subject matter i.e. a dinghy, a buoyancy aid, a safety pack, etc. Use it as often as you can.
  最好的教具是与你主题相关的实物，比如：小帆船、助浮衣、安全包等，尽可能多地使用。
- If the visual is too comprehensive, your audience will switch off from you and read the visual instead.
  如果采用的教具过于复杂，相比你的讲述，观众很可能会更关注教具。
- Whenever possible use pictures, diagrams, graphs and colour rather than lots of writing.
  尽可能多地使用图片、图解、图表和颜色，而不是大量的文字。
- Do not use too many different visual aids as you can end up in a terrible muddle.
  教具的种类不要过多，否则你会很容易搞混。

White Boards/Blackboards
白板/黑板

- The most common form of visual aid.
  最常用的视觉教具。

- Avoid light coloured pens as they are difficult to see at the back of the room.
  避免使用浅色的记号笔，否则在教室后面的人会很难看清。
- Make sure your pens have ink in them!
  确保记号笔墨水充足！
- Practise writing in large letters.
  练习在白板/黑板上写大字。
- Practise drawing diagrams.
  练习画图表。
- Why not use a mobile camera phone to capture the details before rubbing it off, then email it to the students if necessary.
  在擦掉板书前，用手机拍下来，如有必要，可发邮件给学员。

Flip Charts 活页挂纸

- Work well for interaction.
  适用于互动。
- Can be prepared in advance.
  可提前准备好。
- Test your pens on the back of a sheet beforehand.
  在纸的背面提前试一下记号笔。
- Write a note for yourself in faint pencil (audience won't see).
  可用浅色铅笔写一些笔记来提示自己（观众看不到）。
- Bluetack up key sheets on the wall if appropriate.
  如可行，可把关键的页面贴在墙上。
- Pre draw any diagrams in faint pencil, too. Then when the time comes, overdraw them with a marker pen.
  提前用浅色铅笔把图表画下来，讲课时，直接用马克笔描出。

Data Projectors 数码投影仪

- PowerPoint: good for large, formal presentations.
  PPT适合大型的正式场合。
- Useful for key words, images and video.
  对于关键词、图片和视频非常有效。
- Professional effect.
  有专业效果。
- Easy to update.
  容易更新。
- Practise well beforehand.
  提前练习好。
- Avoid too many effects and sounds!
  避免使用过多的特效和声音！

DVDs 视频光盘

- Must be relevant and up to date.
  必须跟主题相关，内容应是最新版。
- Use of video cameras for filming your students and playing footage of their own performance can be very powerful.
  上课时用摄像机记录你的学员，之后播放给学员看，效果会非常好。
- Do not dwell on students' mistakes, no matter how funny.
  不要反复提及学员的错误，即使它非常好笑。
- Use very sparingly.
  谨慎使用。

Models 模型

- Useful for highlighting specific topics.
  有助于强调特定主题。
- Easy to carry and set up.
  便于携带和组装。
- Students can get involved easily.
  很容易激发学员的兴趣，让他们参与进来。
- Usually very 'low tech'.
  通常不需要太复杂的技术。
- Especially good for showing rules of the road and racing rules.
  十分适用于说明航行规则和比赛规则。

The 'Real Thing' 实物

- Better than just about anything else.
  比其他任何东西都更适合。
- Illustrates the point perfectly.
  能非常好地说明要点。
- Students can get 'hands on'.
  学员能够“上手”。
- Saves making diagrams, drawings etc.
  免去制作表格、画图等步骤。

Whichever Method you use, Avoid:
无论用什么方法，避免：

- Too many words.
  说话过多。
- Too much detail.
  细节太多。
- Overcrowded slides.
  演示稿单页信息量太大。
- Bland images.
  乏味的图像。
- Talking to the visual.
  对着教具说话。
- Leaving the visual on display when you have finished with the subject matter.
  讲完相关主题后，没有将教具收起来。

Making your Visual Aids Accessible
让你的视觉教具服务所有人

Every individual has a different perception of what they see and read. The shape and size of words can appear different to each reader. This is especially true when working with young people and students with dyslexia. Consider that 10% of your clients may be dyslexic. Remember that changes you make to accommodate dyslexic people are good practice for everyone.
每个人对他看到和读到的东西，都有不同的理解。文字的形状和大小对看的人来说可能不同，尤其是对年轻人和有读写障碍的人来说。假设10%的学员都有读写困难，记住，你为这些学员所做的课程调整，其实有利于每一名学员。

Adopting some simple strategies can help everyone to get the most from reading written information.
采取一些简单的策略，能帮助每个人最大限度地从读写信息中获取知识。

6 Techniques for Instructing and Coaching
教学和指导技巧

Font Style 字体风格

- Fonts should be rounded with space between letters and reflect ordinary writing. Fonts such as Arial or Comic Sans are good.
  字体之间应该留有适当空间，就像正常书写一样。例如，Arial或Comic Sans就很好。
- Where possible use lower case letters rather than capitals. Using capital letters for emphasis can make text harder to read.
  尽可能使用小写字母，避免大写。大写能起强调作用，但是会增加阅读的难度。

Paper 纸张

- Avoid light text on a dark background.
  避免字体浅，背景深。
- Use coloured paper instead of white. Cream or off-white provides a good alternative.
  相比白纸，有颜色的纸更适合。奶白色或米黄色都是很好的选择。
- Matt paper is preferable to glossy paper, as this reduces glare.
  亚光纸反光度低，比光面纸更适用。
- Ensure the paper is heavy enough to prevent text showing through from the back.
  确保纸张厚度，避免背面的字透到正面。

Presentation Style 排版

- Limit lines to 60 to 70 characters to avoid putting strain on the eyes.
  每行60~70个字，减少用眼压力。
- Use short paragraphs with space between each line and paragraph.
  使用短段落，每句与每段之间留适当空间。
- Use wide margins and headings.
  使用宽页边距和大标题。
- Use boxes for emphasising important text.
  给需要强调的重要文本加框。
- Use bold to highlight words rather than italics or underlining.
  需要强调某些词语时，采用加粗，而不是画线或斜体。
- Keep lines left justified with a ragged right edge.
  每行左对齐，右边可以参差不齐。
- Use bulleted or numbered lists.
  使用项目符号或编号列表。
- Use this page as a guide.
  使用本页作为参考。

Writing Style 文体风格

- Write in short simple sentences.
  语句简短。
- Be conscious of where sentences begin on the page. Starting a new sentence at the end of a line makes it harder to follow.
  注意每页的开头。在一行的最后开启下一句话会增加阅读的难度。
- Try to call the readers 'you': imagine they are sitting opposite you and you are talking to them directly.
  尝试用“你”来称呼读者：想象他们正坐在对面和你交流。
- Give instructions clearly. Avoid long explanations.
  给出明确指示，避免冗长的解释。
- Stop and think before you start writing so you are clear about what you want to say.
  书写前先想清楚，明确想写的内容。
- Use short words where possible.
  尽可能地用精炼的词语。
- Keep your sentences to an average of 15 to 20 words.
  保持每句话平均15~20个词。
- Be concise.
  简洁。

Using Flipcharts 活页挂纸的使用

- Keep essential information grouped together.
  使重要的信息组合在一起。
- Print lower case rather than using joined writing.
  使用小写印刷体，而不是手写连体。
- Write large, it's easier for you and easier to read.
  字体大一些，写起来容易，读起来也容易。
- Flow charts or models are ideal for explaining procedures.
  利用流程图或模型解释操作步骤效果会非常好。
- Use pictures and diagrams.
  使用图片和表格。
- List 'do's' and 'don'ts' rather than continuous text.
  列出“要做”和“不要做”的要点，而不是连续的一段话。
- Use small chunks of information, and plenty of white space, to improve readability.
  使用小段信息和空白来提高可读性。
- Use plain, simple and jargon-free language.
  使用直白、简单语言，避免术语。
- Avoid red, orange or green as they can be hard to read for some people such as those with dyslexia.
  避免使用红色、橙色或绿色，否则可能会增加阅读难度，特别是对有读写障碍的学员。

BRIEFING AND DEBRIEFING
课前简述和课后总结

Sailing instructors are fortunate in that if they are teaching in double handed boats, they can instantly begin teaching their students as soon as they move to the dinghy. This will continue when they go afloat. However, teaching single handers will require a different approach as the majority of teaching input will have to be given ashore, after which the students will go afloat to try the exercise and then practise the skill.
采用双人船教学非常方便。因为教练只要来到船这边就可以开始教学，在水上也可以继续进行。单人船教学则不同，大部分教学在岸上进行，之后学员下水尝试，进行练习。

Teaching and coaching becomes instantly more difficult when it moves to the water, but the prudent instructor will allow for this by using efficient briefing before the task and effective debriefing or feedback afterwards. This will take the place of the immediate teaching input that has been taking place ashore up to that point.
一旦开始水上练习，指导和教学的难度就变大了。但是谨慎的教练会在下水前向学员进行简述，并在上岸后进行总结和反馈。这两个环节取代了岸上教学。

Without both of these elements, learning will only happen either by accident, or if the student is already able to analyse their own performance and then subsequently modify it.
没有这两个环节，整个学习过程就会显得没有计划，或者如果某些学员自己能够分析他们的表现，最后就会改变学习内容。

Brief 课前简述

6 Techniques for Instructing and Coaching 教学和指导技巧

This should occur before every on-water session and before every new skill is introduced. Be careful though, because if it's too long, the students will switch off, becoming disinterested and perhaps miss a vital piece of information which may have a bearing on their performance or safety.
简述应在每次水上训练和每个新技巧讲解开始前进行。但要注意，如果讲的时间过长，学员会失去兴趣，并且有可能忽略对他们的表现和安全都非常重要的信息。

The briefing should include:
课前简述内容应包括：

- The task; what the students should be doing.
  任务：学员需要做什么。
- How to achieve the task with an explanation and demonstration if required.
  如有需要，通过解释和示范说明如何完成任务。
- The duration of the task.
  水上练习的时间。
- The sailing area including the boundaries, how they will be marked and any hazards to be aware of (more relevant to single handers).
  说明航行区域的边界、边界的标记以及潜在危险（与单人船更相关）。
- How and where feedback will take place, if any (single handers).
  如有反馈（单人船），以怎样的形式以及在哪里进行。
- What to do if the students go out of the area (single handers).
  如果学员驶出了航行区域如何处理（单人船）。
- What the students should do in an emergency.
  在紧急状况下，学员应采取什么措施。
- What signals are to be used (including general recall and abandon session).
  使用哪些信号（包括全体召回和停止训练）。

Once this has been given, it's only of real use if it's been understood by the students.
一旦给出了这些信息，只有学员真正理解了才有用。

Please don't fall into the trap of checking understanding by asking the classic wrong question of 'Does everyone understand?' because there will only ever be one answer— 'yes!'
千万不要又问那个经典的无用问题："大家都明白了吗？"你只会听到："明白了。"

Instead, ask questions that relate directly to the information that's just been given,
反而，应该提出与信息直接相关的问题：

'Where are we going to sail?' (single handers)
"我们要在哪里航行？"（单人船）

'What technique or task are we going to perform?'
"我们要练习什么技能或完成什么任务？"

'Which way will the dinghy turn?'
"船会往哪个方向转？"

'How will you make it turn?'
"如何让船转向？"

'What signal will I use to bring everyone back to the beach at the end?' (single handers)
"我要让大家都回到岸边时，会用什么信号？（单人船）"

If the correct answers are coming back, then it's likely that an efficient brief has been given.
如果他们都回答正确了，说明你的简述非常有效。

The classic 'give away' sign is when you move away to start the task, the students get into a huddle and ask themselves 'What do we do, what did the instructor say?'
有一种很典型的现象，教练做完简述后，开始准备下水，学员们却聚在一起讨论："我们要做什么？教练说了什么？"这就说明学员并没有理解教练说的话。

The Task 任务

The task must be chosen to suit the ability of the student. Part of the skill of instructing is to assess the student's ability and provide tuition at a challenging but not impossible level. It is very frustrating for someone

with a natural flair or with some experience to be taught at the pace of the slowest beginner.
学习任务必须符合学员的水平。技术指导工作的一部分就是要评估学员的能力，然后制订出具有挑战性且可实现的课程方案。对于那些有天赋或有经验的学员来说，上课的节奏如果跟教初学者没什么两样，会让他们非常难受。

Once the task has been set, allow the student to feel responsible for it. Do not continually interrupt—if you have briefed well it should be unnecessary. If events start to go wrong a quiet word will allow the student to correct the mistake while still being in control. Never elbow students out of the way to demonstrate your skill: the idea is that they demonstrate theirs.
一旦明确了任务，就要让学员对自己负责。注意不要一直打断他们，如果你在开始就说清明了情况。如果学员出错了，温和地给他们一些提示，使他们改正错误，保持对课程的控制。永远不要让学员让开，急切地展示你的技术。教学的核心是让学员自己操作。

Occasionally, if you can, allow a mistake to be made to illustrate a point, but only do this if you feel it does not compromise safety and it is a good learning opportunity.
在某些情况下，可利用错误的操作来解释要点，但前提是不影响安全且有助于教学。

Debrief 课后总结

Good instructing and coaching allows for students to learn in a variety of ways and is one important element of the instructor's repertoire, but providing good feedback during a debrief will always help the student understand more and maximise that learning.
良好的指导和教学能让学员采用不同的方式学习，同时也是身为教练应具备的重要的素质之一。在总结时，好的反馈能帮助学员更好地理解，同时使学习效果最大化。

Indeed, giving effective feedback is often said to be the one skill that separates the average instructor from the very good instructor.
而且，是否能给出高效的反馈也是区分优秀教练和普通教练的标准之一。

Feedback, to be most efficient, should happen as soon after the event as possible. This implies that it should happen on the water as the student is performing the skill, or just afterwards. If this is possible, then that's where it should happen. However, for many reasons, it probably won't. So it should take place on land once the group are all safely ashore, the kit has been made safe and the students are receptive. This may mean moving to a sheltered spot, getting warmed up/cooled down, having a hot/cold drink and 'paying a visit'. It needs to be more sophisticated than a collective 'Well done, that was great, how does everyone feel?'
总结应在活动结束后立刻进行，才能达到最好的效果。这意味着，理想情况下，应在水上或刚结束练习时总结，但通常因为各种原因其无法实现。所以应在学员全都安全上岸，整理好装备，准备好听讲后再进行。可将学员带到休息区，让大家暖和/凉快一些，喝点热水/冷饮，随意走动一下。总结应具体，而不是泛泛地说：“干得好！海上的表现真不错，大家觉得如何？”之类的话。

Each student ought to be provided with information on what they have achieved, what went well, what didn't go so well and how to put right areas that need improvement.
每位学员都应告知他们的表现，哪里做得好，哪里做得不好以及如何改进。

Any feedback methods will need some common elements to be in place beforehand and they are:
反馈方式都有共性，如下：

- Be clear of what the task is and know how to perform it.
  明确任务内容，以及如何执行。
- Ensure that it is achievable by the students.
  确保学员能完成任务。
- Observe the session/skill carefully.
  认真观察课程/学员的技能。
- Record what has taken place with either a good memory or notes, if necessary.
  如有必要，用脑或用笔记下训练时的情况。
- The instructor always remains in charge of the session, and hence safety, throughout.
  教练始终保持对课程和学员的管理，并确保安全。

Two popular feedback models being used are 'hamburger' or 'traffic light'.
最常用的两种反馈模型是“汉堡包”和“交通信号灯”的方式。

6 Techniques for Instructing and Coaching
教学和指导技巧

The 'Hamburger', 'Sandwich' or 'Layer Cake'
“汉堡包” “三明治” 或 “夹心蛋糕”

It's tried and tested but has been around for a long time now. Also, the students eventually recognise the pattern.
本方法经过长时间实践检验确认有效。而且，学员会逐渐地识别出这个模式。

The top. Give praise for aspects that have gone well. Be specific
上片，表扬学员做得好的方面，并具体说明

The filling. What's not gone well and how to correct it. Be specific and use the 'rule of 3'. i.e. three key things which at this stage will lead to improvement
馅，说明做得不好的以及如何提高。要详尽，使用“3”规则，比如：在现阶段，有三方面需要改进

The bottom. More praise, finishing on a positive note
底片，结尾要正面，以表扬为主

The 'Traffic Light' 交通信号灯

It's along similar lines, but opens up more opportunity for a flowing discussion. This works with most students, but there are some out there who prefer a more direct approach and just want to be told what's going wrong and how they can put it right!
其与“汉堡包”相似，但是“交通信号灯”的方式提供了更多的讨论机会。该方法适用于大多数学员，但也有学员更喜欢教练直接告诉他们哪里做错了，以及如何纠正。

If a student invites this as a coaching solution to the instructor, there's no harm in accepting the invitation, providing it's done with a degree of sensitivity.
如果学员希望如此，只要他能接受，教练直接这样做也无可非议。

Ask – about the task. Who, what, how, when...
问，关于任务的情况。谁、什么、如何、时间……

Discuss – their performance in response to their answer. What went well and what could be improved
讨论□根据他们的回答讨论他们的表现。什么做得好，什么需要改进

Solve – agree on an action plan/route towards improvement
解决，共同制订一个能够提升的改善计划/途径

1. Ask the student about aspects of their performance. Start with open and general questions, then focus in on specific areas of performance.
询问学员的表现，开始可以问一些常见的开放性的问题，然后集中到具体的表现方面。
2. Discuss these areas using the response to the questions given by the student.
根据学员对于问题的回答来讨论这些方面的问题。
3. Solve any problems firstly by encouraging the student to seek the solution. If they can't, the instructor will do this for them. However, the student should always be the one who identifies the problem and then provides the solution with guidance and help from the instructor.
首先，鼓励学员寻找解决办法。如果学员无法做到，则由教练解决。但是，学员应具备发现问题的能力，并能在教练的指导和帮助下解决问题。

By allowing the student to start analysing their performance of the skills being taught, then seeking ways of improving their performance, the students will learn how to continue this process after they have left the environment of the structured session led by an instructor.
通过让学员分析自己的表现，鼓励他们寻找改进的方法，让学员学会如何持续学习，即使在脱离教练安排的课程和环境后也能继续提高。

In effect, the instructor is preparing the student for when the instructor is no longer there. After this training, the student should be able to continue with their own progress using the skills and learning process delivered by the instructor.
实际上，教练是在帮助学员为无人指导的情况做准备。在这次培训之后，学员应能够运用学到的技巧和学习方式，通过自己的练习继续提高。

ASSESSING YOUR STUDENTS' ABILITIES
评估学员的能力

There is an element of assessment in every RYA training course, not just the formal assessment that leads to the award of a certificate but also the more informal assessment that takes place throughout the course, no matter how short or long it may be. Assessment is about understanding how the student is performing against a set of standards or expectations.
每个RYA培训课程中都有测评，除了教练资格认证的正式测评，还包括课程中的非正式测评(或长或短)。测评的目的是，以标准为依据，判断学员的能力。

This might be summarised in three stages:
可为三个阶段：

- Initial assessment. 初步测评。
- Formative assessment. 形成性测评。
- Summative assessment. 总结性测评。

For example, when an instructor or coach first meets their students an 'initial assessment' takes place where the instructor tries to establish what experience and skills the students already have. This initial assessment may be a simple discussion of previous sailing experience or it may be slightly more formal by asking students to set out on paper what they have done previously. The first on-water session is also used to establish the starting point for the course. The benefit of this approach is to enable the instructor to structure the course and the content to suit the students' actual levels of ability rather than their assumed level. There may also be formal checks to be made on pre-course requirements for instructor training.
举例来说，教练或教官初次见到学员时，会对他们进行初步测评，了解学员的经验和水平。初次测评可能是关于过去航行经历的简单讨论，或更正式的，要求学员写出自己的航海经历。第一次水上训练也用来建立课程的起始点。这种方法的好处在于能帮助教练根据学员的真实水平来设计课程，而不是他们对学员的评估。在教练培训中，可能会有正式的课前测评。

As the course progresses the instructor will be carefully monitoring students' progress to see if the pace is too fast, too slow or just right to be challenging, informative and achievable. This can be described as the 'formative assessment' and once again could be either formal or informal. Group discussions, quizzes and one to one discussions may be useful here.
随着课程的进行，教练要仔细观察学员，判断其学习进度是否太快、太慢，还是给学员的挑战刚好，信息量足够，而且可完成。该阶段可被称为"形成性测评"，同样地，可以是正式或非正式的。小组讨论，小测验和一对一讨论等形式都可使用。

Finally, at the end of the course the instructor or coach has to decide, with the help of the Chief Instructor or senior instructor, whether or not the objectives of the training have been achieved. This is the 'summative assessment' and once again could use a range of methods to achieve an objective view of the assessment criteria. Practical tests, such as sailing around a triangular course without an instructor on board, are useful, as are quizzes, oral questions and more formal tests. Ultimately the question may be whether to award the certificate or not. To help you in this the following statements or measures may be of use but never forget that most people are doing this for fun and recognising the progress that your students have made by the award of certificates is more likely to motivate them to continue than withholding the certificate because they cannot perform the task every time!
最后，在课程结束后，教练或教官在主教练或高级教练的帮助下，判定培训目标是否达成。这就是“总结测评”，本阶段也可使用多种方法使评估更客观。可采用实践测试，例如无教练同船指导，航行三角标；或书面测试、口头问答和更正式的测验。最后决定是否颁发证书。以下叙述或措施可帮助你判断，但不要忘记大多数来参加课程的学员是为了娱乐，如果因为学员无法每次都完美地完成任务就不颁发证书会，打消他们学帆船的积极性；酌情给予证书，更有利于激励他们将帆船学习继续进行下去。

CERTIFICATES 证书

RYA certificates provide a great incentive to continue training, providing a clear measure of an individual's progress. However, they can become a discouragement to the weak student as the prospect of gaining a certificate fades. The Chief Instructor will advise on the importance of keeping everyone informed of their progress through the course, and what they can realistically achieve. This could involve breaking the news that a Performance Sailing certificate is not possible by the end of the course. The instructor should explain what can be achieved and agree with the student how to get the best possible value out of the course.
RYA的证书能激励学员继续参与培训，也清楚地说明了个人的进步。然而，没有获得证书的学员可能会很受打击。主教练会建议在课程中，让学员知道他们的学习进展以及他们能达到的程度，并告诉学员课程结束后他们无法获得证书。教练应向学员说明他们能达到什么程度，并与学员达成一致，使课程为他们创造出最大的价值。

From then on, the instructor should set goals, point out strengths and weaknesses and offer encouragement. They should point out how much has been achieved as the course progresses so that by the final debrief both can be satisfied that the course was worthwhile.
接着，教练应给学员设定目标，指出他们的优势和劣势，并鼓励他们。在课程中告知学员的进展，这样在最后总结时，双方都会对课程的效果感到满意。

If students are not kept informed, tension will build up with students discussing amongst themselves whether they are passing or failing. During the final debrief, instructor teaching may be blamed for lack of results. This lack of communication between instructor and student is one of the most common reasons for complaints about RYA courses. Remember that many of the people taught are highly successful and respected in their own field. The only skill the instructor may have that they haven't is the ability to sail and teach sailing. Ensure they retain their dignity and a positive attitude towards their instructor and the sport. This is one of the most skilful aspects of instructing.
如果学员没有及时被告知进展，就会互相讨论自己是否通过，使气氛很紧张。在最后总结时，教练可能会因为没有成果而被责问。这种教练与学员之间缺乏沟通而引起的投诉，是RYA课程中最常见的投诉之一。记住，很多学员都是社会上的成功人士，在他们工作的领域备受尊敬。可能教练唯一比他们擅长也就是帆船以及帆船教学了。教练应注意他们的自尊心，确保他们对帆船运动的积极性，赢得他们的尊重与信任。这是教学中最具技巧的方面之一。

LIBERTY
HELICOPTERS
DOVER

7 The National Sailing Scheme & Youth Sailing Scheme
国家航海计划和青少年航海计划

Stage 1 一级水手

By the end of this introductory course, the student will have a basic understanding of how a boat sails, and some experience of steering and handling the boat. Stages 2, 3 and 4 will complete your introduction to the sport in easy stages.
在此入门课程结束后，学员应能够基本理解帆船的运行原理，且拥有了一些掌舵和控船的经验。在阶段二、三和四会逐步完善对帆船运动的介绍，接受起来会很容易。

Stage 2 二级水手

By the end of this course, the student will have a range of sailing skills and background knowledge, and be well on the way to being a confident small boat sailor.
在此课程结束后，学员应掌握一些航行技巧和理论知识，为成为一名自信的小帆船水手打下坚实的基础。

Stage 3 三级水手

Having completed Stage 3 you will be able to sail in any direction and rig and launch your boat. Your skills and knowledge mean that you can regard yourself as a sailor, not a beginner.
完成阶段三的课程后，你将能够在任何角度航行，并且知道如何装船和下水。你所掌握的技能和知识意味着你已经不是初学者了，而是一个真正的小水手。

Stage 4 四级水手

A Stage 4 certificate means that you have the skills to sail a double-handed boat as crew or helm, and solve a variety of problems afloat. Passing this course is the natural entry point for the advanced courses.
获得阶段四的证书意味着你掌握了使用双人船航行的技巧，以船员或舵手的角色，能解决一系列水上问题。通过该课程就可以开始学习高阶课程了。

Seamanship Skills—See page 116.
航海技术——请看第116页。

Day Sailing—See page 119.
日间航行——请看第119页。

Sailing with Spinnakers—See page 122.
球帆航行——请看第122页。

Start Racing—See page 130.
初级竞赛——请看第130页。

Performance Sailing—See page 137.
高阶航海——请看第137页。

Additional Racing Modules—See page 141.
附加竞赛单元—— 请看第141页。

GAMES TO FACILITATE LEARNING 练船游戏

Youth sailing courses invariably go well when some games are incorporated into the training programme. Games not only provide enjoyment and social interaction but also enable children to practise their sailing skills in a less formal environment. The following are examples of games designed to reinforce sailing skills.
在培训中融入游戏，总是能让青少年航海课程开展得更好。游戏不仅使课程更有乐趣，促进社交，而且也能让孩子们在相对轻松的教学环境下学习。以下是一些专为加强学员航行技巧设计的游戏。

Orienteering Afloat 水上定向赛

As for land orienteering by using buoys marked with code letters.
与陆地定向基本相同，除了使用带有字母的浮标外。

Teaching points: Sailing on all points of the wind.
教学要点：在所有角度航行。

Resources: Buoys coloured or marked with code letters.
游戏器材：不同颜色或用字母标记的浮标。

Tag 海鹰追击

One boat is 'it', raises dagger board half way, throws tennis ball at other boats. If it hits, then struck boat is 'it', retrieves tennis ball, raises dagger board half-way and chases other boats. Useful to play when using different types of boats – Oppies and Toppers.
首先，选一条船作为"老鹰"，该船要将稳向板提起一半，"老鹰"用网球攻击其他船。如击中某一条船，该船就变成"老鹰"，"老鹰"捡回网球，将稳向板提起一半，去追击其他船。在使用不同类型的训练用船，比如用OP和Topper进行练习时，该游戏非常实用。

Teaching points: Use of centre/dagger board, speed control.
教学要点：稳向板的使用，船速的控制。

Resources: Tennis ball, large buoyant sponge, buoyant frisbee.
游戏器材：网球、有浮力的大海绵、有浮力的飞盘。

Relays 水上接力赛

Team event to transport baton/piece of equipment/person from one shore to another. Variations: transport to a boat, race round a slalom course, collect gear required for a task. All of these need very clear instructions about changeover procedures, what and how objects can be carried, time penalties etc.
将一个接力棒/器材/人传递到另一处的团队活动。游戏变型：传递到一条船上，航行障碍航线，收集所要求的装备。每一步都需要非常清楚的指导和交接步骤，如需要携带什么样的物品以及如何携带、时间惩罚等。

Teaching points: Sailing accurately on all points of sailing, landing on lee shore, leaving lee shore.
教学要点：准确地在所有航行角度航行；停靠顺风岸；驶离顺风岸。

Resources: Buckets, tennis balls, corks.
游戏器材：桶、网球、木塞。

All Standing Race 站立航行

Race around a triangular course without sitting down in the boat (tack by walking around the mast or by stepping between boom and sail foot: gybe by stepping around sail clew).
在不坐在船里的状态下，比赛航行三角标（绕桅杆迎风转向，或从帆杆和帆底中间穿过去，绕帆后角顺风转向）。

Teaching points: Boat balance and trim.
教学要点：调节船的左右和前后。

Resources: Three buoys.
游戏器材：三个浮标。

Treasure Hunt 寻宝游戏

Mix clues both onshore and on-the-water. Have each team follow a completely different order of clues. End with a picnic or barbecue when the 'treasure' is discovered. (Have some treasure for everyone, not just the first team.) Add to the fun with pirate costumes!
在岸上和水上均设置"寻宝"线索。给每组的线索顺序要完全不同。成功找到宝藏后，集体进行一次野餐或烧烤（给每组都颁发奖品，不要只奖励第一名）。还可以穿海盗服装增加游戏的趣味性哦！

Teaching points: Accurate and fast sailing, team building.
教学要点：准确快速地航行，团队合作。

Resources: Laminated clue sheets, face paints, box of dressing up clothes, 'treasure'.
游戏器材：塑封的线索卡，脸部涂料，一箱子服装道具和"宝藏"。

HENRI LLOYD

The RYA Teaching Method for Double Handers 8

RYA双人船教学方法

The RYA Method covers the practical techniques of basic boat handling in the Start Sailing, Basic Skills and Better Sailing courses as well as Stages 1—4 in the Youth Sailing Scheme. Whilst the majority of the teaching method is appropriate for all three boat disciplines, some elements may not be e.g. capsize drill for keelboats.

RYA教学方法涵盖了各课程中的基本控船技巧。这些课程有"航海起步""基础技能"和"进阶航海"，以及青少年航海计划阶段1～4的课程。尽管大部分教学方法对三种船型（单体船、双体船、龙骨船）都适用，但有些可能不适合龙骨船，例如正船练习。

The standardised teaching techniques enable Instructors to move from one centre to another and teach any part of the appropriate RYA course. Students can follow a course at one centre with a higher level course elsewhere, and the Instructors will know exactly what has been covered and what needs to be taught next.

标准化的教学技巧使RYA教练能够在不同的培训中心教授RYA课程中的任何部分。学员在一个培训中心学完一个课程后，可在其他的RYA培训中心学习后续课程。教练也能够很清楚地知道学员的水平，以及接下来应教授的内容。

The RYA Method analyses the various elements that make up the activity of sailing a small boat, splitting each element into simple stages. Emphasis is placed on revision and testing to ensure that each stage has been successfully learnt.

RYA的教学方法充分剖析了驾驶一条小帆船需要掌握的内容，并将这些内容分解成一些简单的学习阶段。强调不断地复习与测试，确保学员在每个阶段都完成学习任务。

To maintain motivation, it is important that students succeed at each stage, so the pace of learning and the complexity of the task are adapted to the individual. Students are encouraged to work out solutions from basic 'models' supplied by the Instructor. In educational terms, it is a student-centred method based on experiential learning. When teaching beginners, different centres may use slightly different variations of the Method but all retain the basic philosophy. Thus the RYA Instructor should find no difficulty in adapting to local differences or 'house rules' within the basic framework.

要使学员保持学习动力，关键是让学员在每个阶段都能顺利地通过。因此，学习进度以及任务的复杂程度应视学员的水平而定。要鼓励学员在给出的基本方法上找出解决问题方法。用教育术语来说，就是以学员为本的体验学习法。在教授初学者时，不同培训中心可能会在教学方法上有所调整，但是其基本理念都是一样的。这样，RYA教练就能在RYA通用的基本教学框架下，毫不费力地适应当地的教学差异或"自定规则"。

The instructor course concentrates on the detail of the Method but the overall aim remains the same — to get students sailing safely on their own as soon as possible. Each technique is broken down into easy steps for learning but, once learnt, those steps should disappear as the manoeuvre becomes a continuous flowing action.

教练课程注重教学细节，但是最终目标都是相同的——就是让学员在保证自身安全的前提下，尽快自己驾驶帆船。每一个技巧都被分解成简单的步骤，一旦学会，就看不出明显的步骤了，整个操作就会形成一套连续流畅的动作。

A student who, having mastered a technique effectively, then adapts what he has been taught to suit himself should never be criticised because he has departed from the Method. He should be encouraged to move on and learn more.

有的学员在将某技巧运用自如后，会根据自身情况对操作进行调整。教练不应该批评学员没有遵循标准步骤，应鼓励他们继续学习更多的技巧。

The following outline of the Teaching Method provides the sequence of sessions and the important teaching points. The training course will expand on this framework. When actually using the Method to teach beginners, some sessions may well be run together, but it is worth establishing the principle, that after only 20 minutes or so, the average student's ability to absorb information falls off considerably. A short break, followed by revision and informal testing, makes for much more efficient learning.

以下教学方法概要对课程顺序和教学重点进行了说明。培训课程会在这个框架下扩展。当使用该方法来教初学者时，将其他训练融合在一起会更好。但要注意，在大约20分钟后，学员接收信息的平均水平会大幅度下降。这时候应先暂停，休息一小会，然后进行复习和小测试，会使教学效果更好。

Training in the RYA Method avoids technical terminology. 'Ropes, seats, push and pull' are preferable to instructions which are complicated by unfamiliar terms. Students will be having enough trouble working out what is going on without being told to 'sheet out and bear away'. Some nautical terms in common use come

naturally, however, so they will almost certainly be used and learnt in the first sessions.
RYA教学提倡避免使用术语。采用“绳子、座位、推和拉”等简单用语进行教学会更好，使用学员不熟悉的术语会让教学更复杂。理解教练讲的内容已经不容易了，听到“松缭绳，顺风偏转”等术语只会更头疼。有些航海术语会很常用，所以要确保学员在第一节课就学会这些术语且进行使用。

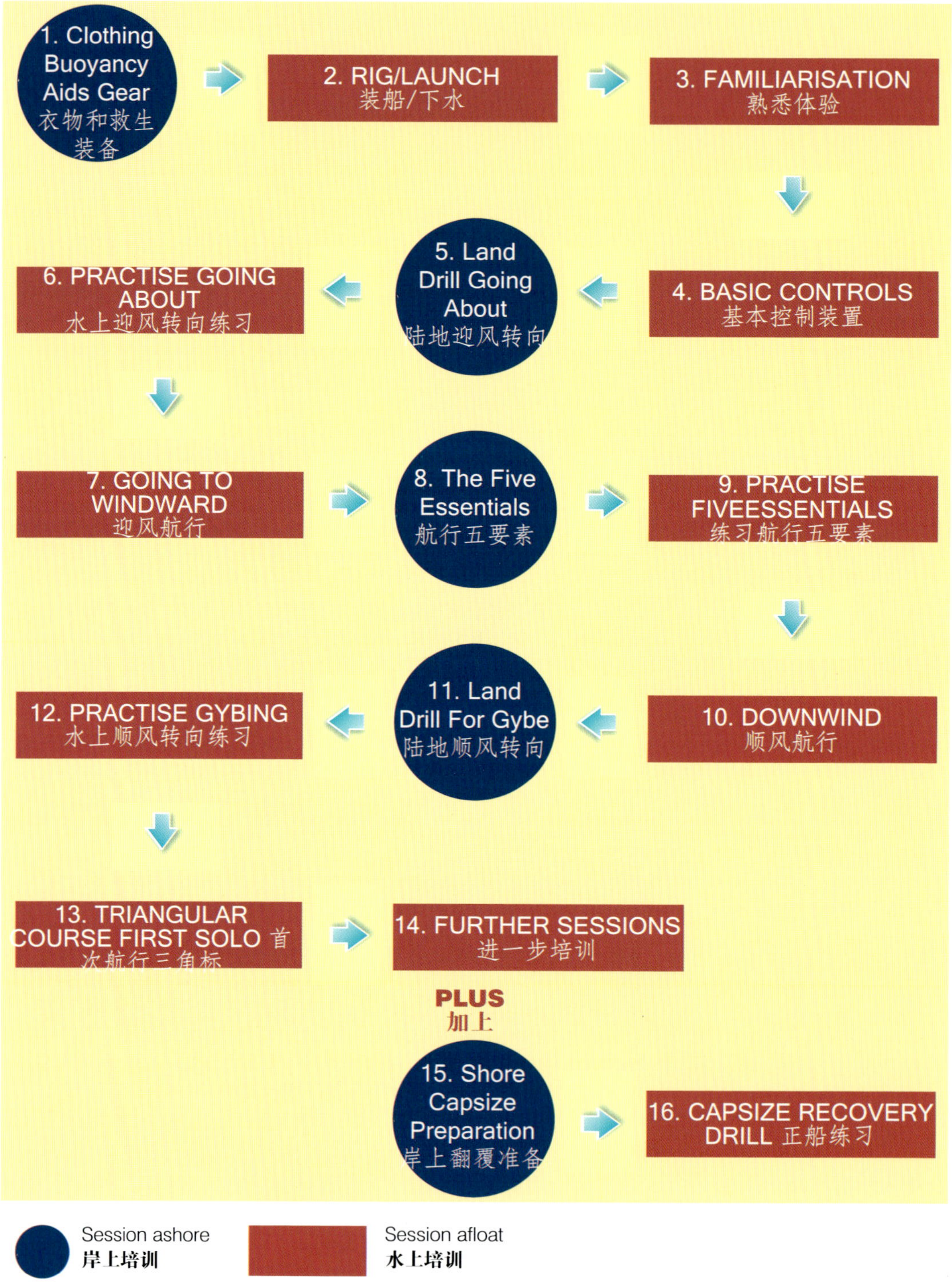

Session 1 训练 1

Clothing/Footwear/Buoyancy aids/Gear collection 衣物/鞋/救生衣/装备

- Appropriate clothing: wetsuit, dry suit, waterproofs.
  衣着合理：湿式保暖服、干式保暖服、防水衣。
- Footwear: wet boots, trainers.
  鞋：下水鞋、运动鞋。
- Buoyancy aid: 50 Newtons, correct size, securely fastened, 150 Newtons life jackets for non-swimmers.
  救生衣：浮力50牛顿，大小合适，穿好扣牢。不会游泳的学员应使用浮力至少为150牛顿的救生衣。
- Gear collection: identify each item briefly.
  装备：简要地识别每件装备。

Session 2 训练 2

Rigging/Launching 装船/下水

Rigging:
装船：

- Rig boat quickly, head to wind. 船头顶风，快速装船。
- Involve students. 让学员一起参与。
- Explain briefly. 简要说明。
- Reef. 缩帆。

Launching and under way: 下水，开始航行：

- Don't waste time. 不要浪费时间。
- Hoist main. 升主帆。
- Keep students dry (where possible). 尽可能不让学员湿身。

Top Tip 重要提示

Most modern boats need jib up first for rig tension.
大多数现代帆船需要先把前帆升起来，使前支索张紧。
Don't let it flog!
不要让帆随风拍打！

Furl/back it while preparing the rest of the dinghy.
在备船时，把帆卷起来或把前缭卡住。

Session 3 训练 3

Familiarisation 熟悉体验

Give your students time to absorb the sensation of being in a sailing boat perhaps for the first time. They should be looking out of the dinghy and not inside, enjoying the new sensation of being afloat. The session demonstrates your skill and, by making no demands of your students, allows everyone to start relaxing.
第一次带学员出海时，给大家一点时间体会在帆船上的感觉。提醒他们朝船外看而不是朝里，享受在水上漂浮的全新体验。这次课程显示了你的航行水平，不要去指挥大家，让大家放松下来。

- Interesting, enthusiastic and enjoyable.
  有趣、热情、愉快。
- Instructor at helm.
  教练掌舵。
- Students allocated tasks.
  给学员分配任务。

- Students balance boat and gain awareness of wind direction and orientation.
  让学员平衡船体，并培养风向及方位意识。
- Short session.
  时间短。
- Calm, relaxed and controlled.
  冷静、放松、控制良好。
- Point out landmarks and wind direction.
  指出陆标和风向。
- Sail a figure of 8 course.
  航行8字标。
- Reef the sails.
  缩帆。

Session 4 训练 4

Basic Boat Controls 基本控船技巧

- Lying-to. Sails flapping (not backed). Hove to.
  飘帆停船。 帆拍打（不是鼓起）。
- Students take helm with target to aim at.
  让学员掌舵，指定航行目标。
- Instructor sits to leeward and forward of the helmsman. Wet elbow position.
  教练坐在舵手下风侧前方、湿肘的位置。
- Instructor keeps hands off the tiller while student is on the helm.
  学员在掌舵时，教练不要动舵柄。

Top Tip
重要提示

Demonstrate good boat control whilst sailing, balance the boat and sails, then take your hand off the tiller to demonstrate that the boat continues sailing in a straight line.
在航行时，演示良好的控船技术，平衡船体和船帆。然后松开舵柄，演示船仍然可以跑直线。

- Simple instructions such as ‘pull it towards you/ push it away’.
  给学员的指示要简单，比如“往自己这边拉/往外推”。

Demonstrate basic boat controls:
演示基本控船技巧：

- From lying-to position pull mainsail to turn boat towards wind.
  在飘帆停船状态，收主帆，直到船顶风。
- From lying-to, pull jib in to turn away from wind.
  在飘帆停船状态，收紧前帆，使船转向下风。

Relate changes in boat direction to the direction of the wind.
将航向改变和风向联系起来。

- Students practise.
  学员实践。
- Discreetly moving your weight may be necessary to guarantee success.
  为了确保学员操作成功，可小心地挪动你的身体进行协助。
- Effect of raising centre board.
  提起稳向板的效果。
- Point out ‘no-go-zone’ when tacking through 180 degrees.
  练习180°迎风转向时，指出不可航行区域。

Session 5 训练 5

Tacking/Going About 迎风转向

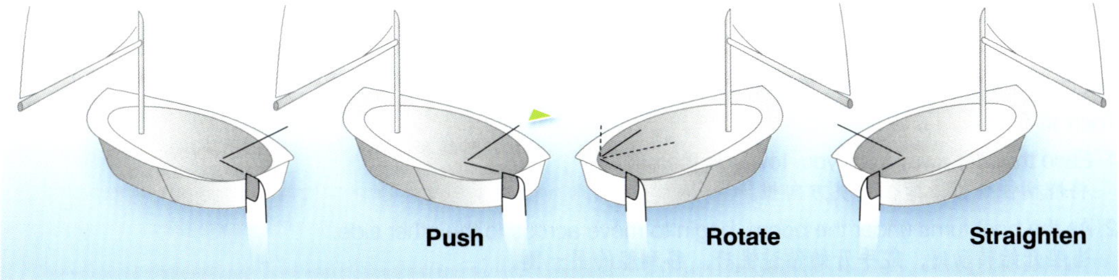

The basics – Turning into the Wind and through 180 degrees.
基本要点——转过顶风，转180°。

- Not all students will require a land drill, which is best done on a boat ashore.
  岸上练习最好用岸上的船来进行，不用要求所有的学员都做。
- Demonstrate using the 'whole-part-whole' method.
  演示使用"整体—分解—整体"的方法。

The process is as follows:
步骤如下：

1. Begin with the boat flat. If the sheeting arrangement is from the transom the helmsman changes hands on the extension and mainsheet.
   在船平稳的状态下开始。如果帆船主缭后置，那么舵手就须先交换拿副舵柄和主缭的手。
2. The turn is initiated by easing the tiller extension smoothly away.
   流畅地推舵，开始转向。
3. As boom nears the centreline, helmsman starts to move across boat, facing forwards if the boat is centre main rigged or aft if transom rigged.
   当帆杆接近中心线时，舵手开始移动，并横跨过船。如主缭中置，脸朝前；如主缭后置，则脸朝后。
4. Helmsman revolves extension away from him forward of the tiller. If the extension is too long to pass between the end of the tiller and the centre falls it will have to be swung towards the stern and over the tiller. This is done by sliding the hand down the extension, swivelling it around, and sliding the hand back up to the end.
   舵手将副舵柄从舵柄前方转到另一侧。如果副舵柄太长，无法通过舵柄和主缭，就得在船尾从舵柄上方转过去。因此需要把手滑到副舵柄下方，把副舵柄旋转到另一侧，然后手滑回副舵柄的尾端。
5. As boom reaches new leeward quarter, helmsman centralises tiller as boat points towards new target and mainsail fills, and sits down. (If the boat is transom rigged, then the turn is complete.)
   当帆杆转到新的下风侧船尾角时，随着船朝向新的方向，舵手回舵，主帆受风，舵手坐下（如果帆船主缭后置，那么转向就完成了）。
6. He then changes hands at this point by bringing the sheet hand back across in front of his body to hold both tiller extension and sheet. He takes the mainsheet with his front hand, releases sheet with back hand, bringing extension under arm to front of body.
   这时，他就可以换手了，拿主缭的手拿住缭绳，换到身体前面，同时抓住副舵柄和主缭。接着，用前手拿主缭；后手松开，将副舵柄从腋下换到前面。

Teaching the basics of tacking 180 degrees through the wind.
180°迎风转向的基本技巧教学。

Very few students will absorb all the information listed above in one go. Teach the skills a little at a time, progressively adding bits in. A 'teaching summary' might therefore be:
很少有学员能一次就接受以上所有的内容。所以，教练应分解教学，一次教授一点，逐步增加内容。因此，可总结为：

Top Tip
重要提示

Choose obvious targets for students to sail towards after tacking.
选择一个明显的物体，作为学员转向后的航行目标。

Going About—the Complete Manoevuvre 迎风转向——完整步骤

Going About Aft Mainsheet 主缭后置帆船的迎风转向

The helmsman faces aft during the manoeuvre and uses the frying pan grip (palm up thumb on top), and before tacking he looks into the area where he is going to tack into to make sure that it is clear, and keeps the boat flat.
舵手在操作过程中面朝后，使用平底锅式握法拿舵（手掌朝上，大拇指在上方）。在转向前，舵手须检查确保周围无障碍物，并保持船体平稳。

1. Helmsman "flicks" the spare mainsheet to the back of the boat under the tiller. Front hand holding the mainsheet, the back hand on the tiller and says "Ready about".
1. 舵手将剩余的主缭从舵柄下方往船后方甩开。前手抓住主缭，后手拿住副舵柄，发出"准备转向"的指令。

2. Crew checks, and if clear says "Ready".

Helmsman changes hands on mainsheet and tiller extension by trapping the mainsheet under the thumb of the rear hand and picking up the tiller extension with the front hand. He places his front foot across the boat.

2. 船员确认周围无障碍后，回复"准备好了"。舵手交换拿主缭和副舵柄的手，前手把主缭放到后手中，然后前手拿住副舵柄，并把前脚往船另一边伸。

3. Helm initiates the turn by easing the tiller away smoothly, saying "Lee oh".
3. 舵手流畅地推舵，并喊"开始转向"。

4. As the boom reaches the leeward stern quarter, the crew releases the jib sheet.
4. 当帆杆到达下风侧船尾处时，船员就松掉前缭。

5. As the boom nears the centre line, the helm starts to move across the boat, front foot leading. About this time the crew can also start to move.
5. 当帆杆接近中心线时，舵手开始移到船的另一边，前脚先迈出。这时船员也要开始移动。

6. Helmsman rotates tiller extension away from him forward of the tiller, and steps fully onto the new windward side. Crew picks up new jib sheet and balances boat.
6. 舵手将副舵柄从舵柄的前方转过去，接下来完全跨到上风侧。船员拿起这一侧前缭并平衡船体。

7. As the boom reaches the new leeward quarter, both helm and crew move to sit down. Helm centralises the tiller as the mainsail starts to fill. Crew sheets in the jib. Helm looks forward to check course.
7. 当帆杆到达下风侧时，舵手和船员都换到船另一侧坐下。随着主帆开始受风，舵手将舵柄回正。船员收紧前帆。舵手往前看，检查航向和航线。

8. Boat sails on, crew balancing the boat, the helm making small tiller/mainsheet adjustments where necessary.
8. 随着船继续航行，船员平衡船体；舵手在适当的时候，对舵或主缭进行微调。

Going About Centre Mainsheet 主缭中置帆船的迎风转向

The helmsman faces forwards through the manoeuvre, not moving too quickly across the boat, helping the balancing action. The helm holds the tiller and mainsheet in the “dagger/dagger” grip.

在整个操作过程中，舵手始终面朝前方，注意在换到另一侧时动作不要过快，并协助平衡船体。舵手用“匕首”式握法拿副舵柄和主缭。

1. Helmsman sails the boat flat, and checks into the area where the boat will be turning into. If it is clear, helm calls “Ready about”. Helm checks that spare mainsheet is untangled. Crew uncleats jib and when ready says “Ready”.

1. 舵手使船平稳航行，查看周围水域，确定无障碍物后，发出“准备转向”的口令。接着，检查确保主缭没有缠住。船员将前缭从夹绳器拿起，准备好后回应“准备好了”。

2. Helm calls “Lee oh” while while pushing away gently. The rear leg is extended across towards the middle of the boat.

2. 舵手喊“开始转向”，缓慢地推舵，后脚伸过船的中心线。

3. As the boat sails up into the wind the crew releases the jib.

3. 随着船逐渐转向顶风，船员松开前帆。

4. Helm rotates the end of the tiller extension forwards, out to the side of the boat and then as the boom moves across to the leeward side, straightens the tiller onto the centreline of the boat steering with the hand holding the tiller behind his back. The helm balances the boat before moving further. The crew sheets in the jib on the new side.

4. 舵手将副舵柄末端往前转到船的另一侧，随着帆杆转到下风侧，将舵柄回正，先不要换手，后手放在后背继续掌舵。舵手先控制好船的平衡，然后再把身体往前移。船员将另一侧前缭收紧。

5. Helm rotates the end of the tiller in the palm of the hand so that the thumb is uppermost and sits down, steering behind his back while facing forwards.
5. 舵手将副舵柄末端在手中转动，大拇指在上，坐下，继续把手放在后背操舵，脸朝前。

6. The helm brings the hand holding the mainsheet up to the tiller extension, thumb extended and trapping the sheet against the extension. The thumbs of both hands point towards each other.
6. 舵手用抓主缭的手去拿副舵柄，大拇指展开将绳子和副舵柄抓在一起，这时两手大拇指相对。

7. Helm releases the tiller with the front hand, and moves the arm back across the front of the body to take hold of the mainsheet, and when in a firm grasp it can be released by the back hand.
7. 然后前手（如左图右手）松开副舵柄，去抓身体前侧的主缭，抓紧后，后手就可以松掉主缭了。

8. With the boat balanced and under control, the back hand holding the tiller can be brought up under the armpit to finish in front of the body. Turning slightly at the waist will assist.
8. 控制好船平稳航行后，就可以将后面抓副舵柄的手从腋窝下面移到身体前面。转动一点手腕部位可以起到帮助作用。

9. The boat sails on under control. Continue to practise until instruction is no longer needed.
9. 继续练习直到不需要指导为止。

Tacking Method – Variations 迎风转向的多种方式

There are several variations for centre mainsheet boats in addition to the basic one outlined previously.
除了前文所述的基本迎风转向方式外，对于主缭中置的帆船，还有其他方式。

Many modern boats have such long tiller extensions that the tiller extension will not fit past the mainsheet hoop/falls (e.g. RS400, Laser Stratos). In this case simply slide your tiller hand down the extension as you move into the boat (preventing over-steering) and rotate the extension around the back of the boat over the transom. After crossing the boat, proceed using one of the following methods.
很多现代帆船的副舵柄很长，导致在迎风转向时，无法从主缭绳圈/滑轮组转过去（例如：RS400，激光Stratos）。遇到这种情况，只需在你移到船内时，将手顺着副舵柄往下滑，然后在船尾梁上方往后将副舵柄转到另一侧。等到人换到另一侧后，采用以下任意一种方式。

With the boat flat, the helm alters the position of the tiller extension so that the end of the extension is pointing up over the rearmost shoulder. All other commands are as for the basic method tack.
保持船体平衡，舵手调整好副舵柄的位置，使副舵柄尾端落到他的肩膀上。其他步骤和基本转向法一样。

As the tiller is pushed away, the helm also starts to rotate the end of the tiller extension out over the transom past the end of the boom until the tiller extension is pointing out over the opposite side of the boat and the helm now stands to cross the boat.
舵手推舵时，转动副舵柄尾端，转过帆杆末端直到副舵柄指向船另一侧，然后舵手开始移到另一侧。

Helm and crew complete the tack as for the normal centre mainsheet tacking method.
然后按照一般主缭中置帆船迎风转向的方式完成转向即可。

Session 6 训练 6

Practise Going About (through 180 degrees) 练习迎风转向（转180°）

After practice the student should be able to sail around a shallow figure of eight course, going about at each end, without any help from the Instructor.

经过练习后，学员应能在无须任何帮助的情况下，航行简单8字标，并且在航线任一端进行迎风转向。

- Go about from reach to reach. Practise often.
  从横风到横风的迎风转向应经常练习。
- Ensure boat is going fast enough to tack through 180 degrees.
  确保船转向速度够快，能够转180°。
- Check crew and jib position.
  检查船员和前帆的位置。
- Consider a land drill if necessary.
  如有必要，考虑先在岸上练习。

Session 7 训练 7

Going to Windward 迎风航行

Going to windward and developing tacking through an increasingly narrow angle until tacking close hauled to close hauled through 90 degrees is achieved.
练习迎风航行，逐步缩小迎风转向的角度，直到能够从一舷迎风航行转90°转到另一舷航行。

In fluctuating winds, sailing on a close reach initially will make life easier for your students.
如果风况不稳定，刚开始训练时后迎风航行，学员会更容易接受。

- Demonstrate that the sails flap as boat turns towards the wind.
  演示当船顶风时，帆随风拍打的状态。
- Demonstrate the no-go-zone again.
  再次演示说明不可航行区域。
- Demonstrate and explain the concept of beating to windward.
  演示并解释迎风段跑Z字形的概念。
- Take the boat downwind. Hand over to the student and ask to be sailed to a point directly upwind.
  将船转到顺风。让学员控船，要求他迎风航行到某个位置。

Many students will now be able to do this unaided so only intervene if you feel that it is really necessary.
在这个阶段，很多学员都能在没有帮助的情况下完成这些操作，因此，除非你觉得确实有必要，否则不要介入。

- Don't worry if the tacking is inefficient.
  如果转向不是很到位的话也不要太担心。
- Use the flapping of the jib luff as an indicator of the edge of the no-go-zone.
  利用拍打的前帆帆前缘，作为在不可航行区域边缘航行的指示标。
- Relate progress to landmarks.
  利用陆标作为参照物。
- Check ability to determine wind direction.
  考查学员的风向判断力。
- Stress that the angle between the sails and the wind stays the same wherever the boat is pointing.
  强调不管船指向哪，帆和风的夹角保持不变。

Tacking will now be through 90 degrees although the novice may tack from close reach to close reach initially. Tacking can be developed further by rolling the boat through the tack.
新手刚开始只会从后迎风转到后迎风，现在应该能转90°了。进一步提高转向技能，还可学习反压舷转向。

- Ensure the boat is flat.
  确保船体水平。
- Crew bring their weight inboard to initiate turn.
  船员将重心移到船内，开始转向。

Top Tip 重要提示

When sailing to windward, sit well forward.
迎风航行时，人要尽量往船前面坐。

- The boat will turn towards the wind as it heels.
  船倾斜时，会往迎风方向转。
- Steer through the wind but discourage over-steering.
  推舵使船转过顶风，注意不要过度推舵。
- Crew's feet are brought under the body as the boat turns.
  随着船偏转，船员将脚收回。
- The mainsail is eased.
  松主帆。
- Helm and crew move across together and sit out.
  舵手和船员一起移到船的另一侧，并坐到船舷外。
- The boat is brought upright and the mainsail sheeted in.
  把船压平，并收紧主帆。

Sessions 8 & 9 训练 8和9

The Five Essentials 航行五要素

The five essentials contain the core skills required to sail a boat properly.
五要素是正确驾驶帆船的核心技能。

1 Sail Setting 调帆

- Restate the point regarding the angle between the sails and the wind.
  再次说明帆和风的夹角。
- Simple board sketch or a working model.
  在白板上画图或者用模型演示。
- Sails should be 'just not flapping'. Ease sails when turning away from the wind and sheet in when turning. towards the wind (which will also aid tacking).
  帆要调到"正好不拍打"的状态。转向下风时松帆，转向上风时收帆。
- Remind students to sheet out when bearing away.
  提醒学员，顺风偏转时要松帆。
- Consider using tell tales.
  考虑使用气流线。

> **Top Tip 重要提示**
>
> The Five Essentials should form a continuous thread at every level. Comment on all five whatever the theme of the session.
> 五要素应贯穿每个级别。任何训练主题都可与五要素结合。

2 Balance 船的左右

- Sail upright for minimum drag.
  在水上航行时，保持船体竖直，阻力最小。
- Demonstrate afloat how heeling makes the boat turn.
  在水上演示船的倾斜是如何促进船的偏转的。
- Every rudder movement slows the boat.
  舵的任何移动都会使船减速。
- Remember 'balance affects turning'.
  记住"船的左右影响偏转"。

> **Top Tip 重要提示**
>
> Sailing downwind, the jib is a useful wind indicator.
> 顺风航行时，前帆是非常有用的风向标。

3 Boat Trim 船的前后

- Show trim for different points of sailing. Explain why the boat goes better close-hauled with weight forward and better off the wind with weight back.
  演示不同航行角度，调节船的前后状态。解释为什么在迎风航行时，人往前坐，船跑得更快；在顺风航行时，人应往后坐。
- Remember 'trim affects speed'.
  记住"船的前后影响速度"。

4 Centreboard 稳向板的位置

- Demonstrate settings for different points of sailing and different classes of boats.
  演示不同航行角度以及不同船型稳向板的位置。

5 Course made good 最佳航线

- Explain different courses that will take you to windward. If the students are ready, introduce the idea that one course may be better than another because of tide, wind shadows or hazards—all in a very basic form.

解释迎风航行的不同航线。如果学员的基础够扎实，可向他们介绍：由于潮汐、挡风或障碍等不同原因，有的航线会比其他航线更好这一概念。讲解形式一定要非常简单。

- Encourage students to make their own decisions based on personal observation.
  鼓励学员根据自己的观察，独立做出决定。

Session 10 训练10

Downwind 顺风航行

- Teach the students how to bear away using a combination of slight windward heel, letting out the mainsheet and avoid over-steering.
  教授学员顺风偏转的操作：向迎风侧倾斜一点，松主帆，不要过度用舵。
- Demonstrate the difference between a training run and a dead run using the jib to indicate the difference between the two.
  运用前帆进行演示，说明顺风和正顺风的区别。
- Allow plenty of room (wind against tide is ideal).
  练习时，下风空间要足够大（风和潮汐流相对时最理想）。
- Students practise running, turning from a beam reach, through a broad reach to a training run and then back to close-hauled.
  让学员练习正顺风航行，从横风转到侧顺风，然后到顺风，然后再转到后迎风航行。
- Any change in direction requires changes in the Five Essentials.
  方向上有任何改变，都要调节五要素。
- Avoid gybing at this stage.
  在这一阶段，要避免顺风转向。
- End this session with a smooth controlled demonstration gybe.
  在本次训练结束时，演示一次控制良好、操作流畅的顺风转向。

Session 11 训练11

Gybing 顺风转向

Similar to tacking, learning the technique can be divided into various component parts:
和迎风转向相似，顺风转向也可分解成几个步骤。

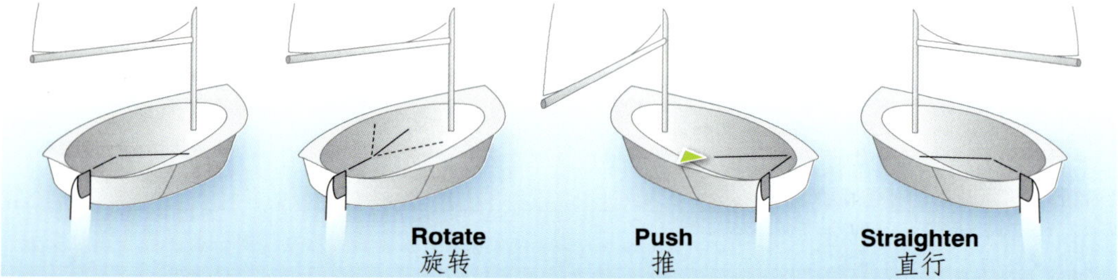

- Explain fundamental difference between tacking and gybing.
  解释迎风转向和顺风转向两者本质上的区别。
- Stress the very clear difference in commands— 'Ready about' for tacking but 'Stand by to gybe' for gybing which avoids any possible confusion.
  强调在指令上的明显区别——"Ready about"用于迎风转向；"Stand by to gybe"用于顺风转向，用语上的差别避免混淆。
- Using smooth and deliberate actions will help success.
  动作清晰流畅，能提高转向的成功率。

Gybing—Aft Mainsheet 顺风转向——主缭后置

Not all students will require a land drill, which is best done on a boat or land trainer ashore.
岸上练习最好是在船上或者模拟装置上完成，但是不用要求所有的学员都做。

Any demonstration should use the "whole—part—whole" method.
演示时，一律使用“整体—分解—整体”的方法。

1.

2.

3.

4.

5.

6.

1. With the boat being sailed flat on a training run, the helm sits forward of the tiller extension. All checks are made to ensure that:
   当船平稳地顺风航行时，舵手坐在副舵柄前方。确保检查以下几点：
- Centreboard is only slightly down 稳向板只往下放一点。
- The jib is just starting to collapse 前帆正要松弛。
- The area in which the boat is about to turn into is clear 航行区域周围无障碍物。
- Helm says "Stand by to gybe" 舵手喊“准备顺风转向”。
- Crew checks and says "Yes" 船员检查后，回复“准备好了”。
- Helm sheets in the mainsail slightly to bring the boom clear of the shroud, if needed. 如有需要，舵手可收紧一点主帆，避免帆杆碰到侧支索。

2. Helm swaps hand on the tiller and mainsheet.
   舵手交换拿副舵柄和主缭的手。
3. Balancing the boat, helm moves to the middle of the boat without altering the steering, one foot either side of the centreboard casing front foot leading.
   调节船的左右平衡，舵手要在不动舵的情况下，移动到船中间。前脚跨到另一侧，稳向板左右两侧各放一只脚，面朝船尾。
4. Before initiating the gybe, the helm swings the end of the tiller extension forwards out over the opposite side to the boom.
   开始转向前，舵手往前转动副舵柄尾端，转到与帆杆相对的一侧。
   Helm calls "Gybe oh" and initiates gybe by pushing the tiller towards where he was sitting and waits for the boom to swing across.
   舵手喊“开始转向”，并把舵推向他之前坐的那一侧，等待帆杆摆过来。
5. As the mainsail clew lifts and starts to travel across the boat, the helm centralises the tiller so that his weight, the boom and tiller are simultaneously in the middle of the boat. The crew changes over the jib sheet, and moves to the centre of the boat. Note that the boat is still flat.
   随着主帆帆后角上升，并摆到另一侧，舵手把舵回正，他的重心、帆杆及舵柄同时来到船中间。船员收紧另一侧前缭，并移到船中间。注意，船依旧是水平的。
6. The helm sits down on the new windward side. The crew sets the jib on the new side.
   舵手坐到新的上风侧。船员收紧这一侧前缭。

Gybing—Centre Mainsheet 顺风转向——主缭中置

The important difference about this drill is that the helmsman takes hold of the falls of the mainsheet to guide the boom across, preventing a violent gybe.
该练习最大区别是，舵手要抓住帆杆下的主缭绳圈，将帆杆拉到另一侧，这样可以控制转向的节奏，避免转向过猛。

1.

2.

3.

4.

5.

6.

1. While on a training run, the helmsman balances the boat as necessary, and checks all around, especially into the area in which the boat is turning through and into. Helm holds the tiller extension in the dagger grip and calls "Stand by to gybe". Crew checks the area and says "Yes".
   顺风航行时，舵手要在必要时帮助平衡船体，检查周围情况，特别是转向后的航行水域。舵手用匕首式握法拿副舵柄，喊“准备转向”。船员检查周围，并回复“准备好了”。
2. Helm steps back foot forward into the middle of the boat whilst at the same time revolving the tiller extension over to the new side whilst still steering a straight course.
   舵手将后脚跨到船中间，同时将副舵柄转到船另一侧，注意保持直线航行。
3. Helm holds the falls of the mainsheet, the crew moves into the centreline of the boat and changes the jib sheets.
   舵手抓住主缭绳圈；船员移到船的中心线，提起另一侧前缭。
4. Helm calls "Gybe oh" and initiates the gybe by pushing the tiller extension towards where he was sitting and waits for the boom to start to move. Helm can assist by guiding boom with the falls.
   As soon as the boom starts to move, the helm centralises the tiller and prepares to sit down on the new windward side. Crew balances the boat.
   舵手喊出“开始转向”，并往他之前坐的那一侧推舵，然后等帆杆摆过来。舵手可拉主帆绳圈辅助转向。随着帆杆开始转，舵手将舵回正，准备好坐到船另一侧。船员调节船的左右。
5. As the boom nears the centreline of the boat the helm, with weight evenly on both feet and the tiller, is in the middle of the boat.
   当帆杆接近船中心线时，舵手来到船中间，两腿用力一样，舵柄回到船中间。
6. As the boom continues on its way over the boat, the helm releases the falls.
   随着帆杆继续往另一侧转动，舵手放开主缭绳圈。

7.

8.

9.

10.

11.

7. Still steering a straight course, the helm transfers his weight over to the new windward side. Crew changes the jib fully onto the new side and prepares to move across to the windward side to assist with boat balance.
保持直线航行，舵手移到新的上风侧。船员把完全前缭换到另一舷，并准备好移动到上风，帮助压舷。

8. Helm sits and steers the boat on its new course (training run) with the tiller hand behind his back.
舵手坐下，手在后背掌舵，在新的航线（顺风航行）航行。

9. Helmsman brings sheet hand back across in front of body to hold both tiller extension and sheet, thumb pointing towards end of tiller extension.
舵手将拿主缭的手从身体前放到背后，去抓副舵柄，大拇指朝向副舵柄尾端。

10. Releasing the tiller with his front hand, he reaches forward and takes the mainsheet, releasing the sheet from his back hand. He can then bring extension under the back arm to in front of body. Facing and momentarily leaning forward will help this action.
前手松掉舵柄，往前去抓主缭，后手就可以松掉主缭了。然后，将副舵柄从腋窝下掏到身体前面。脸朝前，身体往前倾一下，能协助完成该动作。

11. Helm trims the mainsheet and settles on new course.
舵手调节主缭，继续航行。

Gybe – Method Variations 顺风转向——不同的方法

- The variations in handling the tiller extension are the same as for tacking.
  操纵副舵柄的方法和迎风转向时一样。
- With long tiller extensions, slide your hand down the extension before the gybe to reduce the angle through which you push the tiller.
  副舵柄很长的话，在转向前把手滑到副舵柄下方，减少推舵的角度。
- Holding the 'falls' of the mainsheet to help the sail across only works with a 'true' centre main. Aft/Centre combinations can benefit from a pull on the sheet (e.g. Laser) but will not have the same effect.
  抓住主帆绳圈，让主帆转过来，只有在主缭完全中置的帆船才有效。主缭后置与中置结合的帆船，则须拉主缭（例如，激光），但不会有同样的效果。

Session 12 训练 12

Gybing Practice 顺风转向练习

- Consider reefing. 考虑缩帆。
- Allow plenty of room (wind against tide if possible).
练习时，下风空间要足够大（可能的话，在风与潮汐流相对的情况下练习）。
- Check the area to be sailed into. 检查转向后的航行水域。
- Use minimal steering. 舵的幅度要尽量小。
- The helmsman should make a positive movement to initiate the gybe. 舵手平稳地拉舵，开始转向。
- Stress that the mainsail should be brought off the shroud. 强调主帆应与侧支索保持一定距离。

Session 13 训练 13

Triangular Course First Solo 首次独立航行三角标

- Triangular course: with achievable windward leg.
  三角标航线：使用容易完成的迎风段。
- Initially sail with students and then move into the safety boat, but allow them time to 'settle'.
  刚开始，教练和学员一起在船上，然后教练换到安全艇上。给学员一些时间去适应。
- Give instruction where necessary but avoid shouting from the safety boat. Ask them to 'lie-to' to communicate.
  必要时给他们一些指导，但要避免在安全艇上喊叫。让他们运用飘帆停船在安全艇旁停船，进行交流。
- Remember you are still responsible for the safety of the boat and crew.
  记住：尽管你在安全艇上，但是依旧要对船与学员的安全负责。

Session 14 训练14

Further Sessions 进一步培训

The purpose of the 'development exercises' section is to continue to develop the students' boat handling skills through practice, in particular positioning and stopping, which will be useful when the students are returning to base. The instructor should always be afloat in a safety boat and on hand to offer coaching input whenever necessary.
本章节的目的是通过练习，进一步发展学员的控船能力，特别是在控制船的位置及停船技巧方面。这对于学员回岸是非常有用的。教练应始终在安全艇上，在必要时给予指导。

The instructor has introduced various techniques and now the student needs the opportunity to practise these techniques in order to be more skilful.
教练介绍了好几种技巧后，就需要学员去练习，熟练技巧。

The instructor should have a variety of exercises available that help the student practise the techniques they have learned. The use of exercises such as those contained in G100 RYA Race Training Exercises is really helpful. When setting courses for students, remember that you need to be able to communicate with them throughout using some of the techniques explained in the single handers' section.
教练应采用不同的练习，帮助学员练习他们所学到的技巧。G100《RYA竞赛训练》这本书里列出的练习就很有帮助。在给学员设置航线时，要记住使用在单人船章节里讲过的技巧来跟他们解释。

Awareness of other boats will have been part of your teaching in the early stages. Stress it again now. Discuss 'rule of the road' problems as they occur and your solo crew will be less likely to become involved in collisions.

对其他船的意识应在早期教学阶段就涵盖了，现在要再次强调。学员碰到“航行规则”相关的问题时，要进行讨论。单人驾驶帆船发生碰撞的可能性会小很多。

Top Tip 重要提示

Once you step out of the boat, things can go wrong for the student. Give them time to settle.
一旦你迈出船体，学员可能会手忙脚乱。要给学员时间让他们自己稳定下来。

Sessions 15 & 16 训练 15&16

Capsize Recovery Drill (scoop method for dinghy) 正船练习（scoop正船法）

Capsize recovery drill should fit into your programme at the earliest practical moment. Weather, water temperature and other considerations will influence your Senior Instructor's decision, but it is generally agreed that early capsizing is beneficial.
正船训练应安排在早期的实践课程阶段。虽然天气、水温及其他因素都会影响高级教练的决定，但普遍认为尽早教授正船会很好。

The end of a day's sailing provides the best opportunities for drying clothes, personal buoyancy and gear. Students are usually apprehensive about capsizing, and that apprehension can affect their ability to learn. Once capsizing is over, they learn more quickly and are less worried. They are more likely to succeed when they go 'solo'.
一天航海课程的最后是教大家如何将衣服、救生衣及其他装备清洗晾干的最好时机。学员通常会很怕翻船，这种恐惧感会影响他们的学习能力。一旦学员们经历了翻船，他们就会学得更快，而且不会那么害怕了。那么，在他们独立航行时，就会更容易达成目标。

During the capsize drill, the responsibility of the instructor is to enter the water with the students because they have been with students constantly up to this point.
在正船培训期间，教练有责任和学员一起下水，因为他们之前一直就是和学员在一起。

The students would consider it strange if their instructor abandoned them at this stage. Instructors cannot fully control the exercise from a safety boat, although it should, of course, be standing by. The drill must go smoothly and calmly to have the desired effect of building confidence.
如果在这个阶段，教练“抛弃”学员，学员会觉得很奇怪。虽然教练应该完全控制好整个培训，但是在安全艇上是无法做到的。即使如此，教练也要随时待命，在给学员进行该训练时要非常流畅地教学，并保持冷静，循序渐进地帮助学员建立自信心。

- Always ensure that sufficient rescue cover is provided.
  自始至终都要确保有充足的救援。
- Shore briefing or drill using a boat tipped on its side.
  岸上简述或练习：使用一条船，演示侧倾。
- Explain the scoop method.
  解释什么是scoop正船法。
- Check personal and boat buoyancy.
  检查个人与船的浮力。（个人浮力：救生衣等；船浮力：桅顶浮球，船水堵等）
- Check students (contact lenses, glasses, watches and even false teeth!).
  检查学员（隐形眼镜、眼镜、手表，甚至是假牙！）。
- Consider mast head flotation for training purposes.
  考虑清楚桅顶浮球用于培训的目的。
- Your Senior Instructor is responsible for selecting a suitable site for the drill, away from hazards but close enough to base for safety and recovery.
  你的高级教练负责选择一个合适的训练场地，远离危险但离岸边又比较近，这样更安全更容易回岸。

- The instructor is responsible for tipping the boat over (wild swinging on the shrouds is unnecessary: a brisk tack with the mainsail sheeted well in and the crew staying on the old windward side of the boat should cause a gentle capsize).
  教练的责任是让船翻覆，没必要一直拉侧支索把船弄翻，把主缭完全收紧，进行转向，船员保持坐在上风侧不动，就能让船平缓地翻下去。
- Smile, stay calm.
  记住要微笑，保持冷静。
- Encourage students but keep any physical assistance to a minimum.
  鼓励学员，并最小限度地利用身体去帮助他们。
- The students will be much more confident if they have righted the boat without outside help.
  如果学员在无人帮助的情况下，将船正过来，会使他们更有自信。

Repeat the capsize until each student has succeeded but watch out for exhaustion or hypothermia problems after two or three attempts. It is better to stow the boat and gear after everyone has changed rather than risk difficulties with the cold. Maintain constant encouragement.
反复练习直到每个学员都成功为止，但是要注意在2～3次尝试后，学员是否已经精疲力尽了或体温过低了。最好是让大家先换衣服，然后再收船，防止感冒。注意要一直鼓励学员。

Top Tip 重要提示

Allow for free floating in deep water (buoy the mast head). Tethers and mooring ropes can separate students from the boat.
（使用桅顶浮球）船可能会在水深的地方翻船。如果船被拴绳和锚绳系住了，注意不要让学员与船分离。

Step 1 第一步

- Both the crew swim to the stern. This reduces the risk of one becoming trapped if the boat inverts.
  两名船员都游到船尾。如果船完全倒置，这样做能降低被扣在船里的风险。
- Helmsman checks that the rudder is secure and not floating off.
  舵手检查舵叶是否卡好没有飘走。
- Crew finds the end of the mainsheet and gives it to the helmsman who, using it as a lifeline, swims around the outside of the boat to the centreboard and holds it or climbs onto it as necessary to prevent inversion.
  船员找到主缭的末端并交给舵手，舵手把它用作安全绳，从船外侧游到稳向板处，抓住稳向板，或为了防止船完全倒置，直接爬到稳向板上去。
- Crew then swims along the inside of the boat to the centreboard case.
  船员沿着船的内侧游到稳向板槽处。

Following initial immersion, most students are still regaining their breath by the time the crew or helmsman has to go UNDER the mainsheet assembly to get clear round to the centreboard. Many try to swim over the top and some get their personal buoyancy hooked into the various floating bits of rope. Warn them of these difficulties.
第一次翻船落水，大部分学员可能会受到惊吓，需要时间恢复正常呼吸；为了正船，船员或舵手要从主缭绳圈下面游到稳向板。很多学员会试图从主缭绳圈上游过去，有些人的救生衣可能会被浮起来的各种绳子勾住。提示学员们，练习正船时可能会遇到的这些问题。

Step 2 第二步

- The crew checks that the centreboard is fully down.
  船员检查确保稳向板已完全放下。
- Helmsman holds onto it to prevent the boat inverting.
  舵手抓住稳向板，防止船倒置。

If the centreboard is not fully down, warn the crew of the risk of injury to the helmsman from an over-enthusiastic attempt to lower it without warning.
如稳向板未完全放下，务必在将稳向板放下前，通知舵手。过于急切、鲁莽地将稳向板放下，可能会导致在稳向板附近的舵手受伤。

Step 3 第三步

- Crew finds the top (weather) jib sheet and throws it over to the helmsman, checks mainsheet is free.
  船员找到迎风侧前缭并扔给舵手，并检查确保主缭没有被夹住。
- Helmsman confirms that he has it.
  舵手拿到前缭后，告知船员。

Confirmation of receipt is often inaudible, especially if the helmsman has failed to receive it. The centreboard case is a useful slot through which to shout.
有时会很难听清舵手的回应，如果他没有拿到前缭不通知船员，就更难确定情况。通过稳向板槽向对方喊话能使沟通更顺畅一些。

Step 4 第四步

Crew lies in the hull facing forwards and floats above the side-deck, holding on but taking care not to prevent the boat from righting.
船员脸朝前躺在船里，在船舷旁浮起来，抓住船，但注意不要影响正船。

Many students do not, initially, realise the great importance of this point. Some even disregard it, believing that they will be safer by hanging on.
很多学员刚开始没有意识到这一点的重要性。有些人甚至直接忽视这一点，觉得抓住船舷更安全。

Step 5 第五步

- Helmsman either lies back straight in the water with his feet on the boat's gunwale and hauls on the jib sheet or righting lines.
  舵手可以在水里用脚踩在船沿上，抓住前缭，身体直接往后倾。
- Alternatively he climbs onto the centreboard, keeping his weight as close to the hull as possible to avoid breaking the board, and hauls on the jib sheet to right the dinghy with the crew member in it.
  或爬到稳向板上，尽可能保持身体重心接近船体，避免压断稳向板，拉前缭将船正过来（船员在船内）。

Some find it difficult to get onto the centreboard. Any preliminary advice, which you can provide, is worth giving. Heavyweights will be able to right the dinghy by the first method. With lightweights, the advice to keep as close to the hull as possible has to be modified in practice, as their weight is sometimes insufficient to provide the necessary righting moment. Stress the value of straight legs and back for maximum leverage.
有些人发现爬到稳向板上非常困难。有好的建议应提前告知学员。体重较重的船员能够用第一种方式把船给正过来。对于体重轻的船员，建议不要让重心靠船体太近，否则他们的体重可能无法提供足够长的力矩。强调腿和背要直，正船力才能达到最大。

> **Top Tip 重要提示**
>
> Face away from the boat and throw the jib sheet over your head – it's easier.
> 脸朝船外，将前缭从头顶上扔过去——这样更简单。

Step 6 第六步

- With the jib backed the boat is hove-to and the crew is then able to help the helmsman aboard.
  前帆反受风停船。这样船员就能帮助舵手回到船上了。
- Helmsman may find that he can get into the boat as it comes upright.
  舵手可能随着船体的翻转，直接回到船内。

The right place for the helmsman to be brought aboard is beside the weather shroud. Discuss the option of rolling the boat to windward if you have a lightweight crew and a heavyweight helmsman.
舵手应在侧支索旁上船。如果船员体重较轻，舵手较重，船员要帮助舵手回到船上，可以考虑将船往上风压。

In boats with open transoms, it may be more practical to re-enter over the stern. The problem with this method is that the boat tends to bear away around the person hanging on to the stern, so a speedy entry is necessary.
对于船尾没有封闭的船型，从船尾上船会更方便一些。但产生的问题是：人压在船尾，会使船顺风偏转。所以上船速度一定要快。

Many modern boats have the buoyancy built into the floor and sides of the hull. This means that they can invert more readily after capsizing.
很多现代帆船的甲板内侧和船侧都有浮力，这意味着，翻船后更容易使船倒置。

Top Tip 重要提示

If the boat has righting lines the crew need not throw the jib sheet.
如果船体带有正船绳，船员就不需要把前帆索扔出去。

Alternative Method of Capsize Recovery 其他正船方式

- At the point of capsize, the crew nearest the highest point of the hull steps over the gunwale and onto the centreboard as the rig hits the water.
  在船翻覆的时候，船员最接近船体最高点，在桅帆碰到水时，直接跨过船沿，踩到稳向板上。
- Their priority is to keep the mast level on the surface of the water, preventing the boat from inverting.
  首要任务是，让桅杆保持在水面上，防止船倒置。
- At the same time, they check that the other crew member is present and is able to release the mainsheet and kicker to de-power the rig.
  同时，清点船员，并将主缭和斜拉器都松掉，减少船的受力。
- If they can't detect the other crew's presence, their priority is to start bringing the boat upright, using their weight and leaning back against a jib, spinnaker sheet or righting line.
  如果找不到其他船员，首要任务就是把船正起来，利用自己的体重，抓住前缭、球缭或正船绳往后拉。
- If the crew is present, they can also check that the rudder is still attached to the boat, and that they are ready for the righting process to begin.
  如果船员还在，他们也可以检查一下舵是否和船连在一起，然后正船。
- The boat is then righted by the crew member on the centreboard leaning back and holding onto the sheets to help with this.
  船员站在稳向板上往后倾斜，可抓住其他缭绳辅助正船。
- As the boat passes through the point of pivot, the crew on the centreboard can step over the gunwale and back into the boat as the other crew is scooped up by the lower gunwale.
  在船转过惯性中心轴时，稳向板上的船员就可以一脚跨进船里，同时其他的船员也能沿着另一侧较低的船舷进到船内。
- If the rig is pointing into the wind, then the boat needs to be righted slowly to stop it passing through the upright position and capsizing again. This can be achieved by good communication and the crew on the centreboard warning whoever is in the water to lie along the length of the gunwale so that when the boat is brought up, that crew's weight will act as a 'damper', stopping the boat from rolling right over again.
  如果船顶风，就要慢一点正船，防止船被正过来以后又翻到另一侧。良好的沟通能避免该问题，稳向板上的船员应提醒在水里的人沿着船舷躺着，这样当船被正过来的时候，船员的体重能充当“阻尼器”，防止船体继续翻转，再次翻覆。

ADDITIONAL PRACTICAL SESSIONS 附加实践课程

In the course of the previous sessions students will have left and returned to base on several occasions. They can now go on to learn capsize drill, man overboard, picking up moorings, coming alongside a moored boat etc with more guidance and coaching. The instructor will be in and out of the boat, demonstrating particular skills and then watching progress from the shore or a safety boat.
在学员完成了前面的课程后，就可以开始学习正船、落水人员救助、系泊、靠船（船抛锚）等技术，从而获得更多的指导与教学。教练会上船演示一些特定的技能，然后回到岸上或安全艇上观察学员。

A progression of these sessions could be:
课程顺序建议:

- Leaving and returning to shore.
  离岸与返回。
- MOB recovery.
  落水人员救助。
- Picking up a mooring (small, soft, fixed target, with escape route).
  系泊（浮球特性：小而软且固定；操作失败，易解脱）。
- Coming alongside a moored safety boat (large, potentially hard target, with escape route).
  在抛锚的安全艇旁停船（目标特点：大而明显，很可能是硬材质，操作失败，易解脱）。
- Coming alongside and leaving jetty/pontoon (large, hard target, limited escape route options).
  停靠和离开浮码头（目标特点：大而明显，硬材质，不容易解脱）。
- Lee shore landing (large, hard target with no escape route).
  停靠背风岸（目标特点：大而明显，硬材质，无脱离路线）。

The generic skills for upwind approaches will be:
迎风靠岸通用技巧:

- Approaching from the downwind position (tide allowing).
  （如潮流允许）从下风位置靠近。
- Slow the boat in good time by easing the sails early (no brakes).
  提前松帆，使船在适当的时候减速（无制动）。
- Maintain steerage and passage through the water by using small amounts of power from the sails when necessary.
  有需要时，对帆进行微调，以保持舵效和航线。
- On arrival let the sail or sails out completely.
  抵达时，将帆完全松出。

The generic skills for downwind approaches will be (or any of the above with a wind against tide situation):
顺风靠岸通用技巧（或以上任何情况，风与潮流相对）：

- Approach from well upwind, throw the main halyard overboard and ensure that it streams freely.
  从较远的迎风位置靠近，可把主帆升降索扔到水里理顺。
- Turn head to wind, ease the kicker, take off the Cunningham, release the main halyard and drop the mainsail fully into the dinghy, removing the halyard from the headboard of the sail.
  使船顶风，松斜拉器，松下拉索，松主帆升降索，使主帆完全降到船里，把升降索从帆上解下来。
- Bear away and head for the beach (or chosen 'target') using the jib for power.
  利用前帆使船顺风偏转，往沙滩（或选一个“目标物”）航行。
- Prior to arrival, raise the centreboard and release the rudder downhaul.
  在抵达前，抬起稳向板，松掉下舵绳。
- In the shallows, release the jib, round up into wind allowing the crew to step out and secure the boat head to wind.
  抵达浅水处后，松掉前帆，将船转向顶风，使船员能够下船，抓住船体，让船在顶风方向稳定下来。

One of the more challenging skills of coming alongside a pontoon or jetty should be one of the last ones taught, and possibly avoided altogether if boats, crew and equipment could become damaged. This skill is perhaps better suited to being taught in the Seamanship Skills section.
停靠浮码头或码头的技能很有挑战性，应在课程后期教授。如果风险过大，可以先不讲。因为操作不当，会导致船和设备损坏，甚至船员受伤。最好是在航海技术技能单元教授该技能。

Man Overboard Recovery (dinghy):
落水人员救助（小帆船）：

Use dummy (fender and tyre), not a real person.
使用假人（碰垫和轮胎）。

- Regain control immediately and turn onto a beam reach.
  有人落水后，船上的人应立刻重新控好船，并驶入横风航行。

- Maintain visual contact.
  时刻关注落水者。
- Sail away on beam reach for 10/15 boat lengths, but do not lose sight of the MOB.
  横风航行，驶出10～15倍船长的距离，注意保持落水者在你的视线范围内。
- Tack and bear away sharply.
  然后在迎风转向后，直接顺风偏转。
- Position the dinghy so that final approach is on a close reach.
  控制好船的位置后，迎风行驶靠近落水者。
- Spill and fill the mainsail to control boat speed which should be slow on the final approach.
  收放主帆，控制船速，在最后靠近阶段船速要慢。
- Stop to leeward and immediately beside the MOB.
  使船刚好停在落水者下风侧。
- Helmsman goes forward and retrieves the MOB by the windward shroud.
  舵手来到船前方，从上风侧侧支索位置救起落水者。
- A flick to windward on the tiller helps prevent the boat tacking on top of the MOB, who will act as a drogue or sea anchor to keep the dinghy in the basic hove-to position.
  将舵拉向迎风侧，防止船在落水者上方转向，撞到落水者。此时落水者往下压船的力会起到锚的作用，使船保持在反受风停船的位置。
- Repeat with helmsman as MOB, i.e. crew takes control of the boat.
  重复练习救助舵手的操作，即舵手落水后，船员控船。

If it happened for real, the MOB should shout or whistle to gain attention but not swim about or he will rapidly lose body heat. If wearing personal buoyancy with additional oral inflation, he should inflate it, although it may need to be deflated for boarding.
如果真的有人落水，落水者应喊叫或吹口哨来使人注意。但不要游泳，否则体温会迅速下降。如果救生衣有多余的吹嘴，应把救生衣吹起来。上船后，把气放掉。

Outline the aftercare needed for a real casualty.
简要说明如何照料受伤的落水者。

Once your students have mastered the basic principles, encourage more realistic practice by briefing them that it should be the helmsman who 'falls overboard'. When the dummy is dropped over the side, the helmsman should let go of the tiller and mainsheet, move out of the way of the crew and take no further part in the manoeuvre. This results in the crew having to regain full control of the dinghy and achieves better results.
一旦学员们熟练掌握了各项技能的基本原则，就鼓励他们多进行实操。在训练前简述时，说清楚模拟的是舵手"落水"的场景。所以当假人落水时，舵手应松开舵柄和主缭，给船员让出空间，不再参与接下来的操作，使船员学会重新控船，从而达到更好的训练效果。

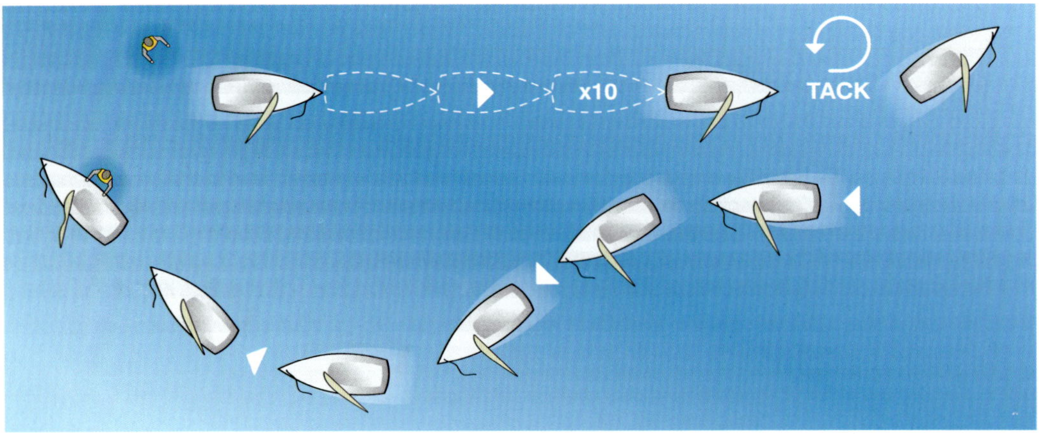

Fun Race 趣味比赛

Some Senior Instructors like to finish a Level 2 course by a practical assessment in which the students sail around a triangular course. Many centres complete the Level 2 course by organising a small informal race, thus encouraging students to consolidate their skills and introducing them to the competitive side of the sport.
有些高级教练喜欢在级别二课程结束时，用三角标来检测他们。很多培训中心会组织一些非正式的小比赛，鼓励学员巩固自己的航行技能，同时介绍帆船运动的竞技性。

Assuming that you have covered the basic rules of the road, the minimum extra knowledge needed by students to complete this satisfactorily is an explanation of the typical port-hand triangular course and a basic starting procedure.
假设你已经掌握了基本的航行规则，如果想圆满地完成比赛，还需要知道绕标时，标位于船的左侧和基本的起航程序。

Top Tip 重要提示

Never force people to be competitive when introducing racing to another course. Allow them to find their own level of competitiveness.
在给学员介绍帆船比赛时，绝对不要强迫他们去竞争。让他们去发现适合自己水平的竞争方式。

9 The RYA Teaching Method—Adaptations for Single Handers
RYA教学方法——单人船

Single handers are used in many centres and instructors should be familiar with the differences in teaching them.
很多培训中心都采用单人船教学，教练应熟悉使用不同船型教学的区别。

General Points 普遍要点

Advantages of using single handers: 单人船教学的优势：

- Students continuously at the helm. 学员能够持续掌舵。
- They learn faster. 学得更快。
- Light. 轻便。
- Simple and exciting. 简单刺激。
- Particularly effective for teaching children. 儿童教学十分有效。
- Less expensive to run. 运营成本更低。
- Durable. 耐久。
- Low skill level required to succeed in some boats (Laser Funboat, Escape Mango). 有些船型技能要求低（激光Funboat, Escape Mango）
- More economical teaching ratio (6:1). 更经济的教学比例（6:1）

Disadvantages of using single handers: 单人船教学的劣势：

- Can be frustrating at first. 学习之初易受挫。
- Students tire easily. 学员很容易疲劳。
- Communication is harder. 与学员交流更困难。
- Group control can be more difficult. 团体管理更困难。
- Students become cold more quickly. 学员很容易感到寒冷。
- Students may quickly scatter over a large area. 学员很容易大范围地分散开。

Sessions should be short and the instructor must always watch for signs of fatigue. Capsizes are more likely in a single hander than in the instructed larger dinghy, so suitable preparation must be made, as outlined below.
培训时间应短一些，教练须时刻注意学员是否有疲劳征兆。在单人船上比在有教练指导的大船上更易翻船，因此必须做好适当准备，基本要点如下：

Teaching Equipment/Sailing Area 教学设备/航行区域

Instructors may have to adapt the equipment and select an appropriate sailing area to achieve the tasks set.
为完成教学任务，教练可能需要采用适当的设备，并选择合适的航行区域。

- Equipment—the right size of boat and sail area for the size of student.
  设备——船只大小与航行区域适合学员的体型。
- Wind strength. 风力。
- Wind direction. 风向。
- Air and water temperature. 气温和水温。
- Sailing area. 航行区域。
- Depth of water (can the foils be full lowered?). 水深（稳向板和舵叶是否能完全放下）。

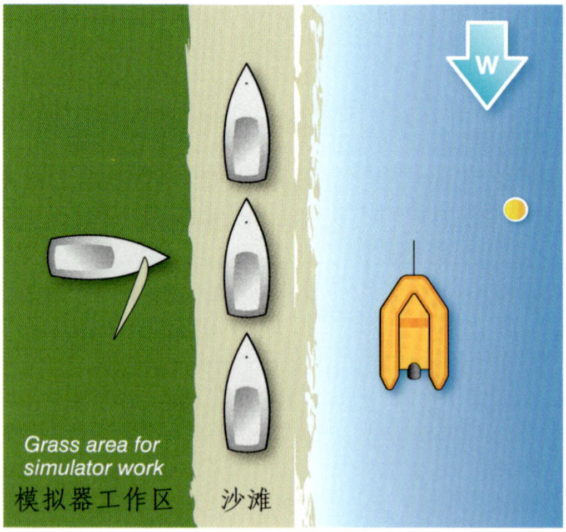

- Starting point (beach/pontoon/bank/slipway). 出发地点（沙滩/浮码头/河岸/下水坡道）。
- Length of sessions (short). 课程时长（短）。
- Any/other hazards. 任何/其他危险。
- Tide. 潮汐。

- Instructor to check all boats before they go afloat. 教练须在下水前检查所有船只。

Group Control 团体管理

- Frequent regrouping and briefings. 频繁地集合大家，进行说明。
- Recall signals (whistle and hand signals). 召回信号（哨声和手势）。
- Awareness of sailing area – diagrams, set course before students go afloat so they can see the boundaries.
  明确航行区域——用示意图说明，学员下水前设置好航线，使学员能看到边界。
- Question students to check understanding. 向学员提问，确认他们是否理解。
- Consider using a 'buddy system' when launching/recovering. 可以在下水与回岸时使用“两人互助”的方式。

What If ... ? 假如……?

Always consider: 总是考虑：

- What is the worst thing that could happen? 可能发生的最糟糕的事情是什么?
- What changes can you make to cope with this? 你能通过什么样的改变来应对这种情况?
- If you are starting to doubt that you can cope, stop and re-assess the session. 如果你不确定自己处理得了，应停止训练，重新评估，做出调整。

Communication 沟通

- Well thought out and structured briefings (include problems that might occur). 在简述前，应深思熟虑，确保简述结构清晰（包括可能出现的问题）。
- Size of sailing area. 航行区域的大小。
- You should not have to shout to your students. 不应对学员喊叫。
- Students stop the boat and you go to them, or students come to you. 让学员把船停下来，你把船靠过去，或者让学员靠到你的船旁边。
- Be aware of the noise from an engine or a sail flapping. 注意发动机或飘帆引起的噪音。
- Keep session short. 保持课程简短。
- Good debrief, which should include feedback to each student. 好的总结应包括对每一名学员的反馈。
- Instructors may sail with the students providing they have the required safety cover available.
  如有救生艇看护，教练可与学员一起航行。

Capsize 翻船

Because your students are on their own and not very confident, you must point out:
学员独自航行，可能信心不足，你必须指出：

- Righting a boat is easy.
  翻船后，把船正回来是很简单的。
- It can be fun. 翻船可以是快乐的。

> **Top Tip 重要提示**
>
> Think 'What's the minimum I need to teach to get them to the next level?'
> 思考“什么是使学员达到下一级别需要的最基本知识和技能？”

- Wearing the right equipment means they will float in the water. 救生衣会让你在水里浮起来。
- Demonstration from instructor first to show how easy it is. 教练先给大家做示范，让大家明白正船其实很简单。
- Even on a hot sunny day your students can get cold once wet. 即使在大热天，学员浸湿后也有可能受凉。
- Try to avoid capsize practice until the end of the day. 尽量在一天结束时，进行翻船练习。
- Try to keep them as dry as possible (consider reefing). 尽可能不让学员湿身（考虑缩帆）。
- Land drill if possible. 可能的话，在岸上进行实践。

Philosophy 教学原则

The basic philosophy of the RYA Teaching Method outlined earlier applies just as much to single-handed teaching as to conventional techniques, but at any stage you should ask yourself two questions:
前文概述过RYA教学法的基本教学原则和传统的教学技巧都适用于单人艇教学，但是在任何阶段你都应该问自己两个问题：

- What do students already know?
  学员已经掌握了什么？
- What is the minimum they need to know before they can complete the next session successfully?
  他们需要至少掌握什么才能成功地完成下节课？

This should save you unnecessary time ashore and save you teaching irrelevant details.
这样能避免你在岸上消耗不必要时间以及与教学无关的细节。

SESSION OUTLINES 培训大纲

The programme given below is just one of many which have been developed successfully. It is not intended to be definitive, merely to provide an introduction to the techniques needed.
下文所列举的大纲只是众多开发成功的培训项目之一，并不是唯一的方式，仅用作技术介绍。

Think of the timing of your shore sessions. You have to cover a lot of teaching material. Usually your students should know how to turn, stop and deal with a capsize before going afloat.
充分考虑岸上培训的时长。你需要讲的内容会很多。通常，学员在下水前就应该知道如何转向、停船以及处理翻船。

Session 1 训练1

Clothing/Footwear/Buoyancy aids/Gear collection:
衣着/鞋/救生衣/装备：

- As for basic Method.
  与前文所述双人艇的基本方法是一样的。
- Consider wet/dry suits and helmets.
  说明湿/干式保暖服的使用以及头盔。
- Correctly fitting buoyancy aids.
  正确穿着合适的救生衣。

Session 2 训练2

Tacking land drill/getting out of irons (with a simulator):
岸上迎风转向/解决帆船顶风问题（使用模拟装置）：

- Establish wind direction.
  确定风向。
- Demonstrate sailing on a beam reach, sheeting in and boat balance.
  演示横风航行，收帆并控制船的左右平衡。
- Swing boat through the wind.
  让船体转过风。
- Demonstrate tacking using the method (centre main or aft mainsheet).
  演示迎风转向（主帆中置或主缭后置）。
- Each student should then practise.
  然后让学员们练习。
- The instructor should then correct any faults.
  教练应及时纠正错误。

Demonstrate getting out of irons (push/push, pull/pull)
演示如何解决帆船顶风问题（推/推，拉/拉）。

Session 3 训练3

Rigging: 装船

- Establish wind direction.
  确定风向。
- Rig one boat first as a demonstration.
  装一条船，给学员做示范。
- Students can then rig their own boats.
  接着让学员自己装船。
- Check each one before they go afloat.
  下水前，检查每一条船。

Top Tip 重要提示

Boats could already be rigged so this can slip to the end of the day.
船只可能已经装好了，所以装船也可以留到一天课程的结束时。

Session 4 训练 4

Practise tacking/Beam reach/
Starting and stopping:
练习迎风转向/横风航行/起速和停船

- Boats rigged. 装船。
- Demonstrate launching one boat.
  演示帆船下水。
- Instructor demonstrates what is to be done, sail out on beam reach, tack and return slowing down and raising the dagger board/rudder close to the beach.
  教练演示操作：横风航行驶离，迎风转向，然后减速返回，在靠近沙滩时将稳向板/舵拉起来。
- Remember, actions are more effective than words.
  记住，实际操作比语言更有效。
- Instructor in the water.
  教练在水里讲解，保证学员的安全。
- Instructor demonstrates capsize drill.
  教练示范翻覆回正。
- Check student's orientation is correct.
  检查确认学员清楚自己的航行方向。
- Before letting go, go through sailing position, starting and stopping, tacking (walk boat through tack).
  在让学员操作前，务必要将所有的航行角度以及起速和停船，迎风转向（在转向时，教练人为地转动船体）为学员演示一遍。
- Once ready send one dinghy off on way to buoy.
  一旦准备好，就让一名学员自己航行，航行到浮标。
- Talk student through tack (student doesn't have to tack around the mark, near it will do).
  在学员转向时，进行指导（不需要绕标转向，近标就可以了）。
- Talk student back to you, stopping the boat by you.
  让学员航行回来，在你的旁边停船。
- Once each student has had a go, set up a beam reach figure of eight course.
  一旦每个学员都试过了迎风转向，就设置一个横风8字标航线。
- Add boats to the course one at a time, once it is clear that the preceding student is sailing/tacking successfully.
  在航线里的学员能够成功航行/转向后，就让其他的船加进去。
- Once the students have mastered the course, lengthen it.
  当学员们都能够熟练地航行本条航线后，就加长航线。

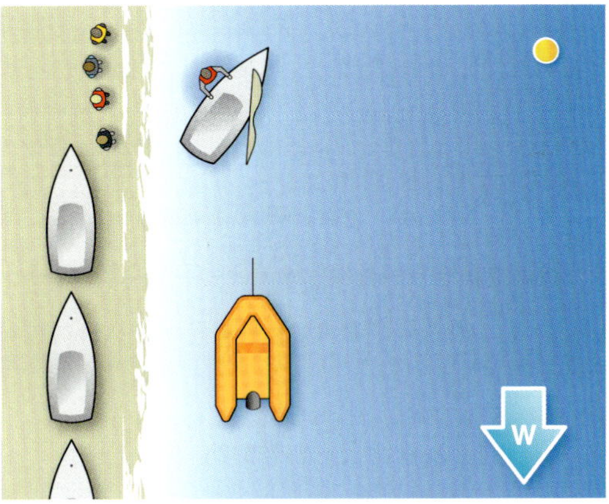

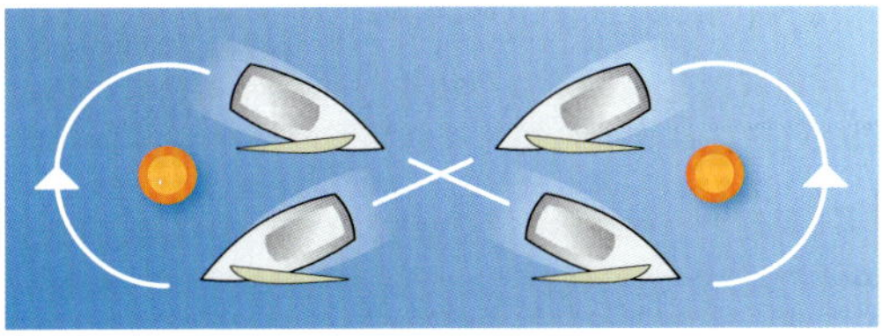

RYA教学方法——单人船

Session 5 训练 5

Turning towards and away from the wind:
转向迎风和远离风：

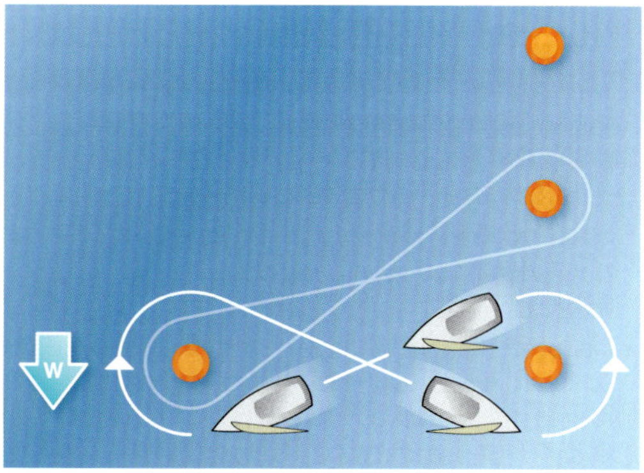

- Lay course as shown. 如右图，设置航线。
- Move buoy further into wind as session continues. 随着课程的进行，将浮标往近风位置移动。
- Brief clearly using board or diagram. 使用白板或图表进行课前简述。
- Demonstrate ashore or afloat the sail positions as boat turns towards and away from the wind. 在岸上或水上演示转向迎风和远离风时帆的位置。
- Reinforce wind direction at each step. 频繁地巩固风向。
- Use easy steps for getting from beam reach to close-hauled. 使用简单的步骤，从横风角度转到迎风角度。
- For bearing away, sheet out, use careful steering and boat balance. 松缭绳，适当用舵，调节船的左右平衡，进行顺风偏转。
- Students practise. 学员实践。
- Move buoy up in stages. 逐渐将浮标往上移。
- Debrief ashore at end of session. 训练结束后，在岸上总结。

Session 6 训练 6

Going to windward/bearing away and sailing downwind:
迎风航行/顺风偏转及顺风航行：

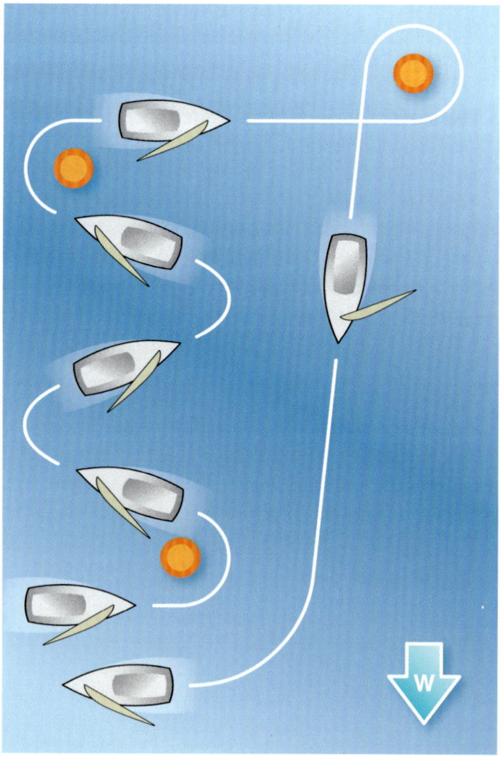

- Lay course similar to illustration, ensuring downwind course is a broad reach. 设置一个类似右图的航线，确保顺风航段是侧顺。
- Brief clearly using board or diagram. 使用白板或图表进行简述。
- Reinforce no - go zone. 强化不可航行区域。
- Demonstrate in water or on simulator. 在水上或使用模拟装置进行示范。
- Effects on sail. 对帆的影响。
- Revise luffing up and bearing away. 复习迎风偏转和顺风偏转。
- Demonstrate. 演示。
- Send off students one at a time at intervals. 让学员一个接一个进入航线。

> **Top Tip 重要提示**
>
> When launching and recovering, get students to work in pairs.
> 在下水与返回时，让学员两两合作。

- Introduce the Five Essentials to this exercise.
  在该练习中介绍航行五要素。

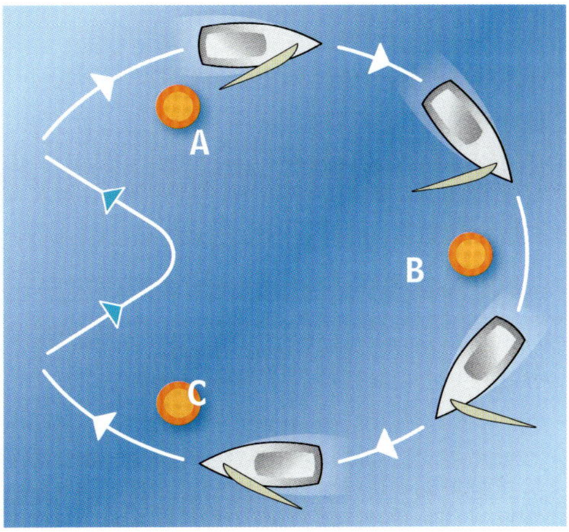

Session 7 训练 7

Gybing Practice: 顺风转向练习：

- Demonstrate on land using the method (centre main/aft main).
  岸上演示（主缭中置/后置）。
- Training run. 顺风角度航行。
- Dagger board position. 稳向板位置。
- Reinforce Five Essentials. 巩固五要素。
- Allow each student to practise.
  让每个学员都进行练习。

Session 8 训练 8

Triangular Course: 三角形航线：

- Lay course as shown. 如图设置航线。
- Demonstrate to students. 给学员做示范。
- Send students off one at a time at intervals.
  让学员一个接一个进入航线。
- Move mark B towards the line between A and C until AB and BC become training runs.
  逐渐将浮标B移动到靠近AC之间的连线，直到AB和BC航段都变成顺风航线。
- Avoid dead runs and 'death rolls' caused by 'sailing by the lee'.
  避免将航线设置成正顺，如果帆与风同舷，很容易翻船。
- Debrief ashore. 在岸上进行总结。

Session 9 训练 9

Follow my leader (behind safety boat, or another boat if helmed by a competent sailor).
跟船（在救生艇或一名有能力的水手后面）。

- Lead boat sails a variety of courses.
  领航船跑出各种不同的航线。
- Following boats should tack/gybe where it turns, not when.
  跟随船应在领航船迎风转向/顺风转向的同一地点进行同样的操作，而不是在同一时间。
- Carry two drop marks in the safety boat.
  安全艇上应配有两个浮标。
- If there are any problems, drop the marks on a beam reach and instruct the fleet to sail a 'sausage course' around them while the problem is dealt with.
  如出现任何问题，在处理问题时，将浮标设置成横风航线，并指导船群绕标跑“香肠”航线。

General Comments 总体评价

- Keep sessions short and intensive.
  保持培训简短且高强度。
- Clear briefings are essential.
  课前简述务必要清楚。
- Debrief each session with effective feedback to individual students.
  每次训练的总结都要给每个学员有效的反馈。
- Lay marks between sessions so your students can see the course before setting off.
  在训练开始前把标布好，这样学员就能在开始航行前看到航线。

In ideal conditions, with above average students and good support, sessions 1 to 8 can be completed in a single long day. It is far more practical, however, to treat this as two days of instruction, which is the usual time taken for an RYA Level 1 course.
在理想的天气状况下，按以上的学员比例，有良好的支持，训练1~8可在一天内完成。这些练习更多的是实践，如果把这些训练用两天来完成，就构成了RYA级别一的课程。

Further Sessions 进一步培训

Coming alongside: 靠泊：

- Same principles apply.
  适用于同样的原理。
- Can only be achieved in wind against tide conditions by releasing the mainsail completely or releasing the clew.
  在风与潮汐流的方向相对时，只有把主帆完全松掉或把帆后角从帆杆上取下来，才能成功靠泊。

Lee shore landings: 停靠背风岸：

- Use similar principles as for double handers, but without the jib.
  与双人艇的原理相似，只是没有前帆。
- It is important that the main is fully released either by unthreading the mainsheet or releasing the clew. Releasing the mainsheet only, reduces wear on the sail.
  关键是把主帆完全松掉，要么把主缭全部松掉，使所有的主缭从夹绳器完全松出；要么把帆后角从帆杆上取下来。只松主缭，减少主帆的磨损。
- Explain when to raise dagger board and rudder.
  解释什么时候抬起稳向板和舵。

Manoeuvres such as collecting objects in the water, using the MOB technique and sailing up to moorings are good boat handling practice.
很多操作，例如在水上收集物体、落水人员救助的技巧和航行到系泊处都是很好的控船操作。

If your students are working towards their Level 2 certificate, you now have several days to consolidate the basic techniques and cover the onshore teaching and exercises etc afloat.
如果你的学员正为了级别二的证书而努力，你可能需要用几天时间来帮助他们巩固基本技术，以及岸上教学和水上练习等。

The RYA Teaching Method—Adaptations for Keelboats 10
RYA教学方法——龙骨船

Teaching in Keelboats 龙骨船教学

The 'method' progression of learning to sail can be successfully taught in keelboats with a few simple modifications. Land drills are inappropriate, but the use of the boat controls for tacking and gybing can be demonstrated on a mooring.

如采用龙骨船教学，为保证帆船学习的顺利，须在教学方法上做一些简单的调整。有些课程不适用在岸上实践的，如迎风转向和顺风转向的操作，可将船系泊后进行演示。

The main differences from teaching in a dinghy are: 与在小帆船上教学的主要区别在于：

- The instructor will probably be teaching on board rather than from a safety boat.
  教练很可能与学员一起在船上，而不是在救生艇上。
- Allow students to take control if they are competent and avoid standing over them at the backstay.
  如学员能力足够，就让他们去操控，不要站在船后面监督他们。

There are usually only four essentials:
航行要素只有四点：

- Techniques for grounding recovery.
  处理搁浅的技巧。
- Use of engine.
  发动机的使用。
- Man overboard technique.
  落水人员的救助。
- Use of harnesses.
  安全带的使用。

With up to five students on board there is less helming time per person, although the crewing tasks are more involved. Move everyone around regularly. Little and often is appropriate for boat handling. For example, the group can practise picking up moorings by approaching on the correct point of sail without actually securing to the buoy. This allows you to teach the principles and gives everyone a try quickly, allowing for slight mis judgements.

如船上有五名学员，平均每个人的掌舵时间就会少一些，但是（每个人在掌舵时间之外）会有其他的任务。应定时让大家轮换岗位。量少次多的方式更适合练习控船。例如，在练习系泊时，确保以正确的航行角度靠近即可，不需要真地系泊。这样有利于你向学员教授操作原理，并能尽快的让每个人都尝试一下，允许小失误的存在。

Man Overboard 落水人员救助

Small keelboats can use the dinghy method but for larger boats (where a man held in the water will not affect the drift of the boat) use one or both of the following:
小型龙骨船也可使用小帆船的救助方法，但是更大的船型（人抓住船舷不会影响船的漂移）就得使用以下的一种或两种方法：

Quick stop with engine: 用发动机快速停船：

- Shout 'Man overboard'.
  呼喊“有人落水”。
- Pointer allocated, immediate tack to go hove-to.
  指定人员，观察落水者，并一直指向他，立即迎风转向，使船反受风停下。
- Drop lifebelt and Dan buoy.
  将救生圈和救生浮标扔给落水者。
- Start engine, check no ropes overboard.
  检查确保发动机周围无绳索，启动发动机。
- Drop jib in hove-to position.
  在反受风停船位置，降前帆。
- Motor sail downwind until wind indicator points at man.
  开发动机顺风航行，直到风向标指向落水者。

- Motor upwind. Release mainsheet.
  然后使发动机转到迎风，松主缭。
- Retrieve man at shrouds, keeping propeller clear. Stop engine when in contact with MOB.
  在侧支索处救人，保持螺旋桨远离落水者。靠近落水者时，立即关掉发动机。

Reach-tack-reach Man Overboard 横风—迎风转向—横风 救助落水者

- Pointer allocated.
  指定人员观察落水者。
- Immediate tack to go hove-to.
  立即迎风转向，使船反受风停下。
- Drop lifebelt and Dan buoy.
  将救生圈和救生浮标扔给落水者。
- Sail away 10 -15 boat lengths on apparent beam reach.
  横风跑出10~15倍船长。
- Tack – can drop jib, furl jib or let flap.
  迎风转向，然后降下前帆，把前帆卷起来或者飘帆。
- Point boat at MOB.
  将船指向落水者。
- Ensure main can flap, if not dip downwind.
  确保主帆飘帆，如不可行，就向下风转一点，再转回来。
- Spill and fill main on close reach aiming slightly upwind.
  后迎风航行靠近落水者，指向落水者上风侧的位置，拉松主帆，保持船的动力。
- Retrieve MOB on leeward side.
  在下风侧救回落水者。

Retrieval of MOB 救回落水者

With larger keelboats you need to have a method of retrieving people from the water. If they are conscious and not hypothermic use a ladder or foothold, e.g. bowline. Otherwise consider:
如使用更大型的龙骨船，须掌握如何把落水者从水里救到船上。如果他们还有意识且无低温症，可利用梯子或立脚点让落水者上到船上。例如，可使用单套结来做立脚点。否则应考虑：

- Boarding ladder. 登船梯。
- Detached mainsheet. 主缭（如主缭可被拆下）。
- Handy Billy from boom or halyard. 辅助滑轮绳组，将其装在帆杆或升降索上。
- Parbuckling with small sail. 用一面小帆做成套拉索。
- Dinghy. 补给船。
- Helicopter harness or equivalent. 直升飞机吊具或同类物品。

Handling under Power 动力操控

- At Level 2 keep the power manoeuvres to simple coming alongside and picking up moorings.
  在教授龙骨船级别二的课程时，重点让学员学习动力靠泊及系泊。
- Demonstrate prop wash effect by engaging astern while secured alongside.
  将船停靠并系住，挂倒挡，演示螺旋桨使船发生的横移效果。
- Practise turning boat under power.
  练习动力转向。
- Prepare for coming alongside—observe wind and tide, secure fenders and warps, position crew, communication, boat control, use of springs.
  准备靠泊——观察风和潮汐流，系好碰垫和系船绳，安排船员的位置，沟通，控船，交叉固定法的使用。

Moorings 系泊

- Wind and tide. 风和潮汐流。
- Preparation (boat hook/warp). 准备（船钩/系船绳）。

- Communication. 沟通。
- Boat control. 控船。

Seamanship Skills 航海技术

Grounding: 搁浅:

- Lee shore dangers. 如在背风岸发生，会非常危险。
- Awareness of state of tide. 注意潮汐状态。

If grounding on windward shore: 如在迎风岸搁浅:

- Ease or drop main, back jib, heel. 松开或降下主帆，前帆反受风，使船倾斜。

If grounding on lee shore: 如在背风岸搁浅:

- If quick you may be able to sheet in main and tack off. If not, drop main quickly to avoid being blown on further.
  如果动作够快，或许你可以收紧主帆，转向脱离。如不可行，尽快降下主帆，防止其被风吹得更远。
- If you have an engine heel boat and motor off.
  如配有发动机，使船倾斜，开发动机驶离。
- With no engine, put out kedge.
  如没有发动机，可抛锚移船。
- If the tide is falling and no help is available, protect side of boat as it dries.
  如正在退潮，且没有其他帮助，随着船侧露出水面，应及时保护起来。

Emergency steering: 紧急掌舵:

Keelboats can be steered rudderless by lashing the helm exactly amidships and using sail trim and, to some extent, balance as in a dinghy. Emergency steering can involve the use of an oar, a spinnaker pole or boathook, or even a bucket attached to each quarter.
龙骨船可在允许范围内进行无舵航行：把舵柄固定在船的正中间，调整船帆，且像在小帆船上一样压舷。紧急掌舵也可使用桨、球帆杆或钩杆，甚至是在两侧船尾角落挂一个桶。

Day Sailing in Keelboats 龙骨船日间航行

One day of a Day Sailing Course should be spent undertaking a day passage. Your planning must be first class. The Senior Instructor or Keelboat Instructor is responsible for the safety of the whole group and should not hesitate to change or abandon the plan if weather or other circumstances dictate.
一天的“日间航行”课程应确保全天的海上航行。计划航行应是第一节课。高级教练或龙骨船教练对整个团队的安全负责，如受天气或其他情况影响，应毫不犹豫地改变或放弃计划。

When planning a trip consider the following: 在做航行计划时，应考虑以下因素:

- Weather • Distance • Student preparation—laminated chartlets, notebook.
  天气 · 航程 · 学员准备工作——塑封小海图、笔记本。
- Tides, streams, tidal gates, heights for entering and leaving harbours or anchorages.
  潮汐、潮汐流、挡潮闸，进出码头水深或锚地水深。
- Extra clothing, drink, food • Extra equipment, tow lines, flares • Radio contact, shore contact.
  备用衣服、饮品、食物 · 备用装备、拖船绳、信号弹 · 无线电通信、岸上通信。
- Emergency plan, refuge port • Danger on route, shipping etc. • Landmarks on route, buoys etc.
  紧急计划、避难港 · 航行潜在危险、海运等 · 航行中的陆标、浮标等。
- Moorings, pontoon, anchorage at destination.
  到达目的地后的停船方式：系泊、停靠浮码头、抛锚。

The problem is to give everyone an experience of pilotage rather than following the boat in front. Try to encourage everyone to become involved in the pilotage but avoid splitting the fleet unless there is an instructor in each boat.
重点是要尽量让大家都具备一些导航经历，而不是跟着前面的船航行。试着鼓励每个人都参与导航工作确定航线，但要避免大家选择的路线过于分散，除非每条船上都有一名教练。

11 The RYA Teaching Method—Adaptations for Multihulls

RYA教学方法——多体船

Rigging/Launching 装船/下水

- Show students where to sit. 告诉学员坐在哪里。
- Demonstrate which items may be used as handholds, and which must not be used.
  说明哪些地方可以抓，哪地方些不能。
- Hoist mainsail first. 先升起主帆。
- Boat must be head to wind to hook on halyard lock (if fitted).
  必须将船顶风，才能使帆卡住升降锁（如配有）。
- Tack down haul must not be tensioned yet, nor mainsheet attached.
  先不要拉紧前帆角下拉索，也不要系主缭。
- Hoist jib and reeve jib sheets if not fitted with a fully furling system.
  如没有完全的前帆卷帆系统，那么在升起前帆后，要把前缭穿过导绳器，但是不要卡住。
- Attach rudders and lock up. 装上舵并卡住。
- Lift bow and slide trolley under. 抬起船头，将船车推到船底。
- Show students how to hold onto the boat, with one hand on the forestay bridle, the other holding the bow.
  向学员示范如何抓住船体，一只手抓住前支索固定架，另一只手抓住船头。
- Trolley boat into water and float off. 把船推到水里浮起来。
- Stow trolley ashore. 把船车拉上岸。
- Warn students of danger of placing feet under hulls in shallow water.
  提醒学员，在浅水区把脚放在船体下面的危险性。
- Crew holds boat head to wind. 缭手抓住船体，使船保持顶风。
- Helmsman attaches mainsheet. 舵手系上主缭。
- Leave windward shore by sailing backwards with the jib furled and rudders up: crew on each hull between bridle and main beam to lift sterns clear.
  离开迎风岸操作：卷起前帆，抬起舵，使船倒退。两人分别坐在两个船体上的固定架和主横梁之间，使船尾翘起。
- Control rate of sternway by backing jib. 前帆反受风，控制倒退的速度。
- The boat can be steered by lowering the appropriate crew's legs into the water.
  缭手可把脚放到水里来控制方向。
- Leave other shores by sailing off gently, lowering windward rudder first.
  若要离开其他类型的岸边，缓慢驶离，先放下上风侧舵叶。
- When in clear water, stop to lower leeward rudder and tension tack down haul.
  到达清楚的水域后，停船，放下下风侧舵叶，收紧前帆角下拉索。

Familiarisation 熟悉体验

- As for monohulls. 与单体船部分“Familiarisation熟悉体验”相同。
- Give a greater feeling of security. 更有安全感。

Orientation/Basic Boat Controls 介绍/基本控船装置

Orientation is as for monohulls, but there are important differences in the basic boat controls session:
与单体船基本相同，但基础控船装置有一些主要区别：

- Point out that multihulls do have brakes—the rudders.
  指出多体船配有制动装置——两个舵叶。
- The mainsail/jib controls used for monohull teaching are very different for multihulls.
  单体船教学使用的主帆/前帆控制索与多体船大不相同。
- Introduce two traveller positions: upwind/reaching (central) and downwind (out).
  介绍滑车的两个位置：在迎风/横风航行时，应将滑车置于中间；顺风航行时，应置于滑轨两端。

Tacking 迎风转向

1. Helm sails close-hauled and looks for a flat patch on the water. Sitting position is back leg bent, front leg straight, tiller over rear shoulder, mainsheet in front hand.
以迎风角度航行到浪小的水域。舵手坐姿：后腿弯曲，前腿伸直，副舵柄放在肩上，前手拿主缭。

The helm calls "Ready about". Crew responds "Ready" and uncleats the jib. Helm calls "Lee oh" and eases tiller away so that the rudders are no more than 45 degrees. In strong winds, sheet in hard as the bows approach head-to-wind.
舵手喊"准备转向"，缭手回应"准备好了"，并把前帆从夹绳器提起。舵手接着喊"开始转向"并推舵，两舵夹角不超过45°。在大风天，当船头接近顶风时，收紧主缭。

2. Helm moves quickly to the centre of the boat and onto both knees, facing aft. The tiller is swung behind the mainsheet falls.
舵手快速移到船中间，双膝跪在蹦床上，面朝船尾。将副舵柄从主缭绳圈后转过来。

3. Still facing aft, the helm places the tiller into the new back hand and prepares to face forward. Crew keeps boat flat and moves accordingly. They may back the jib to assist the tack.
保持面朝船尾，将副舵柄换到另一只手上，准备将身体转向船头。缭手移动自己的重心，保持船体平衡。
可使前帆反受风，辅助迎风转向。

4. Helm pivots and sits looking forward, tiller over rear shoulder, mainsheet in front hand. Crew will join them on the windward side and sheet jib correctly.
舵手转身，面朝前坐，将副舵柄放在后肩膀上，前手拿主缭。缭手也移到上风侧，调整前帆。

5. When the battens 'pop' on their new side, the helm releases a metre of mainsheet to help the boat to bear away. Once on the new course, the helm can sheet in and power away.
当帆换到另一侧时，帆骨发出"嘭"的声音，舵手就松掉1 m的主缭，辅助顺风偏转。一旦船转到新的航向，舵手就收紧主缭，提高动力继续前进。

The RYA Teaching Method—Adaptations for Multihulls
RYA教学方法——多体船

The Five Essentials: 航行五要素：

1. Sail setting—the use of telltales nearest the head of each sail is introduced earlier than in monohull teaching, because of the fully battened mainsail. Introduce the use of the streamer on the forestay bridle as an aid downwind (the streamer should be at 90 degrees to the boat for optimum downwind sailing).
   调帆——对于帆上部风向线的介绍比单体船的教学开展得更早，因为其主帆是全帆骨帆。利用前支索气流线辅助顺风航行（船处于最佳顺风航行状态时，气流线与船成90°）。

2. Balance—stress the different helmsman/crew positions for light and medium winds.
   船的左右——强调中小风天舵手/缭手的不同位置。

3. Trim—check that the boat is level by comparing waterlines forward and aft.
   船的前后——对比船前后吃水线检查船的前后平衡。

4. Centreboard—inappropriate for Darts. Other multihulls may have centreboards used in the same way as in monohulls. Downwind gybing may require small amounts of centreboard for steerage.
   稳向板的位置——该要素不适用于Darts这种船型。其他多体船稳向板的使用方法可能和单体船一样。在顺风转向时，可能需要适当放一点稳向板辅助掌舵。

5. Course sailed—as for monohulls but emphasise the amount of time lost through inefficient tacking. Also stress the importance of gybing downwind.
   最佳航线——和单体船一样，但是其重点强调，迎风转向效率低会浪费更多时间。同时强调顺风转向的重要性。

Gybing
顺风转向

1. With the boat sailing efficiently on a downwind course, with the mainsail out almost to the shroud and the traveller out at least halfway, the helm calls "Stand by to gybe". Crew responds "Yes" and the helm begins steering away from the wind.
   当船在高效顺风行驶时，主帆几乎松到侧支索的位置，滑车至少滑出去一半，舵手喊“准备顺风转向”，缭手回应“准备好了”，然后舵手开始拉舵。

2. The helm immediately moves into the centre of the boat, facing aft, and continues to steer gently. Crew uncleats jib and prepares to move across the boat.
   舵手立刻移到船的中间，脸朝向船的后方，并继续缓慢地转向。缭手提起前缭，准备移到另一侧。

3. The helm, still facing aft, passes the tiller across behind the falls into the new back hand, but continues to steer. Crew prepares to change the jib over.
   舵手依旧面朝船尾，将副舵柄从主帆绳圈后换到另一只手上，继续掌舵，缭手准备将前帆换舷。

4. The helm takes hold of the mainsheet falls with the new front hand and with a positive movement guides the mainsail through the gybe as the back of the boat passes through the wind.
舵手用靠前的手抓住主缭绳圈，随着船尾穿过风，把主帆拉到另一侧。

5. As the mainsail crosses and the battens ‘pop’, the tiller should be centralised. The crew, having crossed the boat, sheets in on the new side.
随着主帆换到另一侧，帆骨会发出“嘭”的一声，舵手应将舵回正。坐到另一侧的缭手把缭绳收紧。

6. The helm pivots and sits, looking forward, and steers onto the new course. Once settled, the boat can be powered up and sailed at maximum speed once more.
舵手转身坐下，朝前看，在新的航向继续航行。调整好船后，就会再次达到最大船度。

Coming Ashore 靠岸

- Lift the leeward rudder first.
  先抬起下风侧的舵。
- Ease the mainsail tack downhaul and furl jib.
  松掉主帆前帆角的下拉索，并把前帆卷起来。
- Sail in slowly with the traveller eased off.
  把滑轮放开，缓慢靠近。
- With an onshore wind the crew can dangle his legs in the water on the windward side, forward of the shroud to slow the boat down.
  如果吹近岸风，缭手可把腿伸到水里，放在上风舷侧支索前面，从而使船减速。
- Crew sits by main beam and chooses right moment to slide off into the water on windward side to hold boat.
  缭手坐在主横梁上，在适当的时候从上风侧滑到水里抓住船。
- An alternative for the lee shore landing is for the helm to go head to wind well off shore, drop the mainsail and remove the halyard. Raise the rudders, then both crew sit on the hulls, forward of the main beam and ‘steer’ the boat as described on page 79.
  背风岸靠岸的另一个方法是：在离岸一定距离的地方使船顶风，降下主帆，拆下升降索。抬起两个舵叶，接着两个船员各自坐在一个船体的主横梁前面，采用第81页所描述的方法控船。
- For an offshore wind the helmsman lifts the windward rudder when close to shore.
  如果吹离岸风，在靠近岸边时，舵手应把上风侧的舵提起来。

- Meanwhile, the crew sits by the main beam and chooses the right moment to slide carefully off into the water on the windward side to hold the boat again, by the main beam.
  同时，缭手坐在主横梁上，在适当时候从上风侧小心地滑到水里，在主横梁旁边抓住船。
- In strong winds with restricted access, the boat is sailed in under jib alone.
  大风天的时候，靠岸空间受限，所以仅用前帆靠岸。

Coming ashore on sandy beaches with an onshore wind and large waves, the technique is different and the multihull is the only boat it applies to:
吹近岸风，大风大浪的情况下停靠沙滩，需要的（停船）技术有所不同，但是其仅适用于多体船：

- De-power the mainsail.
  减少主帆受力。
- Pick the right area and both helmsman and crew sit aft to keep the bows up.
  选择正确的区域靠近，舵手和缭手都坐到船尾，使两个船头翘起。
- At the right moment the helmsman trips the rudders and keeps going straight for the shore.
  在适当的时候，舵手抬起舵叶，保持直线靠近。
- Take care when alighting from the boat and turning it head to wind.
  下船并将船转到顶风。

Further Sessions 进一步培训

The ability to sail around a triangular course marks an important stage in basic instruction, as it shows that the student can tackle all points of sailing.
航行三角标的能力在基础教学里很重要，如果学员能够做到，则表明他能在所有角度航行。

Teaching of man overboard recovery (see page 113) differs fundamentally from monohull teaching. Having regained control, the person left aboard will prefer to gybe rather than tack to get back to the man in the water, as it is quicker and the helmsman is in control throughout the manoeuvre. In addition, the man is recovered from between the hulls and if necessary over the main beam, rather than at the shroud.
双体船落水人员救助的教学方式（参见第87页）在本质上与单体船是不同的。在重新控好船后，还在船上的人会顺风转向，而不是迎风转向，回到落水者旁边，因为这样更快，而且舵手操作更稳定。另外，让落水者从两个船体中间上来，如有必要，从主横梁处救起而不是侧支索。

Teaching Further Skills 教授更多技能

Once the basic techniques have been covered in RYA Level 1, 2 and 3 courses, further multihull training follows the syllabi laid down in the RYA National Sailing Scheme Logbook G4, amended as appropriate with specialist techniques.
一旦在RYA级别1~3课程里学会了基本技能，应按照（RYA国家航海计划）航海计划书G4的大纲进行多体船的进一步训练，特殊技术须做适当修正。

Capsize Recovery 正船

1. As the boat capsizes, the helm and crew must quickly decide on their route into the water. They should avoid the sails, shrouds and mainsheet. Falling from the top sponson can also be a painful experience.
   在翻船时，舵手和缭手必须快速决定落水路线。务必要避开帆、侧支索和主缭。从水面上方的船体掉下去可能会很痛。

   Once in the water, as with all capsizes, both crew should remain in contact with the boat. The stern is a convenient place to meet.
   一旦落入水中，和所有船翻时一样，应保持人船不分，在船尾集合比较方便。

2. The helm and crew then climb out onto the lower hull and begin their tasks. The helm releases the mainsheet and traveller, while the crew releases the jib and finds the righting line, usually at the base of the mast.
然后舵手和缭手爬到下面船体上，并开始正船。舵手将主缭和滑轮松开；同时缭手松掉前帆，找到正船绳，通常绕在桅杆底部。

3. The righting line is thrown over the top hull.
将正船绳从船上方扔到另一侧。

4. Using the righting line, both of the crew can then lean back, using their body weight to begin the righting process. The hull of the boat will have swung downwind of the rig. Consequently, the wind will now be blowing on the trampoline to assist with the righting. However, if this is the case, the crew must be prepared for the boat coming up very quickly.
抓住正船绳，舵手和缭手都将身体往后仰，利用自己的体重开始正船。船体会偏转到桅帆的下风处。随着船渐渐从水里升起，风会作用到蹦床上，辅助正船。注意，在这种情况下，缭手必须做好准备，船会很快起来。

As the rig releases from the water, the boat will begin to right itself quickly.
随着桅帆脱离水面，船会很快翻转过来。

5. To deal with this, the crew get ready to move quickly between the hulls and apply their body weight onto the forward crossbeam...
为了应对这种情况，缭手要准备好在两船体中间快速移动，用体重压住前横梁……

6. Preventing the boat going right over and re-capsizing. This action can be reduced by righting the boat head to wind.
防止正过来的船又再次翻覆。可使船顶风以减少这种情况的发生。

7. Once the boat is righted, the crew can climb back aboard, preferably over the forward crossbeam. Then all sheets and lines can be tidied before sailing away.
船正起来后，缭手就可以爬到船上去了，最好是从前横梁上去，然后整理好绳索，继续航行。

Man Overboard 落水人员救助

1. For this exercise a target (fender) is used, and dropped in the water. The boat is sailed away on a beam reach and the jib is released with the helm noting the position of the MOB.
在该练习中，需要一个“落水者”(防碰垫)。“有人”落水后，先横风驶离，松前帆，舵手留意落水者的位置。

2. Once far enough away (15 boat lengths), the helm gybes the boat.
距离（15倍船长）够远后，舵手顺风转向返回。

3. The helm then sails back to the MOB on a close reach, noting any drift.
然后迎风角度驶向落水者，注意船的横移。

4. Once close to the target, the helm heads up into the wind to slow the boat, aiming to position the MOB between the hulls.
一旦接近目标，就使船头顶风，降低船速，用两船体的中间位置对准落水者。

5. If possible, the boat is sailed head to wind. The boat is stopped this way. The rudders can also be put fully over to help stop the boat. The helm then moves forward ready to bring aboard the MOB. It is preferable that the MOB is brought aboard over the forward crossbeam.
如可行，使船顶风往前移动，最后停下来。也可将两个舵柄都推到底，来辅助停船。然后舵手移到前面，准备把落水者拉上船。最好将落水者从船首梁救起。

12 Teaching the Advanced Modules 高级单元教学

SEAMANSHIP SKILLS 航海技术

Manoeuvres 操作

Many of these are a revision and refinement of skills learnt on a Level 2 course. Nevertheless, during a 2-day course you may only have time to teach the skills required without a great deal of further coaching. Each technique can be broken down into four stages:
这部分的大多数操作都是对级别二课程的复习及精炼。不过，在两天的课程中，你可能只能教授所要求的技能，无法开展进一步的教学。每个技巧都可分成四个阶段：

- **Planning** 计划；
- **Approach** 方案；
- **Manoeuvre** 操作；
- **Escape** 脱离。

A briefing and demonstration or land drill ashore can be used for many techniques.
培训前简述、演示或岸上实践可广泛运用于各种教学中。

Practice doesn't necessarily make perfect—it may serve only to repeat poor technique and hence reinforce mistakes. That's where you come in.
有时候熟并不能生巧——重复练习只会使学员掌握粗劣的技巧，不仅收效甚微，更会加深错误。此时就是你发挥教练作用的时候了。

Ideally, bring all the manoeuvres together once they have been learnt into the framework of a seamanship exercise or a seamanship game.
理想情况下，一旦学员掌握了一些航海技能练习或游戏，就会把这些操作都融合到一起。

The principle is to combine the exercises in a way which will make their practice more enjoyable and their execution more efficient. The golden rule about games is to keep them simple. Don't get bogged down in penalty points and the like, the fun will soon evaporate.
实际上，将练习和游戏融合在一起更有意思，而且学员的操作会更有效率。游戏的黄金规则是，游戏要尽可能简单，不要使学员陷入惩罚的尴尬境遇中，否则就丧失了游戏的乐趣。

If the game is packaged properly, students won't have time to realise that it is simply structured practice. It could be marketed as an obstacle course or treasure hunt full of local interest. It could also be a short triangular course with a different task each lap.
如果游戏设计得合理，学员可能不会意识到，自己做的是结构化的练习。可以设计成障碍赛或充满当地特色的寻宝游戏，也可以是一个短三角标航线，每一圈都要执行不同的任务。

Instructing from a Teaching Boat (Power or Sail) 在教练艇上指导学员（机动艇或帆）

With many of the topics outlined above, the instructor may first be in the sailing dinghy, but then is most likely to be out of it, allowing the students to practise under supervision. As soon as the instructor gets out of the dinghy, communication problems increase.
对于以上所述的主题，教练可能刚开始会和学员一起在船上，之后回到教练艇上进行监督，让学员自己练习。当教练回到教练艇后，交流的难度就增加了。

Reefing Afloat 水上缩帆

Briefing ashore: 岸上简述：

- When to reef—purpose.
  什么时候缩帆——目的。
- Where to reef—away from hazards, starboard tack if possible.
  在哪里缩帆——远离危险，可能的话，在右舷航行时缩帆。
- How—order of events, co-ordination between helm and crew.
  如何操作——操作的顺序，舵手和船员的配合。

- How much—appearance of reefed sail, i.e. efficient shape, boom not drooping, no wrinkles, kicking strap still effective.
  缩多少——缩帆后的状态，例如，受风更好的形状，帆杆不会往下掉，帆上无皱褶，斜拉器仍有效。
- Genoa changed to jib and centreboard raised slightly if necessary.
  有必要的话，将大前帆换成小前帆，稍稍抬起稳向板。

Progression: 下一步：

- Sail around a course once reefed. 一旦缩帆完成，就可以继续航行了。
- 'Timed' reefing/shaking out. 限时缩帆/解开。
- Reef on the whistle. 哨令缩帆。

Anchoring 抛锚

Briefing ashore: 岸上简述：

- Type of anchor and selection of suitable anchorage. 锚的类型及选择合适的锚地。
- Nature of bottom. 锚地类别。
- Shelter. 隐蔽处。
- Depth (changes with tide). 水深（随潮汐改变）。
- Length of warp. 锚绳长度。
- Swinging area. 摆动区域。

Practise afloat: 水上练习：

- Approach on close reach or against tidal stream. 后迎风航行或者顶流靠近。
- Consider dropping jib if possible to provide a clear foredeck. 如可行，考虑降下前帆，前甲板的视野会更清楚。
- Drop main if wind against tide. 如风与潮汐流方向相对，则降下主帆。
- Ensure the warp passes through fairlead or bow strop. 确保锚绳通过导缆器或艇首缆系环。
- Lower anchor when boat stops. 停船，下锚。
- Payout warp. 放锚绳。
- Check holding with transits. 利用参照物，检查锚是否抓地。
- Stow sails when holding. 确认抓地后，整理好帆。

Rigging 装船

- Putting the anchor on the boat. 把锚放在船上。

Being Towed By a Powerboat 拖船

This can be covered best in an informal discussion using the following key points:
通过非正式的讨论，运用以下要点能非常好地解释拖船：

- Good communication. 良好的沟通。
- Approach. 靠船方案。
- Pass tow line. 递拖船绳。
- Drop mainsail. 降主帆。
- Secure tow line. 固定拖船绳。
- Bridle/strong points. 拖索/稳固的点。
- Quick release system. 快速松绳方式。
- Being towed alongside. 靠边拖船。
- Springs. 交叉绳法。
- Being towed stern first. 倒退拖船。
- Centreboard up. 提起稳向板。
- Crew weight aft. 船员重心靠后。
- Steer if possible. 如可行，继续掌舵。

Teaching the Advanced Modules 高级单元教学

Lee Shore Landing 停靠背风岸

- Approach from well upwind, throw the main halyard overboard and ensure that it streams freely.
  从离岸较远的迎风位置靠近，将主帆升降索扔到水中理顺。
- Turn head to wind, ease the kicker, take off the Cunningham, release the main halyard and drop the mainsail fully into the boat, removing the halyard from the headboard of the sail.
  船头顶风，松斜拉器，松下拉索，松主帆升降索，将主帆全部降到船内，从帆顶上解开升降索。
- Bear away and head for the beach using the jib for power.
  顺风偏转，利用前帆向岸边航行。
- Prior to arrival, raise the centreboard and release the rudder downhaul.
  靠近岸边后，首先将稳向板提起来，并松掉下舵绳。
- In the shallows, release the jib, round up into wind and the crew step out and secure the boat head to wind.
  到达浅水区后，松前帆，船头顶风，将前帆卷起来。船员下船，抓住船舷，保持船顶风。

Sailing Without a Rudder (or with an elastic loop over the tiller) 无舵航行（或用弹性绳绑住舵柄）

- Raise centreboard to three quarters down.
  将稳向板抬起四分之一。
- Rudder can be raised rather than removed. Alternatively, a thick loose elastic loop allows some tiller movement.
  可将舵抬起来，不用拆下来。或者，用一条粗弹性绳绑住舵柄，使舵柄能有些许移动。
- Consider reefing the mainsail so as not to overpower the jib.
  可以考虑缩主帆，避免前帆受力过度。
- Jib in, main out to bear away.
  收紧前帆，松主帆，顺风偏转。
- Main in to luff up.
  收紧主帆，迎风偏转。
- To sail on a reach in a straight line, sheet the jib correctly then gently sheet in the main to balance its power.
  横风直线航行，先将前帆收到正确的位置，然后缓慢地将主帆收进来，平衡前帆受力。
- Boats usually have slight weather helm when both sails are filled.
  两面帆都受力后，通常船会略偏向上风。
- If rudder raised keep weight forward.
  如果舵抬起来了，保持重心向前。
- Heel to windward to bear away.
  倾向上风，进行顺风偏转。
- Heel to leeward to luff up.
  倾向下风，进行迎风偏转。
- Slow movements across the boat, but 'anticipate' the boat's movements.
  缓慢地跨到船的另一侧，注意判断船的变化。
- Can be easier if jib sheets tied together and mainsheet reeved as a simple purchase.
  如果将两根前缭系在一起，主缭与滑轮采用简单的组合方式，这样操作能更容易些。
- Following a gybe keep jib to windward until settled on new course to prevent spinning.
  顺风转向后，保持前帆在上风侧，以防止船旋转，直到航行平稳。

Progression: 提高练习：

- Sail around a windward/leeward course.
  迎顺风航线航行。
- Sail the boat more 'freely' when going upwind.
  迎风航行时，不要让船体大面积近风。
- Gybe the main deliberately by passing it over.
  顺风转向时，用手将主帆换过船的另一侧。

Sailing Without a Centreboard 无稳向板航行

- Explain the underwater shape of the boat.
  讲解船底的形状。
- Heeling to leeward helps upwind progress.
  倾向下风，辅助迎风航行。
- Lateral resistance can be increased by moving the crew weight forward.
  船员的重心往前移，以提高横移阻力。

Progression: 提高练习：

- Sail around a windward/leeward course.
  迎顺风航线航行。

> **Top Tip 重要提示**
>
> Rudderless: Set the weight, set the jib – play the main.
> 无舵航行：人在适当的位置，调节好前帆，用主帆控船。

Sailing Backwards 倒退航行

- Explain why, which can be escaping from a crowded mooring or leaving a weather shore/jetty.
  讲解学习倒退航行的原因，如何从拥挤的系泊处或从上风岸/浮码头离开。
- Centreboard at least half down.
  稳向板至少放下一半。
- Bring the boat head to wind and ensure it is stopped.
  船头顶风，确保船停下来。
- Push the boom swiftly to the shroud so that the mainsail backs.
  将帆杆推向侧支索，使主帆反受风。
- As soon as the boat starts to gather leeway, point the tiller away from the boom.
  一旦船开始转向下风，就将舵推离帆杆。
- Steer by looking backwards and keep the rudder movements small (the boat follows the direction that the rudder is pointing).
  掌舵时，脸朝后，小幅度动舵（船按舵指向的方向行驶）。

> **Top Tip 重要提示**
>
> Sailing backwards: At the end, do a J-turn by turning the rudders.
> 倒退航行：最后，利用舵做一个“J字形”转向。

DAY SAILING 日间航行

Navigation 导航

- Small boat navigation is really pilotage.
  小型船只导航是通过观察，利用周围的物体进行航行的。
- You cannot do detailed chart work in an open boat.
  不能在无遮挡的船上进行精细的海图工作。
- Pre-planning is essential.
  务必提前先做好计划。

Charts 海图

- Chart datum.
  海图基准面。
- Measuring distances from latitude scale.
  用纬度比例尺来测量距离。
- Soundings. 水深。
- Drying heights. 干出高度。
- Heights above mean high water springs.
  高于平均大潮高潮。
- Conspicuous features, lighthouses, headlands etc. 明显标志物：灯塔、海角等。

- Common hazards, rocks, wrecks, overfalls etc. 常见危险：礁石、沉船、湍流等。

Compass 罗经

- Compass rose. 罗经刻度盘。
- Variation—corrections. 磁偏差——校正。

Tide and Tide Tables 潮汐和潮汐表

- High and low water. 高水位和低水位。
- Correction for BST. 英国夏令时的校正。
- Springs and neaps. 大潮和小潮。
- Rule of twelfths/percentage rule. 十二分一/百分比潮汐规则。
- Tidal streams and tidal diamonds. 潮汐流和潮汐方块。

Food, Drink and 'Comfort' 饮食与日常排泄

- Suitable clothing • Harbour regulations • Avoiding shipping • Where to moor or beach at destination.
合适的衣物· 港口条例· 避开航运· 到达目的地后，在哪里锚泊或靠沙滩。
- Shoreside facilities.
岸上设施。

Planning and Pilotage 计划及导航

- Sailing a passage, which has first been planned.
按计划的路线航行。
- The time available, ETD, ETA, length of any breaks.
可用时间、预计出发时间、预计抵达时间、休息时间。
- Consideration of tide and weather conditions, traffic etc.
考虑潮汐、天气情况、交通等。
- Use laminated charts and chinagraph pencil.
使用塑封海图和蜡笔。
- Create a 'passage plan' on a separate sheet (easier to look at than a chart).
制作一份单独的“行程计划”（比在海图上更方便易看）。
- Create an expedition sheet including number of participants and other relevant info.
制作一张航行表，包含参与人数及其他相关信息。
- Establish a shore contact and give them the details.
建立岸上联系，并将细节告知他们。
- Consider informing the Coastguard and/or Harbour master.
考虑告知海岸警卫队和/或者港务主任。

Pilotage is usually a visual exercise rather than sailing for long distances on a compass bearing. If you know where you are, with a chart and compass you should be able to identify where to go next.
小型船只导航是依靠视觉进行的，其不同于按照罗经方位进行长距离航行。如果你知道自己的方位，利用海图和罗经，就能确定下一个目的地。

- Courses, distances and time on chart.
通过海图得出航线、距离和时间。
- Sail on transits to avoid being set sideways by tide.
选择参照航线，避免受潮汐的影响而横移。
- At known positions e.g. buoys, confirm position or alter course.
已知位置，例如：浮标、确认位置或改变航线。

Emergencies 紧急情况

- Carry appropriate flares. 携带合适的照明弹。
- Carry a Marine VHF and mobile phone in a waterproof bag.
携带一部海事甚高频无线电和一部移动电话，并放在防水袋里。

- Create a 'Plan B' including alternative safe havens and a plan for darkness.
  制订B计划，包括可供选择的安全港和夜间计划。

Meteorology 气象

Sources of weather information: 天气信息来源：

- Television/Radio—Inshore forecast, local forecast (details in nautical almanac).
  电视/收音机——近岸天气预报，当地天气预报（详细信息请查看航海年历）。
- Weather fax/text forecasts by mobile phone/telephone.
  通过移动手机/电话，获得传真/短信天气预报。
- Internet and email forecasts.
  网络和邮件天气预报。

Terms used in shipping forecasts: 航运天气预报专业术语：

- Beaufort scale and direction.
  蒲福风力等级表和风向。
- Link that with tidal information to determine likely sea state.
  将风力信息和潮汐信息结合，来判定相对的海况。
- Backing and veering.
  逆摆和顺摆。
- Good, moderate and poor visibility.
  能见度，良好、中等和差。

Weather Patterns 天气模式

- Rapid barometric change usually indicates strong winds.
  急剧的气压变化通常预示着大风。
- Anticlockwise wind circulation around lows.
  低气压附近的风是逆时针循环的。
- Clockwise wind circulation around highs.
  高气压附近的风是顺时针循环的。
- Warm front—lowering cloud, decreasing visibility, drizzle, veering winds.
  暖锋——低云，能见度下降，蒙蒙细雨，风顺时针摆动。
- Cold front—veer, cooler, more northerly wind, clear, showery, possible sudden squalls.
  冷锋——风顺时针摆动，温度降低，偏北风加大，能见度良好，多阵雨，可能突发狂风。
- Sea breeze—air over warm land rises, cool sea, air drawn ashore.
  海风——陆地表面空气受热升起，海上的冷空气吹向陆地。
- Fog—advection: warm air over cool sea, or radiation: land cools.
  雾——平流：冷海水表面的暖空气或辐射：陆地温度下降。

Observation afloat: 水上观察：

• Squalls • Gusts • Approach of low pressure—cirrus clouds, hazy sun.
· 狂风 · 阵风 · 低气压来临的现象——卷云、日光朦胧。

Decision Making 决策

• Planning for difficult conditions • Alternative destinations • The effect of wind and tide on sea conditions.
· 为恶劣情况做好计划 · 可选目的地 · 风和潮汐对海况的影响。

SAILING WITH SPINNAKERS 球帆航行

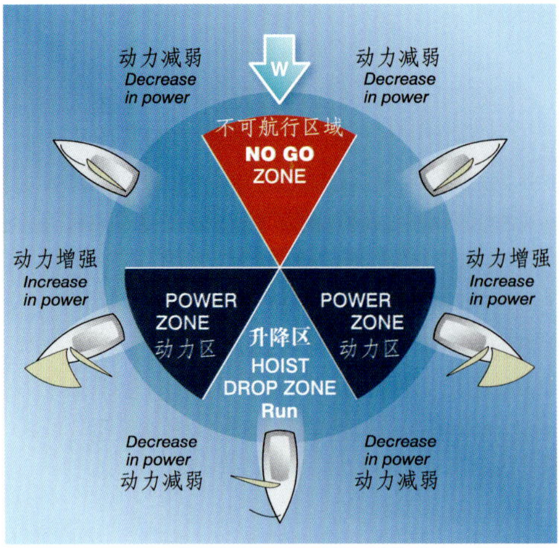

Spinnaker Hoists 升球帆

There are a number of ways to hoist the spinnaker, depending on the situation.
升球帆的方式有好几种，具体采用何种方式视情况而定。

Symmetric Spinnaker—Leeward Hoist (or Spinnaker Chute Hoist)
对称球帆——下风升球帆（或者球帆套筒升帆）

Once helm has sailed boat onto training run (hoist drop zone):
当舵手航行到顺风角度时（升降区）：

1. Crew puts pole on.
   船员装上球帆杆。

Helm hoists spinnaker and balances boat, while steering with tiller between the legs if necessary.
舵手升球帆，平衡船体。如有必要，用双腿夹住舵柄来掌舵。

2. Crew takes the guy and cleats, crew then moves to windward side deck.
缭手接住缆绳并夹住，然后移动到上风侧。

3. Helm sits in appropriate place to balance boat. Crew takes sheet and adjusts as necessary. Adjust pole height to keep both clews level.
舵手坐到适当的位置平衡船体。船员接过球缭，适时调整。调整球帆杆高度，保持两个帆后角在同一水平高度。

Symmetric Spinnaker—Windward Hoist 对称球帆——上风升球帆

1. Crew gathers spinnaker up into a ball and checks that the spinnaker guy is free.
缭手将球帆拢成一个球，并检查确保球缭没有夹住。

2. Crew throws the spinnaker forward as the helm hoists quickly. In most boats this would require the helm to steer with the tiller between the legs. Communication/co-ordination is very important, otherwise the spinnaker will end up under the bow of the boat.
缭手将球帆往前扔出去，同时舵手快速升帆。在大多数船型上，该动作需要舵手用双腿夹住舵来控制方向。沟通/合作非常重要，否则球帆就会从船头掉到水里。

3. Crew puts pole on whilst helm keeps the spinnaker flying by playing the guy and the sheet.
缭手装上球帆杆，同时舵手控制缆绳和球缭，保持球帆充分受风。

4. Crew takes the guy and cleats, sitting to windward.
缭手接过缆绳夹住，并坐到上风侧。

5. Helm sits in appropriate place to balance boat. Crew takes the sheet and adjusts as necessary. Adjust pole to keep both clews level.
舵手坐到合适的位置平衡船体；缭手接过下风缭，适时调整。调整球帆杆，保持两个帆后角在同一水平高度。

Symmetric Spinnaker—Hoist 非对称球帆——升帆

1. Helm bears away until the boat is in the hoist/drop zone (If appropriate, crew passes helm the spinnaker sheet).
舵手使船顺风偏转，直到船到达升降区（如可行，缭手将球缭递给舵手）。

2. Crew launches pole and spinnaker with launch line (some boats use separate lines for each in which case the pole is launched first).
缭手支出球帆杆，升球帆（有些船型控制球帆杆和球帆的绳子不是同一条，所以要先将球帆杆支出去）。

3. Crew hoists spinnaker (if separate).
缭手升球帆（如控制球帆杆和球帆的绳子不同）。

4. Helm 'powers up' by luffing slightly as crew sheets in.
随着缭手收紧球缭，舵手使船稍微往迎风偏转，提高动力。

5. As the boat accelerates the helm bears away and the crew eases the sheet. Communication is paramount to keep the boat achieving maximum VMG (velocity made good) i.e. the crew needs to tell the helm whether the sheet load from the power in the sail is increasing or decreasing. The helm can then steer accordingly. Keep the boat flat by steering towards the mast tip.
随着船加速，舵手使船顺风偏转，缭手松球缭。舵手和缭手的良好沟通是保持船以最快速度航行的关键。就是说，缭手须告知舵手缭绳受帆的拉力是在增加还是减少，然后舵手进行相应的调整。根据桅杆顶部的倾斜控制船的方向，以保持船的平稳。

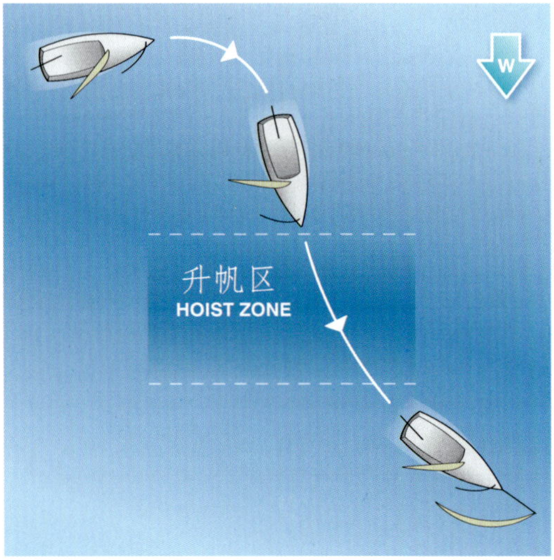

Spinnaker Gybing: Symmetric
对称球帆顺风转向

Again, there are a number of ways to share jobs during the gybe.
同样地，在顺风转向时，也有好几种分配工作的方法。

1. As the helm bears away into the hoist/drop zone, the crew brings the pole back with the guy to set the spinnaker for that point of sailing.
当舵手顺偏到升降区时，缭手用缆绳将球帆杆拉回，将球帆调整到相应的航行角度。

2. Helm calls 'Stand by to gybe'. If crew responds 'Yes' then he gybes the mainsail.
舵手喊“准备转向”，如缭手回答“准备好了”，舵手就开始将主帆换舷。

3. Crew releases guy from the cleat, stands up and hands sheet and guy to the helm. Crew swaps the pole to the new side whilst the helm balances the boat and plays both the guy and sheet to keep the spinnaker flying.
缭手把缆绳从夹绳器上松掉，站起来，将球缭和缆绳都交给舵手。接着缭手将球帆杆换到另一侧；同时舵手平衡船体，并调节缆绳和球缭，保持球帆充分受风。

4. Crew adjusts the new guy and cleats it.
缭手调节好缆绳后夹住。

5. Crew then sits on new windward side taking the new sheet. Helm sits to balance the boat. As a development, the crew may gybe the main with the kicker.
接着缭手坐到船的另一侧，接过球缭；舵手坐下来平衡船体。更高的技术是，缭手通过拉斜拉器，将主帆换舷。

Spinnaker Gybing: Asymmetric 不对称球帆顺风转向

1. Choose a good place to gybe when the boat is travelling fast and in clear water. Crew prepares by gathering slack in new sheet.
在船速够快时，选择一个适合的地点顺风转向，确保航行水域无障碍。缭手先抓住另一侧球缭，做好准备。

2. Whilst the helm is bearing away the crew gradually eases the sheet to assist the spinnaker to slide through the slot in front of the jib, then releases the old sheet and begins pulling on the new sheet.
随着舵手使船顺偏，缭手逐步松球缭，使球帆转过前帆前方的球帆槽，然后松掉这一侧球缭，并开始收紧另一侧球缭。

3. Helm bears away into the hoist/drop zone and gybes the main with the mainsheet falls.
舵手使船顺偏到升降区，然后拉主缭绳圈，使主帆换到另一侧。

4. Helm steers carefully throughout the manoeuvre and into the new hoist/drop zone.
舵手应十分谨慎地掌舵，使船进入升降区。

5. Helm will probably have to luff slightly to fill the spinnaker.
舵手很可能需要使船往上风偏转一点，使球帆鼓起来。

6. If necessary, bear away as the boat speed increases, crew trims as required.
如有必要，随着船速上升，可使船顺偏，缭手根据需要调帆。

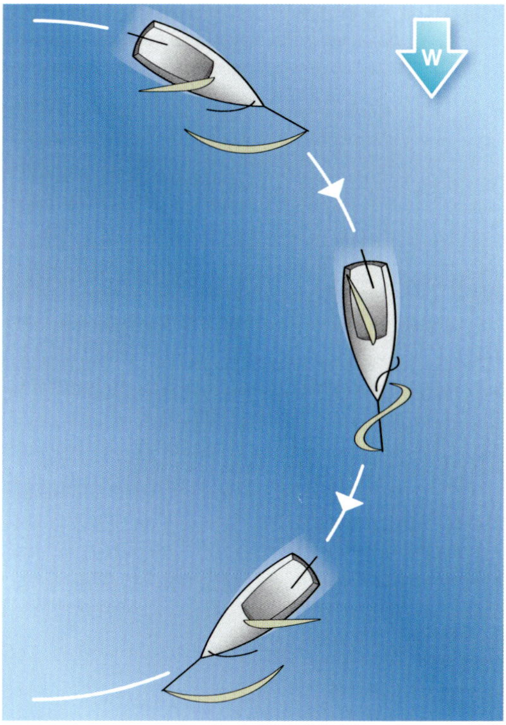

Spinnaker Drop (Windward): Symmetric Spinnaker Drop (Bag)
降球帆（上风）：对称球帆（球帆袋）

1. Crew hands sheet to helm to keep the spinnaker flying whilst pole is being removed. Helm steers with tiller between legs if necessary.
缭手将球缭递给舵手，确保在拆掉球帆杆前，保持球帆的受风。如有必要，舵手可用两腿夹住舵柄来掌舵。

2. Crew takes the pole off the mast and then off the spinnaker clew and stows it.
缭手将球帆杆从桅杆拆下来，然后解开球帆帆后角，塞到帆袋里。

3. On the crew's command, the helm releases the spinnaker halyard and the crew pulls the spinnaker down on the windward side, working up the leech first and then along the foot (this reduces the chance of the spinnaker twisting on the next hoist). Ensure the spinnaker goes under the jib sheet.
在缭手的指令下，舵手松掉球帆升降索，缭手在上风侧将球帆往下拉，先收帆后缘，然后收帆底（这样能减少下次升帆时，球帆缠在一起，无法打开的机率）。确保球帆从前缭下面穿过。

4. Crew then stows it in the bag and tidies up the sheets. Meanwhile the helm is looking ahead.
接着，缭手把球帆塞到球帆袋里，整理好绳索；舵手朝前看，控制好船的方向。

Spinnaker Drop (Windward): Asymmetric Spinnaker Drop
降球帆（上风）：非对称球帆

1. Helm bears away into hoist drop zone.
舵手使船顺风偏转，进入升降区。

2. Crew hands sheet to helm to keep the spinnaker flying until the drop (This keeps the boat moving faster and keeps the spinnaker out of the water during the drop).
缭手将球缭递给舵手，保持球帆受风，直到降帆（这样能确保船持续快速航行，且避免在降帆时球帆落入水中）。

3. Crew pulls in excess retrieval line (to stop spinnaker going under the bow and to speed up the drop).
缭手拉收帆绳松弛的那一段（加快降帆，防止球帆从船头落入水中）。

4. Crew uncleats halyard and pulls down the spinnaker by its retrieval line. If there are separate launch lines, then the pole must be uncleated first.
缭手提起卡住的升降索，通过收帆索，将球帆拉下来。如果升帆索和球帆杆固定绳是分开的，就必须先松掉固定绳。

5. As this is happening, the helm balances the boat and looks ahead.
缭手在进行这些操作时，舵手要负责平衡船体，往前看，注意航向。

START RACING 初级竞赛

The course should include the following characteristics:
该课程应贯彻以下几点：

- An emphasis on racing as fun.
  强调比赛的乐趣。
- Ensuring that starts and rules are not intimidating.
  确保起航和比赛规则不会让人望而却步。
- The provision of enough information for Level 2 standard sailors to get round a club racing course safely, without presenting a hazard to other sailors.
  给级别二的学员提供足够的信息，确保其能安全地完成一般俱乐部的比赛航线，且不会威胁到其他参赛者的安全。
- Encouragement to sailors to start racing, join a club and progress within the sport.
  鼓励学员去参加比赛，加入俱乐部，提高自己的航海技能。

The Course and Starting Sequence
航线和俱乐部起航程序

Club Course
俱乐部航线

Most clubs will have fixed buoys with a system to identify them. The course used will depend upon the wind direction on the day. It will normally be posted as a list of buoys in the order they are to be rounded and which side to leave them on (port or starboard) e.g. SL (Start Line), Ep (Leave buoy E to port), Bs (Leave buoy B to starboard). Also outline the number of laps required.
大部分俱乐部都有固定的浮标和一套辨识的方法。根据当天的风向确定航线。通常，俱乐部会按照绕标的顺序，列出所有的浮标，且说明绕标时，让浮标位于你的哪一舷（左舷或右舷）。例如SL（起航线），Ep（E标在船左舷），Bs（B标在船右舷）。同时，绕航线航行的圈数也会说明。

Trapezoid with Outer Loop
外绕不规则四边形航线

Popular open meeting course, especially with youth classes. These types of course are also extremely good when sailing multiple classes on the same course—different loops can be specified for different classes. This keeps the classes apart on the water.
该航线在公开赛中使用非常频繁，尤其是青少年组别。这些航线也极其适用于同一航线，多个级别同时比赛——要明确不同的级别航行的不同圈数。这样能把各级别的比赛分开。

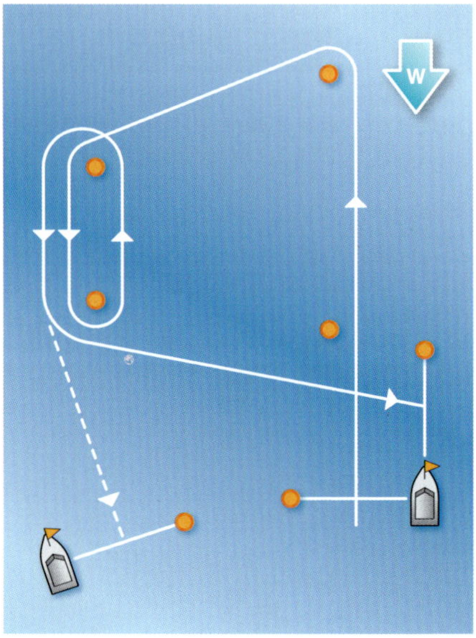

Trapezoid with Inner Loop
内绕不规则四边形航线

Popular open meeting course, as above.
普遍使用的公开赛航线，同上。

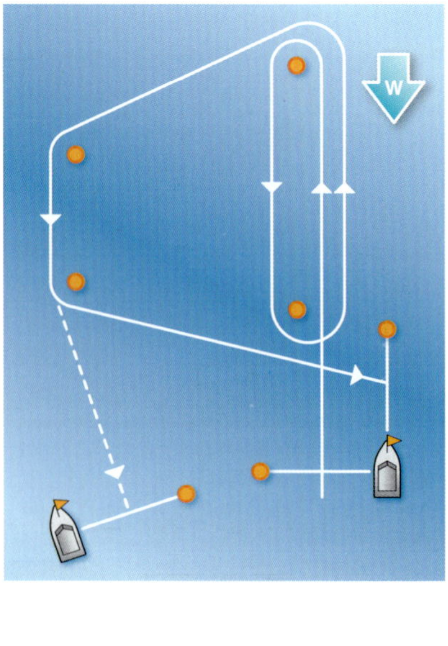

Triangle Sausage Course
三角形香肠航线

Originally called an Olympic triangle, useful with established classes at open meetings and national events.
该航线最早被称为奥林匹克三角形航线，适用于公开赛和全国赛已设立的级别。

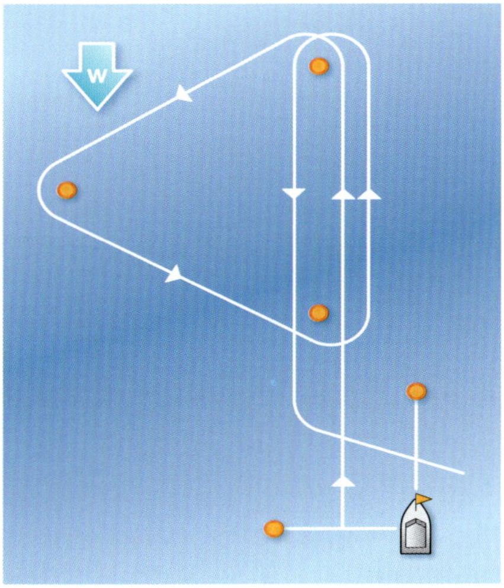

Sausage or Windward/Leeward Course
香肠或迎顺风航线

Very popular with modern asymmetric boats, as they have to go downwind in a series of broad reaches for maximum speed.
该航线在现代非对称球帆船型的比赛中非常流行，因为这些船在跑顺风时，要达到最大速度，需要进行一系列的侧顺风航行。

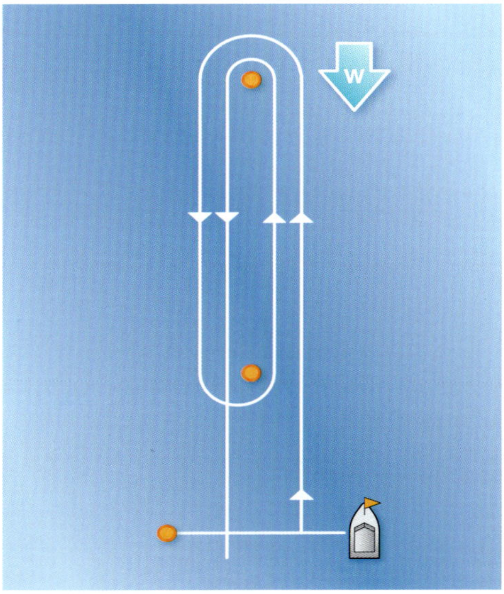

Starting Sequence 起航程序

The starting system used by the majority of sailing clubs consists of a warning signal, a preparatory signal and a start signal. The flags and sound signals used to draw attention to the starting sequence are shown in G12, the RYA Advanced Sailing Handbook. The most common system is five minutes – four minutes – one minute – go.
大多数帆船俱乐部采用的起航程序包括预告信号、准备信号和起航信号。运用旗帜和声音信号，提醒选手注意起航程序。起航程序在G12《英国皇家游艇协会高级航海手册》里有列出。最常用的是，5分钟—4分钟—1分钟—起航。

Other signals relating to starting:
与起航相关的其他信号：

Individual Recall
个别召回
If one or more competitors are over the line at the start then flag X (blue cross against white background) will be displayed immediately after the start with a sound signal. This will be displayed until all competitors have started properly, or up to four minutes after the start, or up to one minute before a following start.
如果一名或多名选手在起航时抢航，那么X旗（白底蓝色十字）将会在起航后立刻被展示，并伴随一次声音信号。旗子要展示至所有选手都按规定起航，或在起航后展示4分钟，或直到下一轮起航前1分钟。

General Recall
全部召回
If several unidentified boats are over the line at the start then the race will be restarted to ensure fairness. Under these circumstances the First Substitute flag (yellow triangle on a blue triangular background) will be flown with two sound signals. The preparatory signal for the next start will normally be one minute after the First Substitute is lowered.
如果多条船抢航且无法确认身份，为确保公正，将会重新起航。在这种情况下，代旗一将会被升起（黄色三角形镶蓝色三角边）并伴随两次声音信号。下一轮起航的准备信号通常会在代旗一降下后1分钟发出。

Starting Penalty Flags
起航惩罚旗
The starting penalty flags are displayed with the preparatory flags and dropped one minute before the start. If any one of these flags is flown then a boat that enters the triangle formed by the two ends of the start line and the first buoy will be penalised as follows:
起航惩罚旗将会和预备旗同时展示，并在起航前1分钟降下。如惩罚旗中的任何一面被升起，那么进入由起航线两端和一标所形成的三角区的船只，将会受到以下惩罚：

Flag I—the competitor must sail to the pre-start side of the line by going around either end of the line.
I旗——选手必须绕起航线的任意一端，回到起航准备区。

Flag Z—the competitor shall receive a 20% scoring penalty.
Z旗——选手被判20%记分惩罚。

Black Flag—the competitor shall be disqualified and shall not be allowed to restart the race if a general recall is necessary.
黑旗——取消选手该轮比赛资格，即使比赛全部召回，也不得参加该轮比赛。

Boat Tuning 船只调整

Tuning a boat can vary between knowing when to ease the kicking strap or pull on the Cunningham in a Laser, to adjusting mast rake and altering the spreaders in a Fireball. The best place to start tuning is to find out what other people who race successfully in the class are doing. Most class associations and sail makers publish tuning guides. Class websites are a good place to start.
调整船只的方式不是一成不变的。对于激光来说，你可能要知道何时松掉斜拉器或收紧下拉索；对于火球级别，就需要调整桅杆倾角和撑臂。学习调整帆船的最好方式是向同级别里的高手请教。多数级别协会和帆厂都会发布调整指南，查询各级别帆船的网页也是一种好方法。

Before experimenting with any rig settings on a boat it is a good idea to set it up to the class average given in the tuning guides.
在尝试设置帆船前，建议设置为调整指南里的平均数据。

Tactics and Strategy 战术与策略

This covers everything from finding the fastest way up the beat using the changes in direction of the wind to manoeuvring at close quarters to gain an advantage on other boats.
该要点涵盖了各类型的技巧，利用风向的改变，找出迎风航段的最快航线；运用策略，近距离抢占优势。

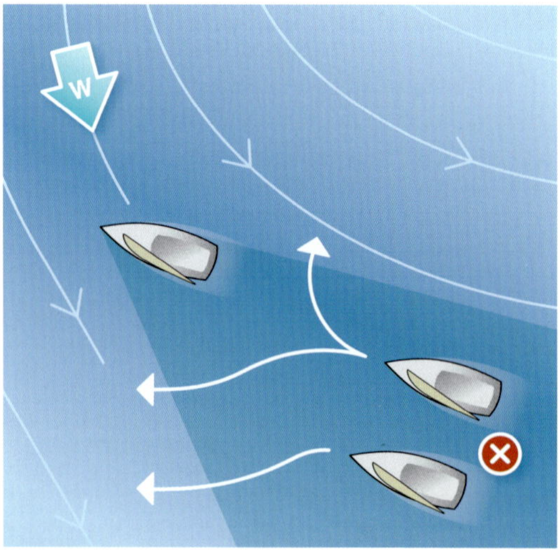

Race strategy 比赛策略

This determines the fastest route around the course dependant on the weather, tidal currents, sea state and surrounding land masses.
利用天气、潮汐流、海况和周围地貌确定最快航线。

Tactics 战术

The course you actually take around the race course must take into consideration other boats and the rules that govern fair sailing. These include sailing

your boat clear of dirty wind, approaching marks using the rules, overtaking slower boats, etc.
在按航线航行时，必须考虑到其他船只和航行规则，确保比赛的公平性。涉及到的战术还包括不要被其他船挡住，在近标处运用规则，超船等。

Dirty Wind 不良受风

The wind to leeward of a dinghy is affected in both strength and direction. To continue on the same tack, to leeward and behind another boat, will result in the boat sailing both lower and slower until it has dropped far enough behind to not be affected.
位于下风的船，其受风在风力和风向上都会受到影响。继续如此，处在下风和在另一条船后，将会导致其航行角度降低，速度更慢。直到落后足够远的距离，才不受影响。

Course Down the Reach
横风航线

A tactical advantage can be gained by sailing very low at the start of a reach as long as there is a gap behind you to prevent your wind being blanketed by other boats. This technique allows for a fast approach to the next buoy on the inside of boats which have gone high.
在横风段，有一个战术可以让你抢占优势，开始横风航行时，跑的角度低一点，但是确保你后面有足够的距离，受风不至于被其他的船遮挡。这样，你就可以在其他航行角度比较高的船内侧，更快地靠近下一标。

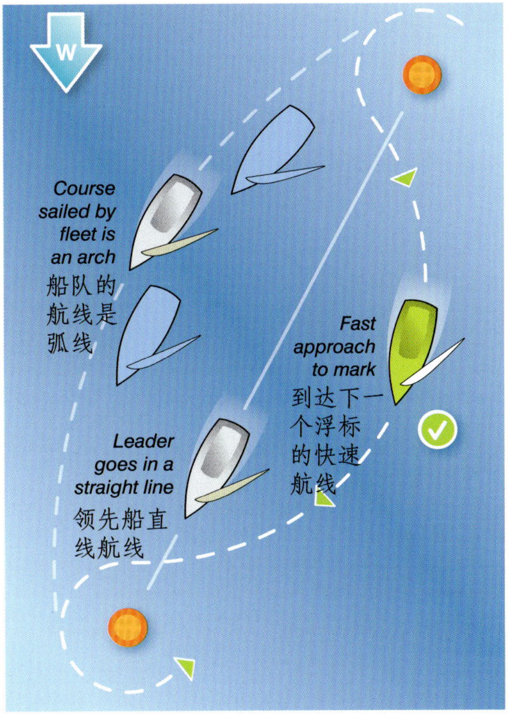

Normal Starting
常规起航程序

Five minutes—Class flag ↑ + sound
5分钟——级别旗↑+声音信号

Four minutes—P flag (or penalty flag) ↑ + sound
4分钟——P旗（或惩罚旗）↑+声音信号

One minute—P flag (or penalty flag) ↓ + sound
1分钟——P旗（或惩罚旗）↓+声音信号

Start—Class flag ↓ + sound
起航——级别旗↓+声音信号

Using Lifts and Avoiding Headers 利用有利舷侧，避免迎风偏转

By studying the water upwind whilst beating, gusts can be seen as dark areas on the water. Advantages can be gained by preparing the boat for the gusts and altering course to make the best use of them. The wind is constantly changing in direction so one tack will always point a dinghy slightly closer to the next mark than the other—this is the lifted tack.
跑迎风段时，仔细观察水面，黑色区域代表阵风区。要想占据有利位置，应做好准备，应对阵风，并改变航线，充分利用阵风。风向是持续改变的，因此，船在某一舷的受风总是比另一舷受风指向的航线更接近下一标——这一舷就是有利受风舷。

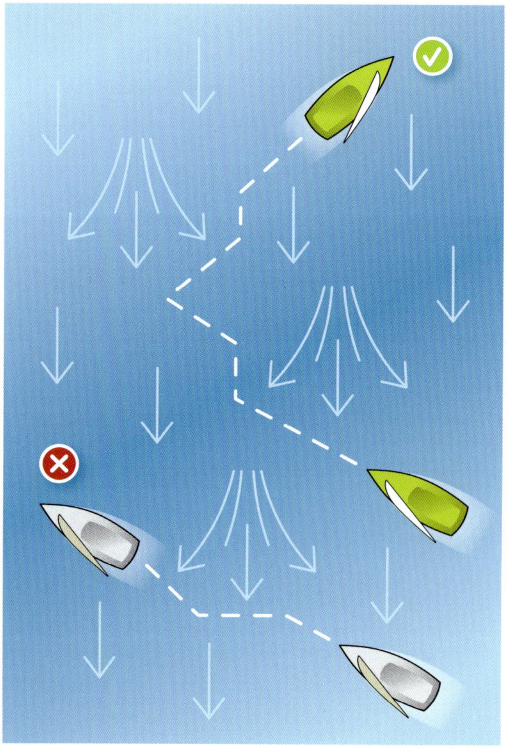

Wind Bends 风的曲线流动

Where the wind bends there can be a significant advantage in sailing towards the inside of the bend. This should result in the boat sailing a shorter distance, as it will spend more time on a lifted tack.
在风曲的内侧航行会有显著优势。能缩短船的航行距离，船位于有利受风舷时间会更长。

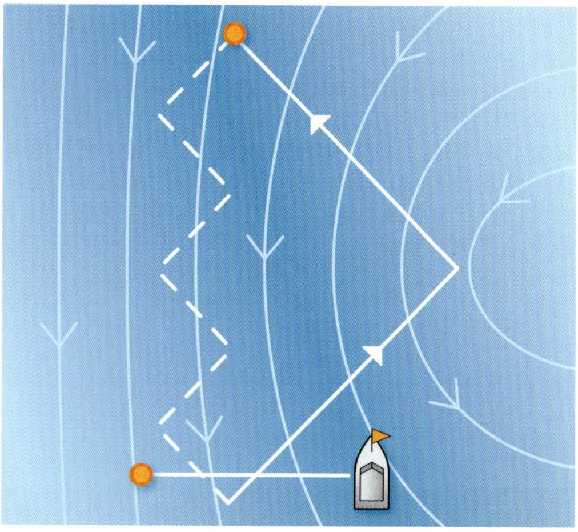

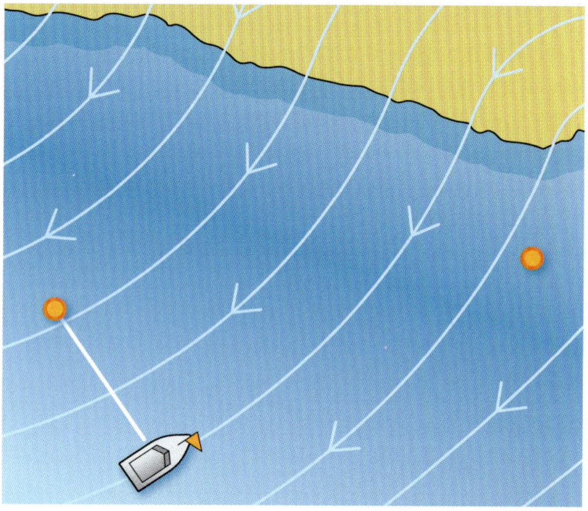

Boat Handling 控船

To be able to apply tactics around the race course good boat handling skills are essential. There are many exercises which concentrate specifically on boat handling, including tacking/gybing on the whistle, follow my leader, start line exercises and racing around a short course.

要能够在比赛中运用战术，其中良好的控船技术是至关重要的。控船的针对训练有很多，包括哨令迎风转向/顺风转向、跟船、起航练习和短航线比赛。

Videoing sailors can be a useful way to provide feedback, which should focus on the key points of the exercise rather than recording everything.

录下学员的航行实况对反馈非常有用，尽管如此，应重点去录控船的要点操作，而不是练习的全过程。

It is generally accepted that to develop boat handling skills it is important to break down a particular manoeuvre into smaller segments. This enables the sailor to focus on particular areas of improvement. Remember, you can't eat an elephant whole.

普遍认为，提高控船技术很重要的一点是，将某个特定操作分解成几个步骤，有针对性地提高学员的操作。

Simple Rules 基本规则

Refer to the RYA Handy Guide to the Racing Rules.

参考RYA竞赛规则指南。

Penalties

惩罚

A boat infringing a rule may exonerate itself by taking a penalty. The penalty is to complete a two turns penalty in the same direction at the earliest opportunity. The boat shall have no rights of way during the manoeuvre.

如果有船违反了第2章中所列的规则，可通过惩罚来解脱自己。惩罚是，在同方向自转两圈，越早越好。正在解脱的船没有航行权。

If a boat fouls a mark she may exonerate herself by performing a 1 turn penalty at the earliest opportunity.

如果船只碰标，可通过自转一圈来解脱，越早越好。

It should be noted that both of these penalties are routinely altered by the Sailing Instructions.

同时也应注意到，这些惩罚条例在航行细则中通常会有变更。

Exercises 练习

By far the most important aspect of teaching people to race is actually racing on the water. Many different exercises can be used to develop sailors' understanding and performance around a course. The race can be broken down as follows and specific exercises used to improve performance.

到目前为止，竞赛教学最重要的方法是，进行水上比赛。通过各种不同的练习提高学员对竞赛的理解和表现。可将竞赛分解成以下具体练习，提高比赛表现能力。

Starting

起航

A good start is measured by: Sailing at maximum speed, in clear air and on or close to the line when the start signal sounds. Starting is a key skill and confidence on the start line is essential if racing is to be enjoyed successfully. Starting exercises should receive major emphasis during a 'Start Racing' Course.

好的起航有这些特征：速度达到最快；受风良好；并且在起航信号发出时，在起航线上或接近起航线。起航是一项非常关键的技术，对于起航有充分的自信至关重要。做好了起航，才能充分地享受比赛。在“初级竞赛”课程中，应重点练习起航。

Timing to be near the start line as the gun goes

当起航信号响起时，控制好时机接近起航线

A simple start line and a short windward leg can be used to practise a number of starts with a short race afterwards. For the purpose of training a shortened two minutes – one minute – go is normally used.

可利用一条简单的起航线和一个短距离的迎风段，练习几次起航，然后进行一次短距离的比赛。为了达到训练目的，通常使用“2分钟—1分钟—起航”的计时方式。

12 Teaching the Advanced Modules 高级单元教学

Holding position and accelerating

控位和加速

Again, a simple start line and windward leg can be used, but the start sequence should involve the start being sounded 15 seconds or so either side of the normal start signal. This encourages people to practise holding position near the start line and accelerating away at the start signal. One of the problems in training with a small number of boats is that the starts are not very realistic—there is rarely congestion at the start line. Boats can practise these skills by hovering next to a buoy for as long as possible before bearing away with the sails, sheeting in slowing and accelerating to full speed. Sailing backwards can also be a useful skill.

该练习也可利用上文所述的起航线和迎风段，不同的是，在最后发出起航信号时，比正常时间提前或晚15秒左右发出。这样能鼓励学员练习在起航线上控制住自己的位置，以及在起航信号发出时加速冲线。如果训练的船只数量很少，很难达到起航的效果——起航线上不拥挤，没那么真实。学员在练习这些技能时，要运用反受风停船，尽可能久地停在浮标旁，然后再顺风偏转、收紧缭绳、减速、加到全速。倒退航行也是一个很有用的技能。

Another useful exercise is 'follow my leader', taking the boats on a close reach and slowing down almost to a standstill before accelerating again.

另一个很有效的练习是"跟船"，使船航行到迎风角度，然后减速到几乎停止，再重新加速。

Line bias

起航线偏差

To raise awareness of the line bias the anchor rope on the committee boat can be periodically lengthened and shortened between starts to alter the bias. This will encourage sailors to regularly check the bias of the start line.

为了提高学员对起航线偏差的意识，可在每轮起航前，将裁判船的锚绳延长或缩短，改变起航线偏差。促使选手经常检查起航线，判断出有利起航的那一侧。

Windward leg

迎风航段

Speed upwind

迎风速度

Start the sailors lying-to in a line across the wind, level and in clear air. This compares speed and pointing. Once they have spread out, regroup and start again.

开始前，让所有学员飘帆停船，排成一条直线，然后同时往上风标航行。每个人的速度和航行角度都不一样。一旦都分散开了，就重新集合所有人，重复练习。

Tactics and lay lines

战术和方位线

After a briefing on tactics a number of short races can be run with a finish between the safety boat and the windward mark. Boats should be encouraged to practise tacking on the lay line and covering other boats up the beat whilst protecting their clear air. They should vary their approach to the mark but always on starboard tack and in clear air.

讲完战术后，进行几个短航线比赛，安全艇和上风标之间为终点线。鼓励学员练习在方位线上转向；确保自己受风良好，遮挡其他船只。靠近上风标的方式有很多种，但一定要保持右舷航行，而且受风良好。

Mark rounding

绕标

Practise bearing away

练习顺风偏转

A small triangular or sausage course should be laid with all the boats sailing around it. The safety boat can then be held near the windward mark to offer coaching advice to the boats bearing away. The emphasis should be on heeling the boat slightly to windward and easing the main, to minimise use of the rudder. You should ask them to consider easing the kicker, Cunningham, adjusting the centreboard and, when windy, getting the crew weight back to assist the turn.

应设置一个短三角形航线或香肠航线，然后让所有的船一起练习。安全艇的位置应在上风标附近，这样学员在标旁顺偏时，教练就可以进行指导。向学员强调，稍微往迎风倾斜，松主帆，尽量少动舵。让他们考虑松斜拉器、下拉索，调节稳向板。风大的时候，往船后坐辅助偏转。

Practise gybing

练习顺风转向

A slalom course can be used to practise reach-to- reach gybing or a whistle to initiate run-to-run gybing.

可设置一个障碍航线，练习侧顺—侧顺的顺风转向或者是正顺—正顺的顺风转向。

Tactics
战术
Start the boats at the windward mark of a triangular course, enabling the boats to arrive at the gybe mark close together. This should allow sailors a chance to think ahead and practise good mark rounding. The safety boat should ideally be positioned inside the course near the gybe mark.
设置一个三角形航线，让所有船同时从上风标开始，使大家到达下风标时距离很近。该练习能促使学员提前思考，练习绕标。理想情况下，安全艇应在航线内侧，下风标附近。

Off wind legs
顺风航段
Speed including spinnakers if applicable
船速（球帆航行也可行）
Start the boats from 'follow-my-leader' on a beam reach, a good distance upwind of a mark. This will allow the boats an equal start with other boats in close proximity. Focus should be on boat speed alone with the boats not attempting to block the wind of others.
从距离下风标较远的地方开始，让所有船跟着你的安全艇跑横风。这样能使船彼此靠得很近，起航就会很公平。这就要求学员集中注意力控制好自己的船速，而不是总试着去挡其他船的风。

Tactics
战术

A similar exercise can be run but this time with the emphasis on gaining position by covering other boats whilst keeping their own air clear. This can be done on a reach or a run.
可进行类似的练习，但是本阶段强调通过挡住其他船来占位，前提是保持自己受风良好。可在横风航行或顺风航行航段练习。

More information on the Portsmouth Yardstick is available on the RYA website.
更多信息请查看RYA官网，朴茨茅斯标准体制。

PERFORMANCE SAILING 高阶航海

Boat Setup 船只设置

This will include general principles and use of rig controls.
包含一些普遍原则和控制索的使用。

Boat Handling 控船

Including use of symmetric and asymmetric spinnakers, trapezing and safety.
包含对称球帆和不对称球帆的使用、悬挂压舷和安全问题。

Coaching 教学

Candidates will be encouraged to develop a positive but relaxed style, which brings about improvement in those being coached.
鼓励候选教练培养一种积极乐观、轻松的教学方式，这样能他们更好地让学员发挥自己的水平。

Use of the Powerboat 机动艇的使用

Safe and effective driving and positioning for coaching and safety.
安全高效的驾驶技术，以及在教学和负责安全时，合理地选择安全艇的位置。

Advanced Instructor candidates should be familiar with the relevant chapters of G12 Advanced Handbook.
高阶教练候选人应十分熟悉 G12 《英国皇家游艇协会高级航海手册》里的相关章节。

Briefing 下水前的简述

The briefing is vitally important because high performance boats could be spread out over a far larger area than a fleet of beginner boats. Make certain of your briefing:
简述非常重要，相比初学者用船，高性能帆船很容易在训练时分散开。所以在简述时要：

- Clear and concise (use pictures and diagrams).
  简洁明了（运用图片和图表）。
- Safety and recall signals understood by everyone.

确保所有人明白安全和召回信号。

- The session aims are clear.
  训练目标要清晰。
- The learning objectives are clear and understood by all students. This is especially important in a group of mixed ability.
  所有学员都清楚学习目标。这一点十分重要，尤其是学员水平参差不齐时。
- The sailing area is suitable for the purpose of the session. Downwind sailing in a breeze will require much more space than roll tacking practise in light winds.
  航行区域要适合培训目标的开展。在小风情况下，练习滚动迎风转向。
- Use bullet points and don't waffle.
  说明要点，不要含糊其辞。
- Use effective questioning to make sure everyone understands what is going to happen on the water.
  有效提问，确保所有学员都清楚要在水上进行什么样的训练。
- Don't try and cover too much in each session—concentrate on 'bite size chunks'.
  不要在一次训练中讲得过多——让学员一次吸收一点，循序渐进。

Land Drills 岸上练习

Due to the nature of the boats and the subject matter involved, the use of land drills is highly recommended. See the notes on land drills on page (?).
对于有些船型和训练主题来说，岸上练习非常适用。

Exercises which can benefit from land drills include:
适合在岸上进行的练习有：

- Spinnaker hoists, gybes and drops.
  升球帆，使用球帆顺风转向以及降球帆。
- Trapeze work (ensure that they are safe).
  悬挂压舷（确保学员的安全）。
- Sail setting and sail controls. This is also an excellent way to make sure that all boats are set up correctly for the conditions.
  调节帆和控制装置，同时也能确保所有船的设置适合相应的天气条件。
- Tacking and gybing practise.
  迎风转向和顺风转向练习。

Demonstrate and then give the students time to practise, using positive coaching all the time. Take care that no one will get hurt falling off a trapeze onto hard ground or falling out of a dinghy whilst dropping a spinnaker.
先示范，然后给学员时间练习，自始至终要保持积极的教学状态。要注意，防止学员从吊索摔到地上，或者在降球帆时从船上掉下来。

Demonstrations 演示

Demonstrations are vital to teach the more complicated advanced skills. This is why it is of paramount importance that you as the Instructor can competently sail performance boats. Areas of coaching that benefit from demonstrations include:
教授更复杂的高级技巧，演示是非常重要的一种教学手段。所以作为教练，必须能够驾驶高性能帆船。适合演示的技术有：

- Tacking and gybing (including rolling).
  迎风转向和顺风转向（包括滚动式）。
- Mark rounding.
  绕标。

- Spinnaker hoist, gybe and drop.
  升球帆，使用球帆顺风转向以及降球帆。

Coaching 指导

Effective coaching whilst on the water is one of the most important aspects of becoming an Advanced Instructor. The ability to assess the performance of a dinghy or student and make a valid contribution to their improvement is fundamental to your role.
能够在水上高效地指导教学，是高阶教练须具备的重要素质之一。高阶教练应具备的基本能力是，评估学员的表现，使学员取得进步。

- Be effective. If you don't have anything useful to say, don't say anything!
  注意效率，如果没有必要的事要说，就什么都不要说！
- Be positive. Sailing is fun.
  保持积极的态度。航海是充满乐趣的。
- Keep it short and simple. Don't overload your students.
  讲解要简短且简单，不要给学员过多的信息。
- Try and reduce stress levels, people perform much better if they are relaxed.
  尽量减少学员的压力，学员放松时的表现会更好。
- Be precise and don't waffle. Tell them exactly how to improve. For clarity use the same words as you used when briefing where possible .
  讲解要准确，不要含糊其辞。向学员说明他们具体要如何提高，尽量与简述时说的话对应起来。
- Don't try and shout across an expanse of water, get them to stop and come alongside—it saves time in the long run.
  不要在距离水上很远时叫喊学员，让他们在你的船旁停下——这比你在水上喊更省时间。
- Make notes whilst on the water to assist your debrief.
  水上培训时做笔记，这有助你给大家做最后总结。

Top Tip 重要提示

Consider using a video camera. Students can see exactly the point being made.
考虑使用录像器材，能使学员更明白你要讲的要点。

Debrief 总结

The debrief is very important as it will probably contain most of the coaching points for improvement. You must give positive feedback from the session on the water. Very often your debrief will be analytical and will deal with a number of small but specific points. It may involve going back to a land drill to demonstrate a point or specific manoeuvre. Always try and involve all of the students and find a positive point for them all.
培训后的总结非常重要，因为很多提高学员表现的要点都是在总结的时候说明的。一定要针对水上的培训，给予学员积极的反馈。通常，要分析学员的表现，提出几个具体的小要点。为了达到目的，可能需要在岸上给学员演示。自始至终要尽力让所有的学员都参与，赞美大家共同拥有的优点。

Debrief points to remember:
总结要点：

- Use the 'Traffic Light' for feedback (see page ?).
  利用“交通灯”方式做反馈。
- Be specific.
  说明要具体。
- Analyse each boat's performance individually and involve all students.
  分析每个学员的表现，让所有人都参与。
- Relate performance to session aims as well as what happened on the water.
  将学员表现与训练目标结合起来，以及水上的情况。
- Be positive. A lot of students will be ecstatic at just having sailed an RS200 with a kite up, so don't pull their

performance to pieces!.
保持积极。很多学员能在RS200上使用球帆航行，就会欣喜若狂。不要去打消他们的积极性。

- Don't be afraid to go back to a land drill – it will reinforce their learning.
如需进行岸上练习，千万不要迟疑——这样会加深他们的学习。

Top Tip 重要提示

When gybing, ensure your students look where they are going and make small adjustments to the helm all the way through—'Steer through the gybe'.
在顺风转向时，确保你的学员注意到航行的方向，注意要对舵进行微调——“顺风转向注意调舵”。

- Remember it's fun. They should want to go back on the water to improve their sailing after the debrief.
记住，保持乐趣。在总结后，学员应该非常想回到水上，提高自己的航行水平。

Safety 安全

Sailing high performance boats always involves capsizing at some point. The ability to capsize, right the dinghy and sail on is an essential skill when racing high performance boats. It is important that you make your students aware of the particular risks which can be involved. Useful issues can include:
驾驶高性能帆船在有些时候总是会翻船。因此，在驾驶这类船型时，正船继续航行的能力十分关键。还有一点十分重要，让学员意识到翻船涉及的危险。一些有用要点是：

- Clothing. Make sure all students have the correct personal equipment required for sailing a performance dinghy: wetsuits or dry suits, good quality gloves, trapeze harness that fits correctly and has a quick release hook if possible, dinghy or wetsuit boots, buoyancy aid that is suitable (i.e. high fit that gives plenty of room for movement).
衣物。确保所有的学员都穿着驾驶高性能帆船所需的个人装备：湿式或干式保暖服，高质量手套；压舷吊索装配正确，如可行，最好有一个快挂；航海靴或下水鞋，合适的救生衣（即高配置装备，能使学员行动灵活）。
- Knife. Advise that they should all carry a knife that can be used to cut themselves clear of the boat or equipment. Ensure that the one in the safety boat is easily accessible.
刀。建议学员佩戴一把刀，在必要时用来切断绳索等，与船或装备脱离。确保在安全艇上也备一把。
- Run a positive safety briefing before your students go afloat. Don't put your students off, but make them aware of relevant issues on the day:
在学员下水前，进行一次安全讲述。注意不要打消学员的积极性，而是让他们意识到相关的安全问题：
  1. The lack of an air pocket under many high performance dinghies when inverted.
  很多高性能小帆船在完全倒置后，船底都没有气囊。
  2. The risk of being caught on rigging with a trapeze harness.
  在使用压舷吊索时，可能会被索具缠住。
  3. The risk of injury during a high-speed wipe-out.
  高速航行时翻船，可能会受伤。
  4. Avoiding inversions.
  避免完全倒置。
- Make sure that all boats being used are safe. Tape up any sharp areas or fittings, make sure that any wire is not fraying, check all fittings and control lines on a regular basis.
确保用船安全。用胶带缠住锋利的地方或配件，确保绳索没有磨损，定期检查所有的配件和控制索。
- Ascertain the ability of all students before going afloat. You can always increase the challenge, but lost confidence is difficult to replace.
在下水前要清楚学员的水平。要增加挑战很容易，但是重新建立孩子们的自信却很难。

Use mast head flotation. It's not 'cool', but it eliminates inversions which are energy sapping to recover.
使用桅顶浮球。看上去不好看，但是它可以防止帆船完全倒置，而且使正船更容易。

TECHNIQUE AND SKILL 技术与技能

One way of looking at how the theory becomes practice is to consider that the RYA Method discussed later in this book is the component part of the RYA Skills Model shown below, and that practice by the student using training exercises shapes those components and develops the techniques to become more skilful.
本书中提到的"RYA教学方法"是如下所示的"RYA技能发展模型"中的一个组成部分。学员通过培训进行技术练习，形成技术的组成部分，继而将这些技术发展成技能。以此可以看出理论是如何转换成实践的。

Technique—The physical movements that make up a manoeuvre.
技术——身体动作形成的操作动作。
Skill—The ability to perform a technique appropriate to the conditions at will and consistently while under pressure. Right skill, right time, right place.
技能——在压力下，能随心所欲的应对不同情况始终如一的展示一项技术的能力。正确的技术，正确的时机，正确的地点。

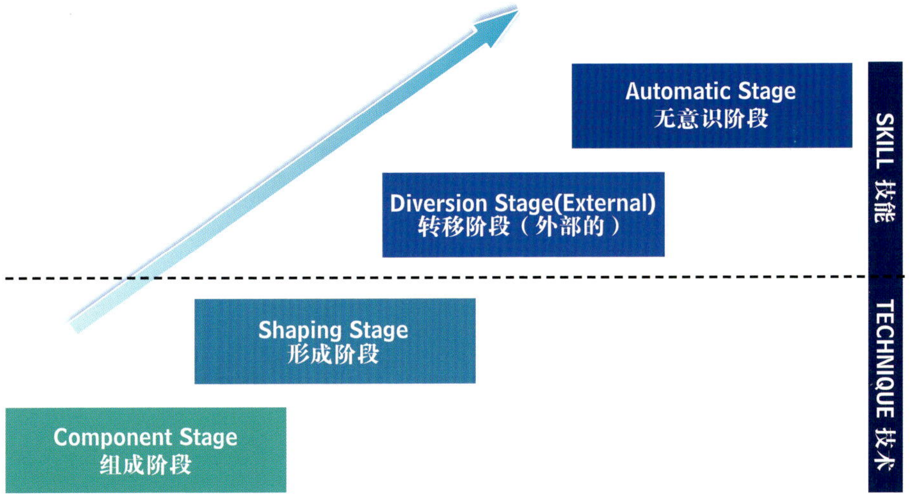

RYA SKILLS MODEL RYA 技能发展模式

Skill Phase
技能板块

Automatic Stage
无意识阶段
Creating consistency of the skill under pressure
在压力下持续做出稳定的操作

Diversion Stage
转移阶段
Switching attention away from the technique, to external factors
把注意力从技术转移至外部因素

SKILL 技能

Key Guidelines
关键指南

- Try to focus externally or away from the technique e.g. tactics, wind, waves
  试着把注意力从技术转移或去注意外部条件。例如，战术、风、浪
- Don't tweak techniques
  不要调整技术

Technique Phase
技术板块

Shaping Stage
形成阶段
Getting the components to work together. Creating a feel, rhythm and flow to the whole technique
把分解的动作组合在一起。给整个技术制造一个感觉、节奏和流畅感

Component Stage
构成阶段
Identifying and developing the components and routines
明确并发展基本操作步骤和程序

TECHNIQUE 技术

Key Guidelines
关键指南

- Minimise verbal intsructions
  最少化口头指导
- Create exercises that give non-verbal feedback
  设计一些练习，能实现无声反馈
- Ask sailor first before providing positive feedback
  先询问水手，在给于他们积极的反馈
- Encourage experimentation
  鼓励学员多实践
- Focused training
  集中培训

Teaching Disabled Sailors 13
残疾学员教学

Teaching a disabled person to sail is exactly like teaching a non-disabled person. You mix common sense with experience and apply safe practice.
教授残疾人学习帆船和教非残疾人是一样的。须将常识与经验结合起来，并采取安全措施。

The overall objective is to learn how to sail effectively, develop confidence, enjoyment, a sense of achievement and to have fun. It is important to encourage maximum participation and activity by people. Do not prejudge a person's competence by their disability, but rather by their experience, knowledge and ability. The first thing you should do is ask!
教学的主要目标是：让学员学会如何有效航行，提高学员的自信与成就感，让他们享受帆船运动的乐趣。首先，非常重要的一点是，鼓励学员最大限度地参与到活动中。不要因为学员的身体缺陷就预判他们的能力，而应先去了解他们的经验、知识和能力。你应该做的第一件事情就是询问！

We are all individuals each with different interests. Someone with a disability has ideas, makes plans, gets excited, even bloody minded. There is no need to adopt a different manner and vocabulary or to feel sympathy or embarrassment. The important thing is to treat a disabled person as you would anyone else.
我们都是独立的个体，各自有不同的兴趣爱好。身体有缺陷的人跟正常人一样，有的人很有想法，有的人善于计划，有的人很容易兴奋，有的人甚至很固执。没有必要用不同的方式和语言对待他们，或是觉得同情或是觉得尴尬。要记住，像对待其他任何正常人一样对待残疾人。

A disability is not a barrier to the successful completion of courses. All participants must be able to demonstrate their ability to complete the whole syllabus, but this can be achieved by proxy. A candidate who cannot perform a task directly must be able to satisfactorily direct a third party to achieve that task on their behalf. It is worth bearing in mind that the candidate has to possess good communication and teaching skills as well as knowing how to undertake the manoeuvre.
身体缺陷并不是学习帆船的阻碍。所有的候选人都必须能展示他们具备整个教学大纲里的所有技能，不过允许有人替代。不能直接达成任务的候选人，必须要能指导第三方，以他们的名义去完成任务。要牢记，学员要具备良好的沟通与教学技能，而且知道如何操作。

How RYA Sailability can Support your Training Needs
RYA残疾人航海项目如何满足你的培训需求

Attitudes to the inclusion of disabled people in sport are forever changing, but we know that the biggest barriers of all are the concerns of non-disabled people. The barriers that these concerns create are often born of ignorance and apprehension, but most significantly from a lack of awareness.
社会上对于残疾人参与运动的态度总是在不断变化，但是如大家所知，最大的障碍是非残疾人的担忧。这些担忧通常是由于非残疾人的忽视和不安而产生的，最主要的还是在意识上对残疾人能力的忽视。

Without the numerous club members and RYA Sailability volunteers there would be no support to organise so many sailing opportunities throughout the country. As groups expand and new ones start up the demand for volunteers grows.
如果没有全国各俱乐部和RYA残疾人项目的志愿者，在全国开展如此大量的帆船活动将会是很艰难的。随着残疾人航海群体的扩展以及新群体的产生，对于志愿者的需求也在逐步增长。

Disabled people want to go sailing and often need a variety of support to enable them to do so. Some are totally independent: others may need help with transport, launching boats etc. Volunteers do not have to be a sailor or paramedic to help someone get afloat, every job is important, but it is essential to identify what job is best for them.
残疾人航海通常需要各种支持。有些残疾人可以完全独立；其他人或许需要运送协助，把船推下水等。志愿者不一定非得是水手或医护人员，才能帮住残疾人去海上玩船。每一项工作都很重要，但是知道什么工作使他们受益最大非常关键。

RYA Sailability offers training packages that can support your groups/clubs in both awareness and volunteer organisation.
RYA残疾人航海项目提供各种培训来支持你的团队/俱乐部，无论是在意识上，还是在志愿者的组织上。

- Depending on the session, position the coach boat in the correct place to enable effective coaching. These are:
根据培训内容，将教练艇停在合理的位置能够提高教学质量。请查看以下说明：

1. Tacking exercise: coach boat to leeward of the fleet.
迎风转向练习：教练艇应在学员船的下风侧。
2. Gybing exercise: coach boat to windward of the fleet.
顺风转向练习：教练艇应在学员船的上风侧。
3. Windward mark rounding: coach boat to windward of the mark.
绕上风标：教练艇应在浮标的上风侧。
4. Leeward mark rounding: coach boat to windward of the mark or use coach boat as the leeward mark.
绕下风标：教练艇应在浮标的上风侧，或将教练艇当作下风标。
5. Trapezing, spinnaker work or boat speed exercise: following individual boats at a safe distance (see above).
悬挂压舷，使用球帆或船速练习：在跟随学员船时，要注意保持一定的安全距离。（参见上述说明）
6. Starting practice: coach boat at windward end of the line and on the line.
起航练习：教练艇应位于起航线两端外侧靠上风的位置。

Top Tip 重要提示

Always wear the kill cord.
始终携带安全绳。

Keep the propeller away from people in the water.
确保螺旋桨远离在水中的人。

During an incident, count heads first.
如发生事故，首先要做的就是清点人员。

Stop the engine on arrival if there is someone in the water.
一旦到达落水者旁，应立即关闭发动机。

- If using a camera, it is highly recommended that someone else drives the boat if it is going to be under way with the engine running.
如果在教学时使用照相机，强列建议让其他人来驾驶，避免发动机在无人控制的情况下运行。

MARK LAYING FOR TRAINING COURSES 设置浮标和航线

When running single handed, improvers or racing sessions, you will need to lay a succession of short, easily moved courses. To avoid problems, remember the following points:
在进行单人艇教学、能力提升练习或竞赛教学时，教练需要设置一系列易改变的短航线。为了提高执行效果，应遵循以下要点：

- Keep marks as simple as possible. 布标应尽量简单。
- Avoid complicated systems with blocks and weights: sinkers are cheaper and less trouble than anchors.
避免使用复杂的滑轮和配重系统：标坠更经济，而且比锚更方便。
- Always lay marks over the windward side of your teaching boat.
始终让浮标位于教练艇的上风侧。
- Have the warp flaked, with the sinker on top ready to go. Retrieve marks in the same way.
将锚绳叠好，把标坠放在最上面，时刻可以抛下水。收标后整理的方法也一样。
- Re-flake neatly as you haul in.
把标坠拉上来后，将绳子重新叠好。
- Don't use warps which float (polypropylene).
不要使用有浮力（如聚丙烯）的锚绳。
- A short length of chain 1m below the mark will help prevent it being 'picked up' by a rudder/daggerboard if a student rounds too closely.
标坠下接1米长的链子，能防止学员在绕标时，离标过近，舵或者稳向板勾到锚绳。
- A range of marks of different colours makes identification easier.
浮标颜色不同更容易辨认。
- It is sometimes easier to lay a mark in approximately the right place, and then tow it into its exact position. Sinkers make this easier than anchors.
有时候更简便的布标方法是：将浮标抛在大致正确的位置，然后拖到你想要的位置。相比锚，该方式更适用于标坠。
- Have a simple communication system if working with a mother ship or committee boat.
如果你在补给船或裁判船上，沟通方式要简单一些。
- Move a course after large wind shifts.
如风摆较大，应改变航线。

Advice and Guidance 15
建议和引导

This document outlines the code of conduct under which all holders of RYA instructor qualifications and RYA training appointments (hereafter referred to as instructors) are required to comply. The code of conduct is intended to make clear to all participants, instructors and RYA appointment holders the high standards to which all are expected to conform. Instructors must:.

本文档概述了所有RYA教练和教官（以下简称教练）必须遵守的行为守则。 行为准则旨在向所有参与者、教练和教官明确要求所有人遵守的最高标准。 教练必须：

1. If working with people under the age of 18 or adults at risk, read and understand the Safeguarding Children and/or Safeguarding Adults policies and guidelines as detailed on the RYA website at www.rya.org.uk/go/safeguarding.

   如果教授18岁以下的人或弱势成年人，请阅读并了解RYA网站www.rya.org.uk/go/safeguarding上详细介绍"保护儿童和/或保护成年人"的规定和准则。

2. Respect the rights, dignity and worth of every person and treat everyone equally within the context of their boating activity.

   尊重每个人的权利，尊严和价值，并在帆船活动中平等地对待每个人。

3. Place the wellbeing and safety of the student above the development of performance or delivery of training.

   学员的健康和安全高于学员的表现和培训要求。

4. Follow all guidelines laid down by the RYA with regards specific training or coaching programmes.

   遵循RYA制定的有关特定培训或辅导计划的所有准则。

5. Not develop inappropriate relationships with students (especially children). Relationships must be based on mutual trust and respect and not exert undue influence to obtain personal benefit or reward.

   不要与学员（特别是孩子）建立不适当的关系。 人际关系必须建立在相互信任和尊重的基础上，不能施加过分的影响以获得个人利益或报酬。

6. Encourage and guide students to accept responsibility for their own behaviour and performance.

   鼓励并引导学员为他们自身的行为和表现负责。

7. Ensure that the activities they direct or advocate are appropriate for the age, maturity, experience and ability of the individual.

   确保指导或倡导的活动符合学员的年龄、成熟度、经验和能力。

8. At the outset, clarify with students (and where appropriate their parents or carers) exactly what is expected of them and what they are entitled to expect.

   在活动开始，就应向学员（其父母或监护人）明确说明你对他们表现的期望以及他们有权获得的期望。

9. Always promote the positive aspects of the activity (eg courtesy to other water users).

   始终从积极的角度评价水上运动（例如，赞扬其他学员）

10. Behave appropriately to ensure the safety of instructors and others under your direction.

    采取适当的措施以确保您指导下的教练和他人的安全。

11. Treat all RYA instructors, appointment holders and other stakeholders with respect.

    尊重所有RYA的教练、教官和其他相关者。

12. Not do or neglect to do anything which may bring the RYA into disrepute.

    不做或不做任何可能有损RYA声誉的事情。

13. Hold relevant up to date governing body qualifications as approved by the RYA.

    持有RYA认可的国家管理机构认证的相关有效证书。

14. Consistently display high standards of behaviour and appearance.

    保持高标准的举止和着装。

15. Act with integrity in all customer and business to business dealings pertaining to RYA training.

    在与RYA培训有关的所有客户以及企业交流时，以诚信行事。

16. Not teach or purport to provide RYA courses or RYA certification outside of the framework of an RYA recognised training centre.

不得在RYA认可的培训中心体系之外教授或支持提供RYA课程或签发RYA证书。

17. Notify the RYA immediately of any court imposed sanction that precludes the instructor from contact with specific user groups (for example children or adults at risk).
立即通知RYA任何法院实施的禁止教练与特定用户群（例如处于危险中的儿童或成人）接触的制裁。
18. Notify RYA Training in the event of any health issues that may affect their ability to carry out their responsibilities.
如果有任何可能影响你履行职责能力的健康问题，请通知RYA培训。
19. Not carry out RYA training, examining or coaching activities whilst under the influence of alcohol or drugs.
有饮酒或吸毒行为，请勿进行RYA培训、检查或指导活动。

Failure to adhere to the RYA Instructor Code of Conduct may result in the suspension or withdrawal of RYA qualifications or appointments.
不遵守RYA教练行为准则可能会导致RYA资格或任命被暂停或撤销。

SAFEGUARDING AND CHILD PROTECTION
安全防护和儿童保护

Introduction 介绍

RYA Recognised Training Centres that teach children and young people aged under 18 are required to have a formal safeguarding and child protection policy which is checked as part of their annual inspection.
教授18岁以下儿童和青少年的RYA认证的培训中心必须制定正式的儿童保护政策，并在年度检查中进行检查。

Adopt a policy statement that defines the organisation's commitment to providing a safe environment for children.
采纳一种政策说明，明确机构承诺为儿童提供一种安全的学习氛围。

Produce a simple code of practice and procedures governing how the organisation runs.
制订基本的实践行为准则和步骤，规定机构的运作方式。

The RYA publishes guidelines to help clubs, training centres and instructors to enable children and adults at risk to enjoy the sports of sailing, windsurfing and power boating in all their forms, in a safe environment. They can be copied or adapted to meet the requirements of the organisation. The document and other best practice guidance can be downloaded from the RYA's website www.rya.org.uk/go/safeguarding
RYA出版各种指南帮助俱乐部、培训中心和教练，使儿童和弱势成人能够在安全的环境下，尽情地享受帆船、帆板和机动艇等各项运动。 各培训中心可复制或直接采用这些指南，来满足自己的要求。如有需要这类文件和其他最佳实践指南，可从RYA官网www.rya.org.uk/go/safeguarding下载。

RYA Safeguarding and Child Protection Policy Statement:
RYA保障及儿童保护政策声明：

This policy refers to anyone under the age of 18, defined as a child by the Children Act 1989. The policy applies to all RYA employees, contractors and volunteers.
根据《1989年未成年法案》中定义的，未成年人指18岁以下的任何人，该政策适用于所有RYA员工、承包商和志愿者。

The RYA is committed to safeguarding children taking part in its activities from physical, sexual or emotional harm, neglect or bullying. We recognise that the safety, welfare and needs of the child are paramount and that any child, irrespective of age, disability, race, religion or belief, sex, sexual or gender identity or social status, has a right to protection from discrimination and abuse.
RYA致力于保护参与其活动的儿童免受身体、性或情感上的伤害、忽视或欺凌。 RYA认识到，儿童的安全、福利和需求至关重要，任何儿童，不论其年龄、残疾、种族、宗教信仰、性别、性取向或社会地位如何，均有权受到保护，免受歧视和虐待的权利。

The RYA takes all reasonable steps to ensure that, through safe recruitment, appropriate operating procedures and training, it offers a safe and fun environment to children taking part in RYA events and activities.
RYA采取所有合理步骤，以确保通过安全招募，适当的操作程序和培训，为参加RYA活动的儿童提供安全有趣的环境。

The child's experience of the sport is our priority. We will create a safe and welcoming environment, both on and off the water, where children can have fun and develop their skills and confidence. We will treat all

children with respect, celebrate their achievements and listen to their views and experiences.
儿童对这项运动的体验是我们的首要考虑的。我们将在水上和岸上创造一个安全而温馨的环境，让孩子们在其中可以玩得开心，并提高他们的技能和建立自信。我们将尊重所有儿童，肯定他们的成绩，并倾听他们的观点和经验分享。

Relevant RYA recognised training centres are required and all affiliated clubs and class associations are encouraged to adopt and implement similar policies and procedures. The RYA will provide them with information and support..
我们要求所有的RYA认可的培训中心、附属俱乐部和相应级别的协会通过和执行类似的政策和程序。RYA将为他们提供信息和支持。

The RYA:
关于RYA：

- Recognises that safeguarding children is the responsibility of everyone, not just those working directly with them.
  认识到保护儿童是每个人的责任，而不仅仅是那些与儿童一起工作的人。
- Carefully recruits and selects all RYA employees, contractors and volunteers in roles involving close contact with children and provides them with appropriate information or training.
  认真招募RYA新员工、与孩子直接接触的承包商和志愿者，为他们提供适当的信息和培训。
- Responds swiftly and appropriately to all complaints and concerns about poor practice or suspected abuse, referring to external agencies as necessary.
  及时并妥善地处理所有关于训练指导不善、疑似或确实的投诉和顾虑，必要时会诉诸外部机构。
- Regularly reviews safeguarding procedures and practices in the light of experience or to take account of legislative, social or technological changes.
  根据经验或顾及到法律、社会或技术的变化，定期审核保护程序和相应做法的正确性。
- Communicates changes and shares good practice with training centres, clubs and class associations.
  与培训中心、俱乐部和相应级别的协会交流变化并探讨良好的改进措施。

This policy will be reviewed by the RYA Safeguarding Steering Group annually and by the RYA Board at least every three years.

这项政策由RYA维护督导组每年审查一次，并由RYA董事会至少每四年审查一次。

The RYA Safeguarding and Equality Manager should be notified of all relevant concerns, allegations or complaints.

应将所有相关问题，指控或投诉通知RYA安全保障与平等经理。

NOTE FOR PRINCIPALS—Good Recruitment Practice
给予培训机构负责人的建议——良好的招聘程序

If a good recruitment policy is adopted, and safeguarding is covered in the organisation's risk assessment and operating procedures, the opportunity for an individual with poor intent towards children to gain access to the organisation or to abuse a position of trust should be minimised. All applications, whether for paid or voluntary work, should be subject to an appropriate level of scrutiny. The level of checking you carry out should be proportionate to the role and the level of risk involved and in line with statutory requirements. The risk is higher if the person will be in regular contact with the same child or children, in sole charge of children with no parents or other adults present, and/or in a role involving authority and trust, such as an instructor or coach.

如果采用了良好的招聘政策，并且在组织方的风险评估和操作程序中涵盖了保障措施，则应尽量减少对孩子怀有不良意图的个人进入组织或滥用信任地位的机会。所有的工作申请，无论是雇员或是志愿者工作，都应被密切关注。关注的程度应根据工作角色以及工作涉及的风险程度而定，并符合法定要求。如果某人与同一个孩子或一些孩子定期接触，而且在没有父母或其他成人在场的情况下单独管理孩子，并且他的角色很权威，被孩子们所信任，那么儿童面临的风险更高。例如，教练或教官。

The organisation should agree a clear policy and apply it fairly and consistently.
组织方应确认一个清楚的政策，并坚持执行它。

Consider: 须考虑：

- Who to check?

谁进行审查？

– paid staff and/or volunteers. (if they have the same level of responsibility and contact, they should be treated in the same way whether they are paid or not).

–带薪员工和/或志愿者（如果他们具有相同的责任和联系级别，则无论是否获得报酬，都应以相同的方式对待他们）。

– those with specific responsibilities (e.g. instructor, centre principal, child protection/welfare officer, coach, head of cadet section) or anyone who regularly helps with junior/youth activity.

–负有特定责任的人员（例如教练、中心负责人、儿童保护利干事、教官、学员区域的负责人）或定期帮助青少年/青年活动的人员。

- The level of check to be conducted for each category:
  各工作类别应执行审查的程度：

  – References. 参考之前的工作经历。

  – Self-declaration(see RYA Guidelines) 自我声明（见RYA指南）。

  – Enhanced Criminal Records Disclosure (and Barred List Check, if appropriate), or membership of the Protection of Vulnerable Group Scheme (Scotland only), if the role is eligible.

  加强犯罪记录披露（以及不良记录检查，如适用），如可能，加入保护弱势群体计划（仅限苏格兰）。

It is a criminal offence in the UK under the Safeguarding Vulnerable Groups Act 2006:

根据2006年《保障弱势群体法》，以下行为是刑事犯罪：

- For a Barred individual to work in Regulated Activity/Regulated Work.

  被禁止从事受管制活动/受管制工作的个人。

- For an organisation to knowingly allow someone who has been Barred to work in Regulated Activity/Regulated work, and

  使组织故意允许被禁止从事受监管活动/受监管工作的人。

- For an organisation to fail to make a referral to the Disclosure and Barring Service/Disclosure Scotland if they have dismissed someone from Regulated Activity/Regulated Work for harming a child or vulnerable adult or placing them at risk of harm, or would have dismissed them if they had not resigned.

  如果某个组织因伤害儿童、弱势成年人，或使他们处于伤害的风险而将某人从受监管活动/受监管工作中解雇，或如果他们没有辞职就会将其解雇，则该组织未能向苏格兰披露和禁止服务/披露处进行转介。

Criminal Records Disclosures

犯罪记录披露

Organisations affiliated to or recognised by the RYA can access the DBS, Access NI or PVG processes through the RYA which is a registered Umbrella/Intermediary Body. The procedure varies according to the home country and legal jurisdiction in which your organisation is located. Full information is available from the RYA website www.rya.org.uk/go/safeguarding or contact the RYA's Safeguarding and Equality Manager at disclosure@rya.org.uk.

隶属于RYA或RYA认可的组织可以通过RYA（安全注册/中介机构）查看相应的犯罪记录。具体操作流程因所在国和所在国的法律管辖区而异。完整信息可从RYA网站获取www.rya.org.uk/go/safessional或者通过disclosure@rya.org.uk与RYA的保障与平等经理联系。

GOOD PRACTICE GUIDELINES 良好的实践指南

Culture 文化

It is important to develop a culture within your organisation where both children and adults feel able to raise concerns, knowing that they will be taken seriously, treated confidentially and will not make the situation worse for themselves or others.

文化的创建十分重要。良好的文化氛围能使孩子和成人放心地提出问题，而且知道问题一定会得到慎重而妥善地处理，并且不会使他们的处境更糟糕。

Minimising risk 风险最小化

Plan the work of the organisation and promote good practice to minimise situations where adults are working

unobserved or could take advantage of their position of trust. Good practice protects everyone—children, volunteers and staff.
计划好组织内部工作，并推进执行，尽量避免成年人在无其他人观察的情况下工作，或防止其利用其他人对自己身份的信任。良好的执行能够保护每一个人——儿童、志愿者和工作人员。

These common sense guidelines should be available to everyone within your organisation.
这些常识性的工作指南需要提供给机构内的所有人。

- Avoid spending any significant time working with children in isolation.
  避免单独与儿童一起工作的时间过长。
- Do not take children alone in a car, however short the journey.
  即便是短途旅行，也不要一个人带孩子上车。
- Do not take children to your home as part of your organisation's activity.
  不要借组织方活动的名义，将孩子带回自己家。
- Where any of these are unavoidable, ensure that they only occur with the full knowledge and consent of someone in charge of the organisation or the child's parents.
  如以上情况无法避免，要确保组织方或孩子的家长完全知晓该情况，并和他们达成一致。
- Design training programmes that are within the ability of the individual child.
  应设计适合儿童能力的培训项目。
- If a child is having difficulty with a wetsuit or buoyancy aid, ask them to ask a friend to help if at all possible.
  如果一个孩子无法自己穿上湿式保暖服或救生衣，尽可能让他们去找朋友帮忙。
- If you do have to help a child, make sure you are in full view of others, preferably another adult.
  如果你必须去帮助一个孩子，确保有其他人在场，最好是成人。
- Restrict communications with young people via mobile phone, e-mail or social media to group communications about organisational matters. If it's essential to send an individual message, copy it to the child's parent or carer.
  禁止通过手机、电子邮件或社交媒体与青年人交流以组织有关组织事务的交流。如有必要发送个人消息，请将其抄送给孩子的父母或监护者。

You should never: 一定不要：

- Engage in rough, physical or sexually provocative games.
  与儿童玩粗鲁的、接触性的或挑逗性的游戏。
- Allow or engage in inappropriate touching of any form.
  允许或进行任何不合理的触碰。
- Allow children to use inappropriate language unchallenged, or use such language yourself when with children.
  让儿童使用不恰当的语言，而不去纠正他们，或者自己在和孩子一起时使用。
- Make sexually suggestive comments to a child, even in fun.
  给儿童性暗示，即使是开玩笑。
- Fail to respond to an allegation made by a child—always act.
  无法回应儿童提出的控诉——务必要采取行动。
- Do things of a personal nature that children can do for themselves.
  替儿童做他们力所能及的事情。

It may sometimes be necessary to do things of a personal nature for children, particularly if they are very young or disabled. These tasks should only be carried out with the full understanding and consent of both the child (where possible) and their parents/carers. In an emergency situation which requires this type of help, parents/carers should be fully informed as soon as possible. In such situations it is important to ensure that any adult present is sensitive to the child and undertakes personal care tasks with the utmost discretion.
有时候可能需要帮助儿童做一些事情，尤其是对于年幼的孩童或残疾人。但必须在得到孩子和其父母/护理员的充分理解和同意后执行。在需要此类帮助的紧急情况下，应通知家长或监护人。对于这种情况，任何进行这项工作的成年人要能敏锐地察觉儿童的需要，且以万分谨慎的态度来承担这样的个人关怀工作。

Responsibilities of Staff and Volunteers
员工和志愿者的职责

Staff or volunteers should be given clear roles and responsibilities. They should be aware of your organisation's safeguarding policy and procedures and be given guidelines on:
要明确地向员工或志愿者说明他们的角色和职责。他们应充分理解组织方的保护政策和操作步骤，并指导

他们:

- Following good practice.
  遵循良好的执行方式。
- Recognising signs of abuse.
  识别虐待的迹象。
- Reporting any concerns to the appropriate person.
  向相关人员报告任何问题。

Identifying Child Abuse 识别虐童

The following brief notes provide a guide to help you identify signs of possible abuse and know what action to take in such cases. The RYA Safeguarding and Child Protection Guidelines on the RYA website cover the subject more fully.
下文的简要说明能帮助你识别可能存在的虐待行为，并帮助你解决这种情况。可查询RYA官网，找到更全面的RYA安全防护和儿童保护指南。

Forms of Abuse 虐童形式

Abuse and neglect are forms of maltreatment of a child. Somebody may abuse or neglect a child by inflicting harm, or by failing to act to prevent harm. Children may be abused in a family or in an institutional or community setting, by those known to them or, more rarely, by others (including via the internet). They may be abused by an adult or adults, or another child or children.
虐待和忽视儿童都是虐童行为。有的人可能故意伤害儿童，或无法保护儿童免受伤害。孩子可能会在家里、公共机构或社区受到虐待，虐童者可能是他们认识的人或其他(包括网络)，被其他人虐待的情况较罕见。也可能是一个成年人或几个成年人，一个孩子或一些孩子。

Physical abuse may involve adults or other children inflicting physical harm:
身体虐待可能会使成年人或其他儿童造成身体上的伤害:

- by hitting, shaking, throwing, poisoning, burning or scalding, drowning or suffocating
  通过殴打、摇晃、投掷、 毒害、燃烧或烫伤、溺水或窒息。
- giving children alcohol or inappropriate drugs
  给孩子喝酒或不适当的药物。
- in sport situations, physical abuse might also occur when the nature and intensity of training exceeds the capacity of the child's immature and growing body.
  在运动中，也可能会对儿童造成身体虐待。如果培训的强度过高，孩子未发育的身体完全无法承受。

Emotional abuse is the persistent emotional maltreatment of a child such as to cause severe and persistent adverse effects on the child's emotional development. It may involve:
精神虐待是一种对儿童精神上的长期折磨，会对儿童的精神成长造成严重影响。这些可以包括:

- conveying to a child that they are worthless, unloved or inadequate.
  传达给孩子，他们是毫无价值的，不被爱或不适当的。
- not giving the child opportunities to express their views, deliberately silencing them or 'making fun' of what they say or how they communicate.
  不给孩子机会表达自己的意见，故意使他们沉默或“取笑”他们说什么或是他们如何沟通。
- imposing expectations which are beyond the child's age or developmental capability.
  施加给儿童超越她/他们年龄或发展能力的期望。
- overprotection and limitation of exploration and learning or preventing the child from participating in normal social interaction.
  过度保护和限制和学习或防止孩子参加正常的社会交往。
- allowing a child to see or hear the ill-treatment of another person.
  允许儿童看到或听到对他人的虐待。
- serious bullying (including cyber bullying), causing children frequently to feel frightened or in danger.
  严重的欺凌行为（包括网络欺凌），使孩子们经常感到害怕或处于危险之中。
- the exploitation or corruption of children.
  对儿童的剥削或腐蚀。

- emotional abuse in sport might also include situations where parents or coaches subject children to constant criticism, bullying or pressure to perform at a level that the child cannot realistically be expected to achieve.
  运动上的精神虐待包括，父母或教官长时间地指责，欺凌或施压，让儿童完成不可实现的任务。

Some level of emotional abuse is involved in all types of maltreatment of a child.
有些程度的精神虐待包含各种对孩子的粗暴对待。

Sexual abuse. involves an individual (male or female, or another child) forcing or enticing a child or young person to take part in sexual activities, whether or not the child is aware of what is happening, to gratify their own sexual needs. The activities may involve:
性虐待是指一个人（男人或女人或另一名儿童）强制或诱惑一名儿童或青少年参与性行为，来满足个人的性需要，无论他们是否有意识到。这些行为可能包括：

- physical contact (e.g. kissing, touching, masturbation, rape or oral sex)
  身体接触(例如，亲吻，触摸，自淫，强奸或口交）。
- involving children in looking at, or in the production of, sexual images
  使儿童参与观看或制作色情画面。
- encouraging children to behave in sexually inappropriate ways or watch sexual activities.
  鼓励儿童进行不当的性行为或观看性行为。
- grooming a child in preparation for abuse (including via the internet).
  为虐待儿童做准备（包括通过互联网）.
- sport situations which involve physical contact (eg. supporting or guiding children) could potentially create situations where sexual abuse may go unnoticed. Abusive situations may also occur if adults misuse their power over young people.
  在运动时，如存在大量的肢体接触（例如，在支持或指导儿童时），可能发生性虐待，且不被注意。如成人在青少年身上错误地使用自己的力量，也可能产生虐待行为。

Neglect is the persistent failure to meet a child's basic physical and/or psychological needs, likely to result in the serious impairment of the child's health or development. Neglect may involve a parent or carer failing to:
忽视儿童是持续/一直无法满足儿童基本的运动和/或精神需求，很可能对孩子的健康或发展产生严重的影响。

- provide adequate food, clothing and shelter.
  提供适当的食物、衣服和住所。
- protect a child from physical and emotional harm or danger.
  保护儿童免受身体和精神上的伤害或危险。
- ensure adequate supervision.
  确保充分的监护。
- ensure access to appropriate medical care or treatment.
  确保获得适当的医疗护理或治疗。
- respond to a child's basic emotional needs.
  回应孩子的基本情感需求。
- neglect in a sport situation might occur if an instructor or coach fails to ensure that children are safe, or exposes them to undue cold or risk of injury.
  在运动时，也可能会产生忽视。如果一个教练或教官无法确保孩子们的安全，或者是让他们受凉或受伤。

Child sexual exploitation is a form of child sexual abuse. It occurs where an individual or group takes advantage of an imbalance of power to coerce, manipulate or deceive a child or young person under the age of 18 into sexual activity in exchange for something the victim needs and wants (e.g. attention, money or material possessions, alcohol or drugs), and/or for the financial advantage or increased status of the perpetrator or facilitator. The victim may have been exploited even if the sexual activity appears consensual. Child sexual exploitation can also occur online without involving physical contact.

儿童性剥削是儿童性虐待的一种形式。当个人或团体利用权力不平衡的优势，胁迫、操纵或欺骗18岁以下的儿童或青少年进行性活动，以换取受害者需要和想要的东西（如注意力、金钱或物质财产、酒精或毒品）时，就会发生这种情况，和/或为了犯罪人或调解人的经济利益或地位的提高。即使性行为是双方自愿的，受害者也可能受到剥削。儿童性剥削也可能发生在网上，而不涉及身体接触。

Extremism includes people who target the vulnerable - including the young - by seeking to: sow division between communities on the basis of race, faith or denomination; justify discrimination e.g. towards women and girls; persuade others that minorities are inferior; or argue against the primacy of democracy and the rule of law in our society.

极端主义包括以弱势群体（包括年轻人）为目标的人，他们寻求：在种族、信仰或教派的基础上在社区之间制造分裂；为歧视妇女和女孩等行为辩护；说服其他人相信少数群体是劣势群体；反对民主和法治在我们社会中的首要地位。

Bullying (including online bullying, for example via text or social media) may be seen as deliberately hurtful behaviour, usually repeated or sustained over a period of time, where it is difficult for those being bullied to defend themselves. The bully may often be another young person. Although anyone can be the target of bullying, victims are typically shy, sensitive and perhaps anxious or insecure. Sometimes they are singled out for physical reasons – being overweight or physically small, being gay or lesbian, having a disability or belonging to a different race, faith or culture. The acronym STOP—Several Times On Purpose - can help you to identify bullying behaviour.

欺凌（包括网络欺凌，例如通过短信或社交媒体）可看作是一种在某一段时间重复或持续的故意伤害行为，且被欺凌者无法保护自己。欺凌者通常可能是其他青少年，虽然任何人都有可能受到欺凌，但受害者的共有特征是：很害羞，又敏感，可能有点焦虑症或是缺乏安全感。他们被盯上，有时候是因为身体原因——体形肥胖、个子矮小、有生理缺陷、同性恋，或是来自不同的种族，有不同的信仰和文化。缩略词STOP——几次故意地——可以帮助你识别欺凌行为。

Bullying can include:

欺凌包括：

- Physical pushing, kicking, hitting, pinching etc.
  身体推、踢、打、捏等。
- Name calling, sarcasm, spreading rumours, persistent teasing and emotional torment through ridicule, humiliation or the continual ignoring of individuals.
  通过嘲笑、羞辱或持续忽视个人来点名、讽刺、散布谣言、持续的调侃和情感折磨。
- Posting of derogatory or abusive comments, videos or images on social network sites.
  在社交网站上发布贬损或辱骂的评论、视频或图片。
- Racial taunts, graffiti, gestures, sectarianism.
  种族嘲弄，涂鸦，手势，宗派主义。
- Sexual comments, suggestions or behaviour.
  性的评论、建议或行为。
- Unwanted physical contact.
  不必要的身体接触。

Recognising Possible Abuse 识别可能存在的虐待

It is not always easy, even for the most experienced carers, to spot when a child has been abused. However, some of the more typical symptoms which should trigger your suspicions would include:

识别孩子是否受到虐待也不是一件易事，即使是对经验丰富的看护者来说。不过，有些或者更典型的症状应该能引起你的怀疑：

- Unexplained or suspicious injuries such as bruising, cuts or burns, particularly if situated on a part of the body not normally prone to such injuries.
  无法解释或令人怀疑的损伤，例如，淤青、割伤或烧伤，尤其是出现在一般不会出现的部位。
- Sexually explicit language or actions.
  使用直白的性语言或有明显的性举动。
- A sudden change in behaviour (e.g. becoming very quiet, withdrawn or displaying sudden outbursts of temper).
  行为上的突变（例如，突然变得很安静、孤僻或者脾气突然变坏）。
- The child describes what appears to be an abusive act involving him/her.
  孙子描述了涉及他/她的虐待行为。
- A change observed over a long period of time (e.g. the child losing weight or becoming increasingly dirty or unkempt).
  孩子在一段时间内的变化（例如：孩子体重减轻，或开始变得很脏或很邋遢）。

- A general distrust and avoidance of adults, especially those with whom a close relationship would be expected.
  对成年人的普遍不信任和回避，尤其是那些以前关系密切的人。
- An unexpected reaction to normal physical contact.
  对一般的肢体接触反应过度。
- Difficulty in making friends or abnormal restrictions on socialising with others.
  交友困难或在与其他人交往的时候有异常限制。

It is important to note that a child could be displaying some or all of these signs, or behaving in a way which is worrying, without this necessarily meaning that the child is being abused. Similarly, there may not be any signs, but you may just feel that something is wrong.
要能注意到儿童表现出以上部分或所有的这些现象，或者行为方式很令人担忧。但是，以上现象并不意味着儿童一定受到了虐待。类似地，可能没有任何迹象，但是你可能感觉到有点不对劲。

If you have noticed a change in the child's behaviour, first talk to the parents or carers. It may be that something has happened, such as a bereavement, which has caused the child to be unhappy.
如果你注意到孩子的行为有变化，首先要和父母或看护人谈谈。可能是出了什么事，比如丧亲导致孩子失落。

Handling an Allegation from a Child 处理孩子们的抱怨

Children may confide in adults they trust, in a place where they feel at ease.
孩子们可能会在他们舒服的环境下，向他们信任的成年人坦露自己的内心。

Always: 时刻注意：

- Stay calm—ensure that the child is safe and feels safe.
  保持冷静——确保儿童的安全，且让他们感到安全。
- Show and tell the child that you are taking what he/she says seriously.
  表现出并告诉孩子你非常认真地对待他们说的事。
- Reassure that child and stress that he/she is not to blame.
  消除孩子的疑虑，向他们解释，不责备他们。
- Be careful about physical contact, it may not be what the child wants.
  注意肢体接触，孩子们可能不喜欢。
- Be honest, explain that you will have to tell someone else to help stop the alleged abuse.
  诚实对待，解释你可能会需要告知其他人，帮助阻止潜在的虐待。
- Make a record of what the child has said as soon as possible after the event, using the child's own words.
  在活动结束后，立刻将孩子们所述的内容用孩子们的语言记下来。
- Follow your organisation's child protection procedures.
  遵守组织方的儿童保护操作程序。

Never: 一定不要：

- Rush into actions that may be inappropriate.
  不假思索地采取错误的行动。
- Make promises you cannot keep (e.g. you won't tell anyone).
  承诺你做不到的事情（例如，不要告诉别人）。
- Ask leading questions（ask 'what happened?', not 'did x hit you?')
  问诱导性的问题（问“发生了什么事？”，而不是“谁谁打了你吗？”）。
- Take sole responsibility—consult someone else (ideally the designated Child Protection/Welfare Officer or the person in charge or someone you can trust) so that you can begin to protect the child and gain support for yourself.
  一力承当——咨询其他人（最好是任命的儿童保护/福利负责人或主管或你信任的人），这样你就可以开始保护儿童，并为自己赢得支持。

- If the module is inappropriate the instructor should discuss realistic aims and gain agreement using tact and diplomacy.
  如果选择的学习单元不适合，教练应运用自己的沟通技能和处事方法与学员商讨并制订一个可行的目标。
- Struggling students are often relieved by this process.
  通过这种方式，学习吃力的学员通常会得到宽慰。
- Performance often improves once the stress has been removed.
  一旦消除了学习压力，学员们的表现通常会得到提高。
- Ensure students are kept informed with regular debriefs.
  确保与学员定期总结。
- Try to spot ‘serial’ complainers early.
  在前期要注意“连锁”投诉。
- Counter them by running the course ‘by the book’.
  向学员说明，自己是“照章办事”，按标准程序来执行的。
- Regularly ask them if they are satisfied, would like any further input and seek agreement. The Principal or Chief Instructor should also give opportunities for feedback as the course progresses.
  时常询问他们对课程是否满意，是否有进一步学习的想法，与学员达成一致。随着课程继续进行，负责人或主教练也应给出反馈。
- Any complaints received should be referred to the SI, Chief Instructor/Principal (in that order).
  收到任何投诉都应告知高级教练、主教练、负责人（按此顺序）。
- Begin with ‘Thank you for bringing this to our attention, how can we resolve it?’
  在应对投诉时，开始应说：“谢谢您向我们提出这个问题，您希望我们如何解决呢？”
- Often, more tuition is all that’s required. It can save a lot of correspondence afterwards.
  通常，需要的就是更多的教学，这样能省去很多不必要的投诉。

If you do not inform people of their progress you are more likely to receive a complaint along the lines of ‘I didn’t achieve the certificate because I wasn’t taught well.”’
如果不告知学员的学习进展，很有可能会被投诉，学员可能会说“我没有拿到证书，是因为教的不好”。

The instructors who receive the fewest complaints are those who are competent, take an interest in their students, and ensure that even the difficult or weak students feel they are an important part of the group. The instructional skills required are well beyond those of just sailing or even just teaching.
不被投诉的教练有这些特征：能力强，愿意去了解学员，还能确保学习困难或较弱的学员感受到自己在集体里的重要性。对于教练来说，不仅要懂航海、会教学，还需要掌握更高的技能。

MANUAL HANDLING 人工搬运工作

Manual handling is any transporting or supporting of a load (including the lifting, putting down, pushing, pulling, carrying or moving thereof) by hand or bodily force.
人工搬运工作是指用手或身体力量（包括抬起、放下、推、拉、搬或移动等）运输或支撑重量。

As an Instructor it is worth being aware that workplace injuries can affect your life and recreation as well as your work, particularly in later years. Injuries sustained while sailing can also affect your students.
作为一名教练，要能意识到在工作场所受伤会影响生活和娱乐，当然还有你的工作，尤其是在晚年。如果学员受伤同样也会影响他们。

This includes sudden injuries in the workplace as well as cumulative wear and tear, commonly caused by poor positioning over a period of time.
这包括在工作场所的突然受伤和积劳成疾，一般是由于长时间使用错误的姿势造成的。

Common risks arise from: 常见风险来源于:

- Excessive or awkward loads for one person.
  一个人搬运大量或无法承受的重量。
- Slippery or uneven surfaces.
  运输道路很光滑或不平坦。
- Repetition or excessive duration of tasks.
  任务重复过多或时间过长。

Slipways, jetties and dragging boats can all give rise to these circumstances. Studies show that the overwhelming proportion of accidents in the workplace are sprains or strains due to manual handling. Of these, back injuries are three times more common than any other injury.
在坡道和码头工作，以及拖船都有可能会导致上述情况的产生。研究表明，大量在工作场所发生的意外，都是因为人工搬运造成的扭伤或拉伤。背部受伤是这三种情况中最常见的。

The Manual Handling Operations Regulations 1992 contain guidance suggesting that manual handling should be included in risk assessments and that employers, employees and volunteers should take sensible steps to minimise the risks.
1992年出版的《人工搬运操作手册管理条例》给出的指南说明了，应考虑到人工搬运的风险性。

Finally, when it comes to moving boats, ensure you have sufficient people to carry out the task safely e.g. pulling a heavy dinghy up a steep slipway.
最后，在需要移船时，确保在安全的前提下，有足够的人员和你一起承担，例如，将一条很重的小帆船从坡道拉上去。

Top Tip 重要提示

Handling tips for instructors:
给教练的处理建议:

1. Widen the base of support whilst lifting/carrying.
   在抬起/搬运的时候，双脚要站开。
2. Keep the load inside the base of support whenever possible.
   时刻保持载重在双脚内侧。
3. Avoid asymmetry, e.g. carrying a heavy fuel can.
   避免不对称搬运，例如，单手提一个很重的油桶。
4. In general before lifting:
   在搬运之前，通常要:

ASSESS: task, load, environment, individual(s).
估计: 任务、重量、环境、个体。

PLAN: task, route.
计划: 任务、路线。

PREPARE: load, self, area.
准备: 搬运、自己、区域。

16 Logbook 航海日志

日期 DATE	地点 LOCATION	体验时间 HOURS' EXP.		活动和天气条件 ACTIVITY AND WEATHER		授权 AUTHORISATION
		角色 ROLE	时长 HOURS	课程或活动类型 TYPE OF COURSE	最大风速 MAX WIND	签字/姓名 SIGN/NAME

日期 DATE	地点 LOCATION	体验时间 HOURS' EXP.		活动和天气条件 ACITVITY AND WEATHER		授权 AUTHORISATION
		角色 ROLE	时长 HOURS	课程或活动类型 TYPE OF COURSE	最大风速 MAX WIND	签字/姓名 SIGN/NAME

17 Recommendations for Coaching Awards
教学认证推荐函

学员姓名 **Candidate Name**

ASSISTANT INSTRUCTOR 助理教练

Training and assessment record 培训和测评记录	Principal's initials 校长姓名首字母
The candidate: 候选人姓名:	
Is aware of safety requirements 良好的安全意识	
Is aware of teaching sequence used when teaching beginners 知道教授初学者的教学步骤	
Is aware of the teaching points for each part of the sequence 熟知每个步骤的教学要点	
Is proficient in teaching shore drills 熟练教授岸上练习	
Is proficient in teaching capsize recovery 熟练教授正船技术	

The candidate has demonstrated competence as an Assistant Instructor to the standards laid down by the RYA, 候选人的能力已达到RYA助理教练的标准

Signed (RYA Principal) 签名（RYA负责人）	
Name in capitals 全名	
Recognised Training Centre 认证培训中心	
Date 日期	

学员姓名 Candidate Name

INSTRUCTOR COURSE AND ENDORSEMENT LOG 教练课程和认证记录

The following Instructor Course and Endorsement Log is a record of course completion and NOT a qualification. This book should always be supported by an Instructor Certificate which will be issued on receipt of notification from the RYA Course Coach/Assessor. Please note it is also a requirement for instructors to hold a valid first aid certificate of a type approved by the RYA, and a Powerboat Level 2 certificate before progressing to the instructor training course.
以下教练课程和认证记录只是对于候选人完成课程的一个记录，并不是证书。负责课程的RYA教官/测评官确认候选人通过后，本书将与教练证书一起发给候选人。请注意，在参与教练培训课程前，教练应持有RYA认可的有效急救证书和机动艇级别二的证书。

RYA DINGHY/KEELBOAT/MULTIHULL/INSTRUCTOR
RYA小帆船/龙骨船/多体船教练

Pre-entry Assessment Completed 完成课前测评

Venue 场地

Date 日期

Type of boat 船型 — 小帆船/龙骨船/多体船 DINGHY/KEELBOAT/MULTIHULL

Approved by (RYA Coach/Assessor)
批准人（RYA教官/测评官） — 签字 Signature

Name in capitals 全名

Training Course Completed 完成培训课程

Venue 场地

Date 日期

RYA Coach/Assessor RYA教官/测评官签名 — 签字 Signature

Name in capitals 全名

Assessment/Moderation Completed 完成测评/审核

I confirm that the candidate has demonstrated competence as an Instructor in a DINGHY/KEELBOAT/MULTIHULL (delete as appropriate) to the standards laid down by the RYA.
我确认该候选人的能力已达到RYA小帆船/龙骨船/多体船（不适用请删掉）教练的标准。

Venue
场地

Date
日期

Approved by (RYA Coach/Assessor)
批准人（RYA教官/测评官） — 签字 Signature

Name in captals
全名

Recommendations for Coaching Awards
教学认证推荐函

学员姓名 Candidate Name

ADVANCED INSTRUCTOR ENDORSEMENT 高阶教练认证

Endorsement Completed 完成认证

I confirm that the candidate has demonstrated competence as an Advanced Instructor to the standards laid down by the RYA. 我确认该候选人的能力已达到RYA高阶教练的标准。

Venue
场地

Date
日期

Approved by (RYA Coach/Assessor)
批准人（RYA教官/测评官）

签字 Signature

Name in capitals
全名

KEELBOAT INSTRUCTOR ENDORSEMENT 龙骨船教练认证

Endorsement Completed 完成认证

I confirm that the candidate has demonstrated competence as a Keelboat Instructor to the standards laid down by the RYA. 我确认该候选人的能力已达到RYA龙骨船教练的标准。

Venue
场地

Date
日期

Approved by (RYA Coach/Assessor)
批准人（RYA教官/测评官）

签字 Signature

Name in capitals
全名

MULTIHULL INSTRUCTOR ENDORSEMENT 多体船教练认证

Endorsement Completed 完成认证

I confirm that the candidate has demonstrated competence as a Multihull Instructor to the standards laid down by the RYA. 我确认该候选人的能力已达到RYA多体船教练的标准。

Venue
场地

Date
日期

Approved by (RYA Coach/Assessor)
批准人（RYA教官/测评官）

签字 Signature

Name in capitals
全名

学员姓名 Candidate Name

DINGHY INSTRUCTOR ENDORSEMENT 小帆船教练认证

(For those whose initial instructor award is in keelboats or multihulls)
（对于已获得龙骨船或多体船教练认证的候选人）

Endorsement Completed 完成认证

I confirm that the candidate has demonstrated competence as a Dinghy Instructor to the standards laid down by the RYA. 我确认该候选人的能力已达到RYA小帆船教练的标准。

Venue
场地

Date
日期

Approved by (RYA Coach/Assessor)
批准人（RYA教官/测评官）

签字 Signature

Name in capitals
全名

RACING INSTRUCTOR ENDORSEMENT 竞赛教练认证

Endorsement Completed 完成认证

I confirm that the candidate has demonstrated competence as a Racing Instructor to the standards laid down by the RYA. 我确认该候选人的能力已达到RYA竞赛教练的标准。

Venue
场地

Date
日期

Approved by (RYA Coach/Assessor)
批准人（RYA教官/测评官）

签字 Signature

Name in capitals
全名

Recommendations for Coaching Awards
教学认证推荐函

学员姓名 Candidate Name

SENIOR INSTRUCTOR 高级教练

Recommendation 推荐函

I confirm that the candidate is competent to plan, organise and run a course within the RYA National Sailing Scheme. 我确认该候选人已具备计划，组织以及执行RYA国家航海计划课程的能力。

Signature (RYA Chief Instructor/Principal/RYA RDO/RYA Regional Coach/RYA-appointed Coach Assessor/Trainer)
签名（RYA 主教练/负责人/RYA 区域发展官员/RYA区域教官/RYA任命的教官考核员/培训员）

签字 Signature

Name in capitals
全名

Recognised Training Centre
认证培训中心

Date
日期

Training Course 培训课程

I confirm that the candidate has successfully completed the course and has demonstrated competence in all the areas required. 我确认候选人已成功完成本课程，且充分表现了其在各方面所需的能力。

Venue
场地

Date
日期

RYA Coach/Assessor 1
RYA教官/测评官1

签字 Signature

Name in capitals
全名

RYA Coach/Assessor 2
RYA教官/测评官2

签字 Signature

Name in capitals
全名

学员姓名 Candidate Name

COACH/ASSESSOR 教官/测评官

Recommendation 推荐函

I confirm that the candidate has the experience and technical competence to be trained as a Coach/Assessor with the RYA National Sailing Scheme.
我确认该候选人已拥有足够的经验和技术能力担任RYA国家航海计划的教官/测评官。

Regional Development Officer/Coach
区域发展负责人/教官

签字 Signature

Name in capitals
全名

Training Course 培训课程

I confirm that the candidate has successfully completed the course and has demonstrated competence in all the areas required.
我确认该候选人已成功完成该课程，并充分表现了其在各方面所需的能力。

RYA HQ Training Chief Instructor
RYA总部培训主教练

签字 Signature

Name in capitals
全名

Details of dates, venue and conditions must be entered in the Personal Log on page 158—159.
具体日期、场地和条件必须在个人信息记录第160页到161页上填写清楚。

Task Experience 任务经历

I confirm that the candidate has assisted with an RYA Instructor Course and Assessment.
我确认该候选人协助过RYA教练课程和测评。

RYA Coach/Assessor
RYA教官/测评官

签字 Signature

Name in capitals
全名

The candidate has completed all the requirements and is hereby appointed as an RYA Coach/Assessor.
该候选人已满足所有被任命为RYA教官/测评官的要求。

RYA HQ Training Chief Instructor
RYA总部培训主教练

签字 Signature

Date
日期

18 Glossary 航海术语表

ABACK 反受风	The sail pressed backwards by the wind. 帆被风向后压。
ABAFT 船后	Behind the boat. 船后.
ABEAM 正横	At right angles to the line of the boat. 与船中心线垂直。
ADRIFT 漂浮	Afloat, but without a propulsive force. 在水上漂，没有任何推动力。
AFT 船后	Towards back of the boat. 向船的后面。
AGROUND 在岸	On the ground and not afloat. 在陆地上，不是漂浮的。
AHEAD 船艏	The area in front of the boat. 船前方区域。
AMIDSHIPS 船中间	In the middle of the boat. 船中间的区域。
AWASH 淹没	The boat being full of water. 船充满了水。
BACKING 逆摆（动词）	The wind changing direction in an anti-clockwise direction (against the sun). 风的方向逆时针改变（与太阳的转动相反）。
BALANCE 船的左右	How level the boat is. 船在水平方向的状态。
BEAM 船侧	The side of a boat. 船的侧面。
BEARING AWAY 顺风偏转	Changing direction away from the wind. 改变船的方向，使其远离风。
BELAY 栓绳	Twist a rope around something to make fast. 将绳子绕在什么东西上，使绳子固定。
BELLY OF THE SAIL 帆腹	The fullness of the sail. 帆受风鼓起来。
BIGHT 绳圈	A loop. 一个环。
BLANKETING 遮挡	To take the wind from another craft which is to leeward. 挡住位于下风船的风。
BOTTLE SCREW 松紧螺旋扣	A means of attaching and adjusting shrouds. 一种固定和调节侧支索的装置。
BROACHING 横移	To turn sideways onto the wind and heel over. 船发生横移，转向迎风并侧倾。
BURGEE 三角旗	A flag. 一面旗子。
BY THE LEE 同舷受风	Sailing with the wind on the same side of the boat as the mainsail. 在航行时，风与主帆在同一侧。
CABLE 链	A nautical measurement being 200 yards or 100 fathoms. 航海计量单位，200码或100英寻。
CARS 滑车	Adjustable fairleads on tracks, to adjust sheet angle. 一种在轨道上，可调节的导缆器，用来调节缭绳角度。
CASTING OFF 出发	Leaving the moorings. 离开系泊处。
CATSPAWS 波纹（猫爪）	Ripples on the surface of the water showing a gust of wind. 在水面上的涟漪，显示阵风。
CHAIN PLATE 桅侧支索牵条	Metal plate to which the shrouds are attached at their base. 固定在侧支索底部的金属板。
CLAWING OFF 迎风离岸	Sailing off a lee shore. 航行离开背风岸。
COAMING 舱口栏板	The built up woodwork around hatches etc to exclude water. 绕着舱门的木板等，防止水进入。
CRINGLE 索圈	The metal ring used to reinforce any holes in the sail. 安装在帆上的金属环。
CROSS TREES 撑臂	Horizontal spreaders which hold the shrouds away from the mast. 横向的支杆，将侧支索从桅杆往外支出。
CUNNINGHAM 下拉索	System for tensioning luff of sail. 张进帆前缘。
DISPLACEMENT 吃水	The amount of water that a boat displaces (Archimedes' Principle). 船在水里排开的水量（阿基米德定律）。
DOWNHAUL 下拉索	See Cunningham. 参见Cunningham
EASE, TO 松	To slacken. 使松弛。
EBB 落潮	A tide is on the ebb when it is falling. 正在退下去的潮。
EDDY 漩涡	A current flowing in a different direction to the main stream. 向不同方向流动的涌流，与主流方向不同。
FAIRLEADS 导缆器	Permanent fixtures on a boat which are designed to guide a rope. 一种固定在船上的装置，用来引导绳子。
FAIRWAY 航路	A clear passage for navigation. 导航路线。
FALL 绳圈	The loose end of a rope. 绳子松弛的末端。

Glossary 航海术语表 18

FATHOM	A measurement of depth (1 fathom = 6 feet).
英寻	一种深度单位（1英寻 = 6英尺）。
FLOOD	A flooding tide is a rising one.
涨潮	正在上涨的潮汐。
FREEBOARD	The amount of boat above the water line.
干舷	船体在水线以上的高度。
GHOSTING	To move when there is no recognisable wind.
	在没有可识别的风时，使船移动
GNAV	Lever above boom, function same as kicker.
帆杆上斜桁	位于帆杆上方的杠杆装置，和斜拉器的作用一样。
HEADWAY	Forward momentum.
前进	向前的动力。
HEAT SEALING	Tidy end of rope by melting together.
热封	
HOUNDS	The fixture of the mast to which the shrouds are attached.
	桅杆上的固定装置，用来固定侧支索。
IN IRONS, STAYS	The boat lies head to wind, sails flapping.
顶风，停留	帆船顶风，飘帆。
JURY RIG	This is an emergency rig, having undergone temporary repair.
应急装置	一种临时装置，在原装置坏掉时使用。
KICKER	(Kicking strap) pulley system between boom and mast designed to tension leech of sail.
斜拉器	位于帆杆和桅杆之间的滑轮系统，用来张紧帆后缘。
LUFF	To change the boat's direction towards the wind.
迎风偏转	朝风的方向，改变船的航向
MAKE FAST	To secure.
把…拴紧	固定。
MAST STEP	The slot into which the mast heel fits.
桅座	桅杆底部放入的槽。
OUTHAUL	System for tensioning foot of sail.
横拉器	张紧帆底的装置。
RACKS	Metal or carbon extensions to side of boat.
侧翼	船侧伸出的金属或碳支架。
RAKE	Angle of mast to vertical.
桅杆倾度	桅杆与水平方向的夹角。
ROCKER	Amount of curve on the longitudinal axis at bottom of boat.
凹度	船底的弯曲程度。
SPLICE	To tidy end of rope by weaving through itself.
捻接	将绳端编到绳子里，整理末端。
TELL TALE	Wool or lightweight tape used to detect airflow.
气流线	由绒线或较轻的带子制成，用来指示气流状态。
TRIM	Fore and aft adjustment of weight in boat.
修理	船上重量的前后调整。
VANG	See KICKER.
斜桁支索	参见斜拉器
VEERING	The wind changing direction in a clockwise direction (with the sun).
顺摆	风顺时针转动（与太阳的偏转方向一致）。
WARP	Rope used for anchoring or mooring.
锚绳	用来抛锚或系泊的绳索。
WEIGHING	Raising the anchor.
起锚	将锚拉起来。
WHIPPING	End of rope tidied by winding twine around it.
缠接	在绳端缠一圈小绳，使绳端整齐。

黑版贸审字 03-2020-109
Simplified Chinese rights arranged through Shenzhen Vanhang Sailing & Yachting Sport Cultrue Dev Co.Ltd.
（本书中文简体版权经由深圳万航帆艇体育文化发展有限公司取得。）

内容简介：

本书用专业的视角和通俗的语言，介绍了如何成为一名合格的 RYA 助理教练、教练或教官，以及讲解了 RYA 单人船、龙骨船和多体船的教学方法。本书可作为 RYA 教练培训教材。

图书在版编目（CIP）数据

国家航海计划教练手册 / 英国皇家游艇协会著 ； 黄乙能， 杨玉译 . -- 哈尔滨 ： 哈尔滨工程大学出版社， 2020. 4
ISBN 978-7-5661-2625-2

Ⅰ . ①国… Ⅱ . ①英… ②黄… ③杨… Ⅲ . ①帆船运动－教练员－手册 Ⅳ . ① G861. 425-62

中国版本图书馆 CIP 数据核字（2020）第 054071 号

选题策划 史大伟 薛 力
责任编辑 唐欢欢
特约编辑 顾 禹
封面设计 李海波

出版发行 哈尔滨工程大学出版社
社　　址 哈尔滨市南岗区南通大街 145 号
邮政编码 150001
发行电话 0451-82519328
传　　真 0451-82519699
经　　销 新华书店
印　　刷 武汉精一佳印刷有限公司
开　　本 787 mm×1 092 mm 1/16
印　　张 10. 75
字　　数 210 千字
版　　次 2020 年 4 月第 1 版
印　　次 2020 年 4 月第 1 次印刷
定　　价 100. 00 元
http：//www. hrbeupress. com
E-mail：heupress@hrbeu. edu. cn